MW01125554

UTOPIAS OF ONE

Utopias of One

Joshua Kotin

PRINCETON UNIVERSITY PRESS
PRINCETON & OXFORD

Published by Princeton University Press,
41 William Street, Princeton, New Jersey 08540

In the United Kingdom: Princeton University Press,
Street, Woodstock, Oxfordshire OX20 1TR

press.princeton.edu

Jacket art: Henry Francis Walling, 1825–88. Map of the town of Concord,
Middlesex County, Mass. Library of Congress, Geography and Map Division

An earlier version of chapter 3, "Osip and Nadezhda Mandel'shtam's Utopian Anti-Utopianism," appeared as "Osip and Nadezhda Mandel'shtam and Soviet Utopianism" in *Modernism/modernity* 24.1 (January 2017), copyright © 2017 The Johns Hopkins University Press.

An earlier version of chapter 5, "Wallace Stevens's Point of View," appeared in *PMLA* 130.1 (January 2015), published by the Modern Language Association of America.

An excerpt from an earlier version of chapter 6, "Reading Ezra Pound and J. H. Prynne in Chinese," appeared as "Blood-Stained Battle-Flags: Ezra Pound, J. H. Prynne, and Classical Chinese Poetry," in *News from Afar: Ezra Pound and Some Contemporary British Poetries*, edited by Richard Parker (Bristol: Shearsman Books, 2015).

Library of Congress Cataloging-in-Publication Data

Names: Kotin, Joshua author.
Title: Utopias of one / Joshua Kotin.
Description: Princeton : Princeton University Press, 2017. | Includes bibliographical references and index.
Identifiers: LCCN 2017007977 | ISBN 9780691176710 (hardback : alk. paper)
Subjects: LCSH: Utopias in literature.
Classification: LCC PN56.U8 K68 2017 | DDC 809/.93372—dc23
LC record available at https://lccn.loc.gov/2017007977

British Library Cataloging-in-Publication Data is available

This book has been composed in Miller

Printed on acid-free paper. ∞

Printed in the United States of America

10 9 8 7 6 5 4 3 2 1

for Rachel

Thank Heaven, here is not all the world.

—HENRY DAVID THOREAU, *WALDEN*

CONTENTS

INTRODUCTION

Utopias of One

1

The word "utopia" is now almost entirely meaningless.[1] Its "definitional capabilities have been completely devoured by its connotative properties," writes Jacques Rancière. "Sometimes it refers to the mad delusions that lead to totalitarian catastrophe; sometimes it refers, conversely, to the infinite expansion of the field of possibility that resists all forms of totalizing closure."[2]

Yet all utopias share at least one basic feature: failure. The word's etymology makes the point: Thomas More invented the word "utopia" in 1516 by combining "eu-topia" (good place) and "ou-topia" (no place). Failure is inevitable—whether the aim is a social structure that harmonizes individual and collective interests or freedom without limit.

Not all utopias fail in the same way, of course. Some end in mass death. Others remain fixed to the pages of novels and manifestos. The reasons for failure also vary. Some utopias rely on violence. Others are quixotic. Most are simply unable to overcome the class interests of an elite or the inertia of everyday life.[3]

Failure can be redeemed as social critique. "Utopia," argues Jay Winter, "is a fantasy about the limits of the possible, a staging of what we take for granted, and what is left unsaid about our current social conventions and political cultures."[4] From this perspective, all utopias (even the most catastrophic) testify to the inadequacy of the status quo—and to humankind's enduring desire for a better world. As Ernst Bloch writes, "the essential function of utopia is a critique of what is present."[5]

This cursory account of utopia connects Fruitlands and the Soviet Union, William Morris's *News from Nowhere* (1890) and B. F. Skinner's *Walden Two* (1948), and Jean Baudrillard's "Utopia deferred . . ." (1971) and Anahid Nersessian's *Utopia, Limited* (2015).[6] An unrealized, unrealizable ideal; the consolations of social critique—this is utopia.

2

Utopias of One departs from this account of utopia. The book follows eight writers—Henry David Thoreau, W.E.B. Du Bois, Osip and Nadezhda Mandel'shtam, Anna Akhmatova, Wallace Stevens, Ezra Pound, and J. H. Prynne—as they respond to the failures of utopia by constructing utopias of one. These utopias do not fail. But their success comes at a cost: they cannot serve as models for readers hoping to perfect their own lives or remake their communities. Utopias of one are exclusive—and, in most cases, inimitable.

This book tracks the emergence of these utopias within and against modernity's two most ambitious attempts to harmonize individual and collective interests: liberalism and communism. My approach is comparative and transnational. The book's chapters move from antebellum America through the end of Jim Crow, from Stalin's Russia through the Soviet reform period known as the "Thaw," and from England and America at the dawn of World War I through the end of the Cold War and the emergence of neoliberalism. Together, the chapters capture how writers from diverse contexts create lived and perfect worlds—for themselves alone.

From one perspective, utopias of one are unremarkable. In *Charles Olson: A Scholar's Art* (1978), Robert von Hallberg criticizes American poets who attempt "to change American culture by establishing common knowledge and values" but then settle for "the achievement of a personal order."[7] In *Dreamworld and Catastrophe* (2000), Susan Buck-Morss laments the rise of "personal utopianism," which she associates with "the abandonment of the larger social project" and "political cynicism."[8] From this perspective, utopias of one simply reaffirm my earlier account of utopia and failure: a utopia of just one person is a contradiction in terms—and thus no utopia at all.

But from a different perspective, utopias of one represent a limit case of literary efficacy—*what literature can and does make happen*. (Efficacy: "Power or capacity to produce effects," to quote the *Oxford English Dictionary*.) The texts I examine are not merely occasions for imagining or promoting alternatives to the status quo or for representing totality—what Joshua Clover calls "the inner dynamic of social existence and its forms of appearance."[9] The texts are not primarily critical, analytical, aspirational, inspirational, sentimental, or even representational.[10] Their efficacy is real, direct, and dramatic—yet isolated and isolating, singular and specific.

This is my first overarching claim: the texts I examine create perfect worlds. My second overarching claim is related: the texts I examine create perfect worlds by refusing or failing to present models of perfect worlds. Efficacy and divisiveness go hand in hand. For the writers I discuss, the dissolution of community is the first step toward establishing an alternative to community. The book, in this way, offers an account of utopianism that does not default to an account of failure and social critique.

Despite the book's complexity and breadth, it explicates a basic sequence of events. A writer responds to the failure of utopia—America in the aftermath of Reconstruction, the Soviet Union in the 1930s, the world under neoliberalism—by devising his or her own utopian project. The project is precarious. It risks solipsism at one extreme and mere critique at the other. Ultimately, its effects are asymmetrical and highly improbable: a perfect world that cannot be replicated or shared.

Utopias of One attempts to illuminate these "asymmetries"—how texts benefit writers and neglect (and even harm) readers. Occasionally, the asymmetries (and the utopias that result) are intentional. Writers develop techniques to estrange readers: irony, obscurity, invective, cliché. But in many cases, the asymmetries are unintentional. Writers do not intend to abandon "the larger social project" (to quote Buck-Morss again), yet discover that they are unable to reverse the divisive effects of powerful institutions: legal segregation, government censorship and surveillance, class. In such cases, writers save themselves and leave readers behind.

The utopias I discuss are thus morally ambiguous. They reflect and reinforce the atomization of modern life. But they also demonstrate literature's power to create lived and perfect worlds. In light of this moral ambiguity, the book does not promote narratives of redemption or wrongdoing. My aim is not to celebrate or indict a subgenre of literature—or to identify heroes and villains. My aim is to describe the construction and significance of utopias of one. If read with a sense of political optimism, the book may seem cynical; if read with a sense of political pessimism, the book may seem consoling, even hopeful.

Utopias of One attempts to address a series of questions at the intersection of aesthetics and politics—questions about dissent and complicity, personal and aesthetic autonomy, genre and world-making, and the meaning and value of perfection. (The book will, I hope, provide a framework for understanding the efficacy of other texts, and for understanding how utopian desire survives the failure of utopia.) In the process, the book confronts a vexing hermeneutical problem: If utopias of one are, by definition, exclusive, how can we, as readers, identify and evaluate them?

3

The first utopia of one I discuss is Thoreau's "experiment of living" at Walden and in *Walden* (1854).[11] When Thoreau moved to Walden Pond on July 4, 1845, his goal was to maximize his independence. America, from his perspective, had failed. The government (at all levels) had betrayed its own liberal ideals. Slavery and imperialism defined everyday life. Reform seemed impossible. Voting (for those who could vote) was an act of complicity. The abolitionist movement was in disarray.[12] The utopian community at Brook Farm was breaking down.[13] Fruitlands had collapsed a year and half earlier.

To maximize his independence, Thoreau radically reduced the size of his world. As I discuss in the first chapter: he minimized his social and financial obligations, and chose to live in an artificially circumscribed environment. He also developed a practice of writing and rewriting that refined his perception of his environment. Writing became an instrument of attentiveness and suppression—a way to improve his vision and restrict its range. At Walden and in *Walden* there was little or no conflict between receptivity and sovereignty. Thoreau could be open to his surroundings and in control—vulnerable and secure.

This was the beginning of Thoreau's utopia of one: a world small enough to be received in its entirety. To revitalize certain liberal ideals, he deprioritized or abandoned others. Personal sovereignty took precedence over popular sovereignty—or, to be more precise, personal sovereignty and popular sovereignty became one. This is one reason that *Walden* is such an innovative and radical book. Thoreau did not respond to the failures of utopia by proposing a new way to harmonize individual and collective interests. He dissolved the difference, transforming *the* world into *his* world.

Thoreau's utopia of one puts readers in an awkward position. How should we relate to his carefully tailored world? The options are all problematic. We could take *Walden* as a model and attempt to cultivate our independence. But to do so would be self-defeating—an act of dependence, not independence. Alternatively, we could "stand aloof" (the phrase is Thoreau's) and cautiously evaluate the project's strengths and weaknesses.[14] But to do so would be to ignore the project's allure and the intimacy of Thoreau's address. Finally, we could reject the project altogether—as narcissistic, even dangerous. But to do so would be to ignore the project's moral seriousness and Thoreau's virtuosity. The best response might be all and none of the above—to adopt and abandon roles constantly: to become a disciple, then a disinterested critic, then a skeptic, then a disciple, ad infinitum.

Walden's reception history testifies to this awkwardness. The book is one of the most celebrated and reviled books in literary history. Some readers struggle to adopt and abandon a range of roles—an impossible task, especially in the long run. ("The writer keeps my choices in front of me," Stanley Cavell writes, "the ones I am not making and the ones I am. This makes me wretched and nervous.")[15] But most are happy to ignore the book's complexity—and thus the book itself—and adopt a single role.[16]

This awkwardness was a deliberate effect. Thoreau did not want to become responsible for the lives of his readers. Why, then, did he publish *Walden*? Why address readers at all? As I argue in chapter 1, he recognized that to maximize his independence, he had to confront his imbrication in social norms.[17] *Walden* is the most prominent site of that confrontation.

Thoreau thus describes the construction of a utopia but not *how* to construct a utopia. This omission represents a significant shift in the history of utopian literature. Traditionally, utopian literature presents models or blueprints for constructing perfect worlds. More's *Utopia*, for example, models three general principles: "equality of all good and evil things among the citizens . . . ; a fixed and unwavering dedication to peace and tranquility; and utter contempt for gold and silver."[18] Readers are meant to adopt (or imagine adopting) these principles in their communities. (The leaders of the October Revolution, for example, did just that—almost four hundred years after the publication of *Utopia*.) Thoreau's project is an exception. Its exclusivity and inimitability are essential characteristics.

Thoreau's utopia of one, in this way, threatens the very idea of utopia. In *Utopia and Anti-Utopia in Modern Times* (1987), Krishan Kumar writes:

> Thoreau's two-year experiment in solitary living around Walden Pond can almost be considered the epitome of American utopianism. It breathes its spirit through and through. It carries to a logical extreme the utopian promise of America to grant every single individual the right and opportunity to pursue his own vision, however idiosyncratic, of the good life. The paradox, of course, is that it is also the *reductio ad absurdum* of American utopianism. One man does not make a community, even a utopian community.[19]

Yet this is exactly what Thoreau wanted to do: make a one-man community—a utopia of one. To ask whether his project should count as a utopia is to ask about the capaciousness of a specific word. But it is also to ask about perfection itself. Is perfection still perfection when it cannot be shared?

I do not know for certain how Thoreau would have answered this question. Despite his narcissism, he rarely describes his inner life at Walden. (As E. B. White notes, Thoreau "disguised most of the facts from which an understanding of his life could be drawn.")[20] Readers observe Thoreau's utopia from the outside. We can track its construction but not confirm its effects. This is not an accident, of course—it is a way to protect his independence.

In the conclusion to *Walden*, however, Thoreau intimates that the project's most significant shortcoming was its unsustainability, not its exclusivity:

> I left the woods for as good a reason as I went there. Perhaps it seemed to me that I had several more lives to live, and could not spare any more time for that one. It is remarkable how easily and insensibly we fall into a particular route, and make a beaten track for ourselves. I had not lived there a week before my feet wore a path from my door to the pond-side; and though it is five or six years since I trod it, it is still quite distinct. It is true, I fear, that others may have fallen into it, and so helped to keep it open.[21]

These lines are ambiguous, but they suggest that when Thoreau decided to leave Walden in September 1847, he did so for two reasons. First, he had begun to imitate his own behavior. ("[I]mitation is suicide," Ralph Waldo Emerson writes in "Self-Reliance" [1841]. Self-imitation is still imitation.)[22] Second, Thoreau's contemporaries (who would have learned about his project from various sources, including Thoreau himself) had become too proximate—their paths had begun to converge with his own.[23] Thus, the problem was not that his utopia of one was, in fact, a utopia of one, but rather that it could not remain so.

4

Utopias of One does not identify a genealogy of projects influenced by *Walden*. The book focuses instead on a process and a concept. The other writers I discuss develop their own projects, which reflect their own goals and contexts. Du Bois responds to the failure of Reconstruction. The Mandel'shtams and Akhmatova respond to the failure of Soviet communism. Stevens responds to the failure of humanism, and Pound and Prynne to the failure of what both might describe as global capitalism. (Stevens is the outlier: he does not respond to the failure of a political or economic system; he responds to the failure of a system of thought.) Yet the basic sequence or paradigm holds. The failure of utopia leads to a utopia of one. Language becomes a medium of independence, and independence an opportunity for perfection.

What is independence? The word has many synonyms or near-synonyms: autonomy, sovereignty, freedom, free will, liberty, agency, self-determination. These concepts all have their own dictionary definitions and context-dependent connotations.[24] Yet in most modern accounts, they entail two seemingly complementary ideas. To be independent (or autonomous, sovereign, free, etc.) is to be beyond the control of others and in control of oneself.

In "Two Concepts of Liberty" (1958), Isaiah Berlin calls these ideas "negative liberty" and "positive liberty," respectively, and argues that they, in fact, are not complementary at all. "Negative liberty" reflects an ideal of noninterference: "I am normally said to be free," he writes, "to the degree to which no man or body of men interferes with my activity."[25] "Positive liberty," in contrast, reflects an ideal of mastery: "Freedom is self-mastery, the elimination of obstacles to my will, whatever these obstacles may be—the resistance of nature, of my ungoverned passions, of irrational institutions, of the opposing wills or behaviour of others."[26] Negative liberty is thus incompatible with positive liberty. To maintain an ideal of noninterference, one must avoid interfering in the lives of others—and, perhaps, in one's own life as well.

Hannah Arendt complicates matters further. In "What Is Freedom?" (1958–61), she argues that freedom and sovereignty, and freedom and free will, are both mutually exclusive:

> Politically, this identification of freedom with sovereignty is perhaps the most pernicious and dangerous of the philosophical equation

> of freedom and free will. For it leads either to a denial of human freedom—namely, if it is realized that whatever men may be, they are never sovereign—or to the insight that the freedom of one man, or a group, or a body politic can be purchased only at the price of the freedom, i.e., the sovereignty, of all others.[27]

Arendt is making two arguments. First, sovereignty is an illusion. Individuals and groups are never fully in control of their surroundings or themselves. Second, sovereignty is socially undesirable—a zero-sum game of power and powerlessness. For Arendt, freedom has little to do with control. It is, instead, an act that interrupts the "automatism . . . inherent in all processes."[28]

In *Scenes of Subjection* (1997), Saidiya V. Hartman links this zero-sum game to a history of racism:

> Prized designations like "independence," "autonomy," and "free will" are the lures of liberalism, yet the tantalizing suggestion of the individual as potentate and sovereign is drastically undermined by the forms of repression and terror that accompanied the advent of freedom, the techniques of discipline that bind the individual through conscience, self-knowledge, responsibility, and duty, and the management of racialized bodies and populations effected through the racism of the state and civil society.[29]

In this account, independence always entails its opposite. Racism is a barrier to independence and a consequence of independence. In an endnote, Hartman quotes Étienne Balibar, who draws attention to the contradiction in the meaning of the word "subject": "why is it that the very *name* which allows modern philosophy to think and designate the *originary freedom* of the human being—the name of 'subject'—is precisely the name which *historically* meant suppression of freedom, or at least an intrinsic limitation of freedom, i.e., *subjection*?"[30]

On closer examination, the list of synonyms or near-synonyms of independence devolves into a list of irreconcilable and contradictory concepts. The desire to escape domination leads to various forms of domination, including self-domination. Sovereignty is, at once, an impossible ideal and not an ideal at all. The history of independence is a history of slavery and racism.[31]

This impasse would not have surprised Thoreau. His particular solution was to construct an artificial environment in which he could be sovereign and nonsovereign—powerful and powerless. At Walden and in *Walden*, he consolidated what C. B. Macpherson would call his "possessive individualism" and what Leo Bersani would call his "authoritative selfhood," while making such defense mechanisms unnecessary.[32] In the process, he was able to maximize his independence without eliminating the world or denying his receptivity, or seriously injuring others or himself.

The other writers I discuss embrace different solutions to this impasse—or ignore it altogether. Du Bois, for example, attempts to evade the "lures of liberalism" by developing a practice of freedom that does not lead to oppression. Osip Mandel'shtam, in contrast, accepts these lures—despite the antiliberalism of the Soviet Union. He develops the most radical project of all: composing a poem that links his independence to his death. His performance of an epigram mocking Stalin in 1933 anticipates Berlin's claim that the "logical culmination of the process of destroying everything through which I can possibly be wounded is suicide."[33] Mandel'shtam's performance led to his arrest in 1934 and his death in a Gulag transit camp in 1938. "Total liberation in this sense," Berlin laments, "is conferred only by death."[34]

Ultimately, the ability to solve or mitigate the impasse is an index of relative safety. In extreme circumstances, a zero-sum game of power and powerlessness might seem justifiable—even desirable.[35]

5

Apart from identifying a genealogy, there are three ways to write a book about the efficacy of utopian literature. First, one could select a single case study—such a book might examine Thoreau's utopianism. Second, one could select a series of case studies based on their similarity—such a book might examine utopian responses to the failure of Soviet utopianism. Third, one could select case studies based on their complementarity—such a book might (and, of course, *would*) resemble *Utopias of One*.

This third way has specific risks. The case studies might prove disparate. The pursuit of complementarity might lead to discontinuity: a collection of essays, instead of a greater-than-the-sum-of-its-parts monograph. The case studies might also sacrifice depth for breadth and thus alienate readers. Finally, and most significantly, the case studies might lead to false generalizations.

But there are benefits as well: depth and breadth, a diverse audience, genuine theoretical insights. Ideally, the pursuit of complementarity would lead to a multifaceted account of a single phenomenon while challenging critical assumptions about national context, periodization, and genre. More dramatic, a rigorous comparative and transnational study, attentive to the importance of historical and political context, might lead to a *nonnational* study that exposes a long-ignored facet of literary efficacy.[36]

Utopias of One, I hope, avoids these risks and realizes at least some of these benefits. The book investigates a series of different yet complementary case studies. The chapter on Du Bois, for example, focuses on his *Autobiography* (1962, 1968) and his defense of communism, especially Soviet communism. The next chapter—on the Mandel'shtams—focuses, in part, on Nadezhda Mandel'shtam's memoirs and her attack on Soviet communism. The coincidence is not an occasion to take sides—to argue that Du Bois was right about communism and Nadezhda Mandel'shtam was wrong, or vice versa. Instead, the coincidence is an occasion to interrogate how a single ideology and a single genre can lead to such divergent opportunities for self-making and world-making.

The comparison between Du Bois and Nadezhda Mandel'shtam is particularly fascinating. Both wrote autobiographies in the late 1950s, and both were unable to find publishers at home. (*Autobiography* was first published in Moscow in 1962—in Russian translation. The initial volume of Nadezhda Mandel'shtam's memoirs was first published in New York in 1970—in English translation and Russian.) Both writers also had to negotiate de-individualizing traditions of autobiographical writing. Du Bois had to confront the history of African American autobiography. ("If the goal of autobiography is the assertion of individuality," writes Henry Louis Gates Jr., "the typical black memoir is assigned the contrary task: that of being representative.")[37] Nadezhda Mandel'shtam, in turn, had to confront the history of communist autobiography. ("Communist autobiography," writes Igal Halfin, was "the standard by which entrance into the brotherhood of the elect was determined.")[38] Together, the two autobiographies illuminate the resources of a genre.

But the book's case studies are not only comparative; they are also transnational. The chapter on Du Bois begins in Washington, DC, and travels to New York, Moscow, Beijing, and Accra, among other locations. The chapter on the Mandel'shtams begins in Karelia in northwest Russia and travels to Moscow, Oslo, New York, Ann Arbor, and Princeton, among other locations. The book's other chapters are similarly global, traveling from Saint Petersburg to Oxford and back again, Cambridge to Hartford, and London to Tokyo to Cambridge to Guangzhou. By attending to these itineraries, *Utopias of One* captures how the transnational circulation of texts influences their efficacy.

This transnational approach reflects a trend in scholarship but also a sincere attempt to understand utopia. Utopian projects violate national borders and undermine the coherence and hegemony of nation-states. Yet utopian projects also consolidate national borders and nation-states. Consider, for example, the American Revolution or the October Revolution—or any revolution—or the African American civil rights movement. A strictly national or international approach to any of these projects would be inadequate.

Utopia is also transhistorical.[39] Yet utopia has a different status after the Industrial Revolution—and, especially, after the Green Revolution and the bombings of Hiroshima and Nagasaki. In *Aesthetic Theory* (1970), Theodor W. Adorno makes the point: "This is the true consciousness of an age in which the real possibility of Utopia—that given the level of productive forces the earth could here and now be paradise—converges with the possibility of total catastrophe."[40] The conditions that make utopia possible also make total catastrophe possible. The paradox is detectable, already, in Thoreau's anxieties about the railroad, which carried ice from Walden Pond to ships traveling to "Charleston and New Orleans, [and] Madras and Bombay and Calcutta."[41] The paradox is explicit, finally, in Du Bois's participation in the antinuclear peace movement in the early 1950s, at the height of McCarthyism. To understand utopia is to understand its special significance in modernity.

Utopia, in this way, justifies the book's comparative and transnational approach, and its historical framework. But what justifies its focus on poems and memoirs instead of stories and novels, and, especially, science fiction, the genre most frequently associated with utopia? My answer: nonfictionality. The worlds that poems and memoirs represent are not fictional—they are part of our world, the world. The worlds that stories and novels represent, in contrast, are fictional—separate, counterfactual.[42] For poets and memoirists, worldmaking is an act of remaking the world they already inhabit.

This distinction between nonfiction and fiction is imprecise.[43] But two examples help clarify my argument. First: when Wallace Stevens makes the following claim in "Sunday Morning" (1915, 1923), he is addressing his own anxieties about materialism:

> Death is the mother of beauty; hence from her,
> Alone, shall come fulfilment to our dreams
> And our desires.[44]

The claim would resonate differently if Stevens were already a committed and satisfied materialist—or if he were representing the anxieties of a fictional character named "Wallace Stevens." The claim would also resonate differently if its truth-value mattered to Stevens alone—or if its truth-value in the poem were distinct from its truth-value in the world. But "Sunday Morning" represents (or better, presents) a real person confronting a real problem in the real world. By addressing his anxieties in the poem, Stevens is attempting to address them in the world—our world—as well.[45]

A second example—this time from a radically impersonal poem by the contemporary English poet J. H. Prynne. When Prynne writes the following lines in *The Oval Window* (1983), he is most likely not representing his own anxieties:

> Sideways in the mirror and too slow
> to take up, it is the point of death. Not
> lost from the track as passing its peak
> but the cycle burns out on the axle,
> quenching a thirst with lip salve slicked
> on the ridge of its porridge bowl. Still
> spoilt by bad temper the screen relives
> a guessed anxiety: wounds were his feast,
> his life to life a prey.[46]

Prynne—the historical Prynne, who recently retired from the University of Cambridge after almost sixty years of teaching—is not the speaker of this poem. But it would be a mistake to assume that the speaker must then be fictional. The poem might not have a speaker—at least not a consistent, identifiable speaker. Regardless, the world of the poem is still our world. As Prynne writes, "It has mostly been my own aspiration . . . to establish relations not personally with the reader, but with the world and its layers of shifted but recognisable usage; and thereby with the reader's own position within this world."[47] Again, "this world"—our world.

Many poems are wholly fictional, of course—the *Odyssey*, Goethe's *Faust* (1808, 1832), Robert Browning's "My Last Duchess" (1842), Ezra Pound's "The Beautiful Toilet" (1915). "Sunday Morning" includes fictional characters: the woman who "feels the dark / Encroachment of that old catastrophe," the "ring of men."[48] Some memoirs might be novels, and vice versa.[49] Herman Melville's *Typee* (1846) might be a memoir and a novel.[50] But the distinction between nonfiction and fiction, however fuzzy, helps explain the efficacy of poems and memoirs, on the one hand, and stories and novels, on the other. Stories and novels present counterfactuals that model (and involve readers in) alternative social arrangements, and invent characters that simplify complex ethical and psychological problems. (As Candace Vogler notes, "With any luck, *no* human being will be knowable in the way that *any* literary character worth repeated readings is knowable.")[51] As a result, novels and stories are especially suited to social critique.[52] To state my argument as baldly and precariously as possible: poems and memoirs create utopias; stories and novels depict utopias.[53]

Do my case studies lead to any theoretical insights? The case studies, taken together, suggest a new theory of literary efficacy. Standard theories assume that literature changes the world (if it changes the world) by motivating or educating readers. Consider Julia Ward Howe's "The Battle Hymn of the Republic" (1861) or Nikolai Chernyshevskii's *What Is to Be Done?* (1863) or Rachel Carson's *Silent Spring* (1962). The memoirs and poems I discuss, in contrast, change the world by ostracizing readers. If *Utopias of One* had a subtitle, it might be *The Antisocial Utility of Literature*.[54]

The case studies also suggest a new theory of aesthetic difficulty. Standard theories associate aesthetic difficulty with defamiliarization, political resistance, elitism, prophecy, and attempts to solve (or simply represent) difficult conceptual problems.[55] The memoirs and poems I examine are difficult for these reasons. But they are also difficult because their effects are singular. The utopias they create are available to their authors alone.

These theories of literary efficacy and aesthetic difficulty are interrelated. Indeed, they connect two parallel discourses about autonomy. The first concerns personal autonomy—how individuals maximize their independence. The second concerns aesthetic autonomy—how texts resist the contexts of their production or reception or both. Lisa Siraganian, in *Modernism's Other*

Work (2012), provides one account of the connection: "The freedom of the art object not from the world generally but from the reader's meaning specifically presents a way to imagine an individual's complicated liberty within yet enduring connection to the state."[56] For Siraganian, aesthetic autonomy is a metaphor for personal autonomy. (She identifies a homology between the two kinds of autonomy.) In *Utopias of One*, in contrast, aesthetic autonomy is an instrument of personal autonomy, which, in turn, is an instrument of utopia.[57]

6

The book has three parts, each focused on a distinct geopolitical context or keyword. Part 1 examines two responses to the failure of American liberalism and the enlightenment ideals of America's founding fathers. Chapter 1 concerns *Walden*'s pedagogy. What, I ask, can we, as readers, learn from reading the book? What does Thoreau learn from writing it? What is the connection between these scenes of pedagogy (or anti-pedagogy)—between our experience of *Walden* and Thoreau's experience of Walden and *Walden*?

Chapter 2 concerns Du Bois's utopianism during the last fifteen years of his life, after his final break with the National Association for the Advancement of Colored People (NAACP). I track his increasing commitment to Soviet communism and examine the difficulty and efficacy of his *Autobiography*. How, I ask, did Du Bois's utopianism lead, finally, to a utopia of one?

Du Bois's political commitments foreshadow the book's shift, in part 2, to the Soviet Union. Chapter 3 concerns two anti-Soviet texts: Osip Mandel'shtam's so-called Stalin epigram and his widow's memoirs. Chapter 4 examines Anna Akhmatova's two great late poems *Реквием* (1935–62) (*Requiem*) and the famously difficult *Поэма без героя* (1940–65) (*Poem without a Hero*). These two chapters, together, investigate the efficacy of utopian literature within a failed and failing utopian state, and the connection between dissent and complicity.

The book's third and final part departs from these contexts. Its focus is, at once, more global and more local. Chapter 5 examines Stevens's repeated attempts to use his poetry to establish a livable form of secularism—to find value in a world of fact. Independence, here, is not a matter of escaping political oppression but of self-regulation. Chapter 6 examines Ezra Pound's and J. H. Prynne's use of Chinese poetry to understand the problem of motivation—and the incentive structures that govern modern life. How, I ask, does difficult poetry illuminate the difficulty of motivating social change?

The book's conclusion, "Utopias of Two," concerns the challenges and value of reading such difficult texts. The book, here, comes full circle, examining the work of Thoreau's near-contemporary Emily Dickinson. (Dickinson becomes the ninth writer in the book's archive.) Why, I ask, should we, as readers, attempt to access utopias of one?

Utopias of One, as a whole, responds to my frustration with critics who read utopian literature exclusively as an instrument of social critique. For these critics, utopianism is either quixotic or ironic. I adopt a less settled approach and attempt to evaluate the practical effects of utopian literature. Failure and social critique, I argue, are not utopia's only fate. Utopianism can (and occasionally does) have concrete, utopian consequences.

But *Utopias of One* does not respond to a frustration with social critique itself. Indeed, the book is fully invested in various forms of critique—in correcting standard accounts of canonical authors, in challenging frustratingly abstract scholarship on aesthetics and politics, in making political arguments. The book is future-oriented in a way that many of my central texts are not. The authors I discuss want utopia now—and get a version of it. I just want to get the authors right.[58]

PART I

The United States of America

CHAPTER ONE

Learning from *Walden*

1

"*Walden* is a work that sets about offering specific advice about ways in which the individual can achieve both microcosmic and macrocosmic fulfillment."[1] This is a strong version of a claim that informs most readings of the book. *Walden* is a "guide," a model of "moral prose," a "tract of political education," an "effort to educate [its] audience in the 'deep' art of living," and a "framework for developing virtue ethics."[2] Yet despite this near-consensus, there is much confusion about what, specifically, the book teaches.

The confusion predates the publication of *Walden* by six years. On April 2, 1849, the *New-York Daily Tribune* published an anonymous review of Thoreau's lecture "Economy."[3] The reviewer summarized Thoreau's experiment and offered an account of its pedagogical value: "Mr. Thoreau," he wrote, "is a young student, who has imbibed (or rather refused to stifle), the idea that a man's soul is better worth living for than his body. . . . If all our young men would but hear this lecture, we think some among them would feel less strongly impelled either to come to New-York or go to California."[4] For the anonymous reviewer, the lecture taught its auditors how to prioritize self-cultivation over material gain.

Five days later, the *Tribune* published a letter from a puzzled reader, along with a response from Horace Greeley, the newspaper's editor. The reader questioned whether Thoreau's lecture could teach its auditors anything at all. "Having always found in The Tribune a friend of sociability and neighborly helping-each-other-along," the reader wrote, "I felt a little surprise at seeing such a performance held up as an example for the young men of this country. . . . [N]obody has a right to live for himself alone."[5] Greeley, in response, defended the reviewer's original position. "Nobody," he explained, "has proposed or suggested that it becomes everybody to go off into the woods, each build himself a hut and live hermit-like, on the vegetable products of his very moderate labor." The point, instead, is more general: Thoreau has "set all his brother aspirants to self-culture, a very wholesome example, and shown them how, by chastening their physical appetites, they may preserve their proper independence without starving their souls."[6]

The exchange in the *Tribune* captures the complexity of Thoreau's exemplarity—and *Walden*'s pedagogy, more generally. How, we might ask, has Thoreau taught us to chasten our appetites? If we purge *Walden* of its detail—of its specific means of "self-culture"—what is left but platitudes? As Leo Marx has noted, "For centuries writers [have suggested] that men might enrich their contemplative experience by simplifying their housekeeping."[7] How is *Walden* special or especially compelling? How can we learn from Thoreau's example if we cannot follow his example? What, in other words, does his utopia of one have to do with us, his readers? This, ultimately, is the subject of this chapter: our relation to Thoreau's utopia of one, and its relation to us.

2

What Would Thoreau Do?

—MOTTO ON T-SHIRT[8]

Walden teems with advice. Thoreau tells readers what to eat and wear, what to read and how. Yet as many readers recognize, this advice is inconsistent. "[T]rade curses everything it handles," Thoreau writes in "Economy."[9] In "Sounds," he remarks, "What recommends commerce to me is its enterprise and bravery" (118). In "Higher Laws," he condemns eating meat, including fish. In the next chapter, "Brute Neighbors," he prepares for a fishing trip. In "Where I Lived, and What I Lived For," he denounces the railway that cuts across the southwestern edge of Walden Pond. In "Sounds" he celebrates the railway's grandeur, comparing "the passage of the morning cars" to "the rising of the sun" (116). As Robert D. Richardson Jr. writes, the book "can be cited on both sides of many issues, and rather easily."[10]

But inconsistency is not the only obstacle to identifying (or following) *Walden*'s advice. Thoreau deploys an array of parables and aphorisms—many of which are intractably ambiguous. "Through our own recovered innocence we discern the innocence of our neighbors," he advises in "Spring" (314). But as he knows, to discern innocence is to lose it: "What is chastity?" he asks in "Higher Laws," "How shall a man know if he is chaste? He shall not know it" (220). In "Reading," he counsels that "Books must be read as deliberately and reservedly as they were written" (101). But how does one know how "deliberately" a book was written? What does it mean to read "reservedly"? Should we reserve judgment or read skeptically, standing in constant judgment of a book's claims? In "Economy," he declares, "We might try our lives by a thousand simple tests; as, for instance, that the same sun which ripens my beans illumines at once a system of earths like ours" (10). How is this a test? What does this sentence even mean? As Barbara Johnson notes, "It is paradoxical that a writer who constantly exhorts us to 'Simplify, simplify' should also be the author of some of the most complex and difficult passages in the English language." "The perverse complexity of *Walden*'s rhetoric," she adds, "is intimately related to the fact that it is never possible to be sure what the rhetorical status of any given image is."[11]

When Thoreau's advice is consistent and unambiguous, it often is clichéd or empty. "Explore thyself," he recommends (322). "It is never too late to give up our prejudices" (8). "Set about being good" (73). This is not advice but the outline of advice—maxims that require readers to supply their content and justify their relevance. "But I would say to my fellows, once for all, As long as possible live free and uncommitted" (84). Thoreau, here, follows his own advice by tentatively withholding it from readers: the conditional mood marks his refusal to commit to his aphorism.

But this line of inquiry, one could argue, is misguided. Indeed, *Walden*'s inconsistencies, ambiguities, and clichés might not be meant as advice at all. They are provocations.[12] The book, from this perspective, does not follow a "'banking' concept of education"—to cite a phrase from Paulo Freire's *Pedagogy of the Oppressed* (1968).[13] Knowledge is not "a gift bestowed by those who consider themselves knowledgeable upon those whom they consider to know nothing."[14] Thoreau is not an exemplary figure—a model for readers to emulate. Instead, *Walden* is an occasion for readers to think for themselves. "I would not have any one adopt *my* mode of living on any account," he writes. "I would have each one be very careful to find out and pursue *his own* way, and not his father's or his mother's or his neighbor's instead" (71). "Who shall say what prospect life offers to another?" (10).

When read in this way, *Walden* asks us to take responsibility for how we live—by asking us, first, to take responsibility for what we read. Contradictions are opportunities to assume opposing points of view. Ambiguous sentences invite us to adapt the book to fit our individual lives. Clichés motivate us to question social norms. Thoreau cultivates critical readers—not disciples.

One could push this argument even further. To encourage critical thinking, Thoreau relies on an array of literary and nonliterary techniques—irony, puns, monotony, aggression. Consider his use of "relish" in the following passage from "The Bean-Field." The historical context is the buildup to the Mexican-American War. Thoreau describes the influence of hearing "some waifs of martial music" emanating from Concord on "gala days":

> But sometimes it was a really noble and inspiring strain that reached these woods, and the trumpet that sings of fame, and I felt as if I could spit a Mexican with a good relish,—for why should we always stand for

> trifles?—and looked round for a woodchuck or a skunk to exercise my chivalry upon. (160–61)

The passage warns readers about art's influence: the "noble and inspiring strain" inspires a fantasy of killing a Mexican soldier. But the pun on "relish" undermines the warning by emphasizing Thoreau's control and self-awareness. ("Relish" is at once a description of pleasure and a garnish. Thoreau is joking about roasting and eating the soldier.) The passage, in this way, catches readers in a web of contradictory effects—we are repulsed by Thoreau's joke, impressed by his verbal dexterity, confused by his warning.

This line of inquiry suggests that Thoreau's aim in *Walden* is to teach self-reliance. What is self-reliance? For Emerson, it is a practice of perspectivism and receptivity. The "self," in his view, is not an individual's discrete nature but a relationship to an impersonal "common nature."[15] As Sharon Cameron writes, "what self-reliance turns out to mean for Emerson is a strong recognitional understanding of the inadequacy of any person: other persons *or* this person. And what the preacher and the American Scholar know how to do is to break out of the tyranny of egotistical self-enclosure."[16] To be self-reliant, in other words, is to constantly defy one's own point of view while developing a connection to what Emerson calls, in the "The Over-Soul" (1841), "that Unity, that Over-soul, within which every man's particular being is contained and made one with all other."[17]

Emerson attempts to teach self-reliance in two seemingly contradictory ways. First, he helps readers "break out of the tyranny of egotistical self-enclosure" by packing his essays with incompatible ideas and points of view. To read his work is to adopt and abandon a series of disparate subject positions. Second, he invites readers to identify with his point of view. By accepting this invitation, we participate in his practice of perspectivism and receptivity, and, in the process, learn to see the world anew, from a common subject position. His world becomes our world—or, more accurately, our worlds become one.

Does Emerson's version of self-reliance illuminate *Walden*'s pedagogy? Yes and no. Thoreau also encourages us to adopt and abandon a series of disparate subject positions. But he does not present a world we can hold in common. As I noted in the introduction, Walden is an artificially circumscribed environment, tailored to reduce and reveal the needs of a single individual. As a result, it cannot easily serve as a site of collective action. (Indeed, I think *Walden* presents an implicit critique of Emerson's pedagogy. For Thoreau, Emerson's practice of perspectivism and receptivity is rarely sustainable over long periods of time. One cannot live in the world and remain radically vulnerable to the world. Walden and *Walden* are Thoreau's attempt to change that—to construct an artificial world that would support a genuine and durable practice of self-reliance.)

Perhaps Thoreau's own concept of "awakening" better captures the book's pedagogical aims. (Variations of "to wake" appear thirty-four times in the book;

"self-reliance" does not appear at all.) "*Walden*'s great achievement," argues Johnson, "is to wake us up to our own lost losses."[18] "*Walden* makes up for the absent cock-crow," notes Walter Benn Michaels.[19] "I do not propose to write an ode to dejection," Thoreau himself declares, "but to brag as lustily as chanticleer in the morning, standing on his roost, if only to wake my neighbors up" (84).

But what does it mean, in *Walden*, to be awake? In "Solitude," Thoreau describes a "doubleness by which I can stand as remote from myself as from another" (135). "However intense my experience," he explains, "I am conscious of the presence and criticism of a part of me, which, as it were, is not a part of me, but spectator, sharing no experience, but taking note of it; and that is no more I than it is you" (135). To be awake, in this account, is to regard one's life from first- and third-person perspectives.[20] "This doubleness may easily make us poor neighbors and friends sometimes," he concludes (135). Elsewhere in *Walden*, to awake is to lose perspective entirely. In "The Village," he writes, "Every man has to learn the points of the compass again as often as he awakes whether from sleep or any abstraction" (171).

Wakefulness, in this way, is yet another ambiguous concept in the book. "Moral reform is the effort to throw off sleep," Thoreau writes in "Where I Lived, and What I Lived For" (90).[21] Yet later in the chapter, he ridicules men who wake every half hour to hear the news. "We have the Saint Vitus' dance, and cannot possibly keep our heads still" (93). Stanley Cavell asks, "How do we replace anxious wakefulness by a constant awakening?"[22] But first, we should ask: What is the difference? To further complicate matters, recall who does the waking in *Walden*: Chanticleer. In the Chanticleer and the Fox story (famously adapted by Chaucer in the "Nun's Priest's Tale"), Chanticleer dreams about being captured by a fox. Against his better judgment, he disregards the dream and is captured midsong—literally as he brags lustily to his neighbors. To be awake, in this case, is to sleep—dreaming, for Chanticleer, is a way to see the future and safeguard the present.

"Literary anarchy"—this is how Michaels describes *Walden*'s ultimate effect.[23] Thoreau refuses to model a coherent practice of right action or self-reliance or wakefulness. Indeed, he refuses all forms of authority. Reading *Walden*, we confront a series of crises—concerning capitalism, animal rights, environmental degradation, erotic desire, reading, patriotism, religious experience—but we do not receive any guidance about how to respond to them.

This refusal of authority can itself be turned into a lesson. Laura Dassow Walls, for example, argues that *Walden* devises a radical, nonhierarchical communitarianism:

> By dissociating himself from a determinative "law" or *logos* as the cohering center, Thoreau devised an alternative, decentered, and relational world constructed on the ethic of interaction rather than dominance, knowledge not through control but through "sympathy" and the

intimacy of sensual contact, action not alone but through the cooperation of the community's individual members.[24]

This is an attractive way to understand the book's anarchy. But it is also problematic. Thoreau may reject a "determinative 'law' or *logos*," but he does not represent a decentered world: his experience anchors the book. Moreover, he does not offer a happy portrait of intimacy. Consider his relationships with Alek Therien (the Canadian woodchopper and post-maker), John Field, and William Ellery Channing—his three most prominent interlocutors in the book. These relationships do not present a portrait of "cooperation"—a fact I discuss in section 3 of this chapter.

But even if we ignore these facts, we should ask: Is Walls's account an ideal or yet another cliché? A "world constructed on the ethic of interaction rather than dominance" is an easy fantasy. (It is a fantasy common to the community at Brook Farm and many humanities departments today.) In "Economy," Thoreau critiques such fantasies, telling a story of two travelers, one with means, one without: "It was easy to see that they could not long be companions or coöperate, since one would not *operate* at all. They would part at the first interesting crisis in their adventures" (72). The story highlights the importance of class, revealing the economic barriers to cooperation. But the story does not show us how to address them—or even suggest that we should. Thoreau simply notes, "the man who goes alone can start today; but he who travels with another must wait till that other is ready, and it may be a long time before they get off" (72).

Thoreau's life at Walden is meant to spur us to find our own Waldens. This seems to be the only way to describe the book's charge to readers. But even this extremely weak account is not satisfactory. Cavell asks but does not answer a vital question: "Does the writer of *Walden* really believe [that] one could find one's Walden behind a bank counter, or driving a taxi, or guiding a trip hammer, or selling insurance, or teaching school?"[25] The answer, one presumes, is no. *Walden* seems to require more than a shift in attitude or understanding. The book asks us to take responsibility for our lives, but it does not give us the tools or the authority to evaluate our success.

Ultimately, a weak account of what *Walden* teaches readers is unsatisfying, while a strong account is incoherent. The book pressures us to become new men and women, yet refuses to tell us how. In the context of *Walden*, the question "What Would Thoreau Do?" is unanswerable and wrongheaded, yet omnipresent.[26] We know that the book has something important and specific to teach us about how to live, but we cannot articulate it. Is there a way to escape this impasse—to make sense of the book's power and emptiness?

One way would be to stop reading *Walden* as a guide. In "Percept, Affect, Concept" (1991), Gilles Deleuze and Félix Guattari claim that aesthetic experience does not admit disparate subject positions: teacher and student, writer and reader. "By means of the material," they write, "the aim of art is to wrest the percept from perceptions of objects and the states of a perceiving subject, to wrest the affect from affections as the transition from one state to another: to extract a bloc of sensations, . . . pure of being sensations."[27] "The composite sensation," they add, "deterritorializes the system of opinion that brought together dominant perceptions and affections within a natural, historical, and social milieu."[28] For Deleuze and Guattari, aesthetic experience frees us from ourselves and from each other, and from the countless factors that determine our perception of the world.

This unorthodox account of aesthetic experience leads to a very different—yet, to my mind, equally unsatisfying—conception of *Walden*'s pedagogy. Without subjects, there is no Thoreau to question—and no one to do the questioning. Indeed, art does not convey ideas and impressions from artist to audience. Art is not a medium of communication. "Perhaps the peculiarity of art," Deleuze and Guattari write, "is to pass through the finite in order to rediscover, to restore the infinite."[29] The restoration of the infinite—this is one way to make sense of *Walden*'s power and emptiness—its contribution to "the deep art of living."

3

Dew yew figger Mr Thoreau wuz a onanist or an eunuch? or wot ministered to his pleasures thaaaar in th' wildurness?

—EZRA POUND[30]

What is lost in this investigation of *Walden*'s pedagogy or anti-pedagogy or whatever? Thoreau spent two years and two months living at Walden Pond, and nine years writing and rewriting *Walden*, producing seven discrete drafts.[31] What did he learn? How did living at Walden and writing *Walden* change his life? How did he construct his utopia of one?

In the year preceding Thoreau's move to Walden Pond on July 4, 1845, Congress had approved the annexation of Texas, laying the foundation for the Mexican-American War, and Frederick Douglass had published his *Narrative*, detailing the horrors of slavery. Major rifts were developing in the abolitionist movement over black civil rights, the legitimacy of the United States Constitution, and even the urgency of emancipation itself. Alternative forms of community had failed or were failing. In 1844, Fruitlands had dissolved and Brook Farm had started to charge its members to sit at the "meat table," an early sign of unsustainability.[32]

Thoreau's experiment in independence was, in part, an attempt to escape this culture of failure—the failure of American utopianism. "That moment of origin," Cavell notes, "is the national event reenacted in the events of *Walden*, in order this time to do it right, or to prove that it is impossible."[33] As I wrote in the introduction: to establish his independence, Thoreau radically reduced the size of his world. He minimized his personal and financial obligations. He built his own house and grew much of his own food. He worked as little as possible. "For myself," he writes in "Economy," "I found that the occupation of a day-laborer was the most independent of any, especially as it required only thirty or forty days in a year to support one" (70).

But these practical measures were just the beginning of Thoreau's project. He not only had to establish his independence, he also had to learn how to exploit it. Walden was a refuge and a space for reflection. In "Higher Laws," he describes the effects of his practice of receptivity:

> I have found repeatedly, of late years, that I cannot fish without falling a little in self-respect. I have tried it again and again. I have skill at it, and, like many of my fellows, a certain instinct for it, which revives from time to time, but always when I have done I feel that it would have been better if I had not fished. I think that I do not mistake. It is a faint intimation, yet so are the first streaks of morning. There is unquestionably this instinct in me which belongs to the lower orders of creation; yet with every year I am less a fisherman, though without more humanity or even wisdom; at present I am no fisherman at all. (213–14)

In the passage, Thoreau does not embrace vegetarianism; he is embraced by it. Moral sentiments appear as faintly and naturally as "the first streaks of morning." Receptivity, here, is pedagogical—a way to accept a lesson in nonconformity. Thoreau does not become wiser or more humane; he becomes vulnerable to conscience.[34]

How else does Thoreau learn to exploit his independence? It is difficult to say. *Walden* presents a detailed portrait of his environment and daily chores but rarely describes his development or inner life. As E. B. White notes:

> Thoreau said he required of every writer, first and last, a simple and sincere account of his own life. Having delivered himself of this chesty dictum, he proceeded to ignore it. In his books and even in his enormous journal, he withheld or disguised most of the facts from which an understanding of his life could be drawn.[35]

Walden is the source of this "dictum" and the site of its most blatant repudiation. The book obscures many of the most important aspects of Thoreau's life between 1845 and 1854: his work on *A Week on the Concord and Merrimack Rivers* (1849), his frequent trips to Concord, his interactions with his family and friends. Emerson, the greatest intellectual influence on his life and the owner of land around Walden Pond, is mentioned only once and not by name: "There was one other with whom I had 'solid seasons,' long to be remembered, at his house in the village, and who looked in upon me from time to time; but I had no more for society there" (270).

Why does Thoreau suppress these contexts? My hypothesis is that suppression is an instrument of independence. By suppressing his contexts in *Walden*, he hopes to escape them at Walden (and after he leaves Walden). Consider the book's account of his famous act of civil disobedience:

> One afternoon, near the end of the first summer, when I went to the village to get a shoe from the cobbler's, I was seized and put into jail, because, as I have elsewhere related, I did not pay a tax to, or recognize the authority of, the state which buys and sells men, women, and children, like cattle at the door of its senate-house. I had gone to the woods for other purposes. But, wherever a man goes, men will pursue and paw him with their dirty institutions, and, if they can, constrain him to belong to their desperate odd-fellow society. It is true, I might have resisted forcibly with more or less effect, might have run "amok" against society; but I preferred society should run "amok" against me, it being the desperate party. However, I was released the next day, obtained my mended shoe, and returned to the woods in season to get my dinner of huckleberries on Fair-Haven Hill. (171)

In the passage, an argument about political representation cedes to a matter of real import: a solitary dinner of huckleberries. Jail is a mere interruption, not an occasion for heroism or reform or didacticism or charisma. Indeed, the book's account elides the complex sociality of Thoreau's arrest and its aftermath.[36] In the face of slavery and solidarity, he withdraws. "I had gone to the woods for other purposes," he declares.

This practice of suppression encompasses other aspects of Thoreau's life as well. Ezra Pound asks a question that must have occurred to generations of *Walden*'s readers: "Dew yew figger Mr Thoreau wuz a onanist or an eunuch? or wot ministered to his pleasures thaaaar in th' wildurness?" *Walden*, it seems, ignores sex from the start. But reading the journals and *Walden*'s drafts, one discovers that this is not the case. Sex is purged—not ignored. Robert Sattelmeyer highlights a deletion from the fifth draft: "I do not know how it is with other men, but I find it very difficult to be chaste."[37] The deletion is a kind of resolution: Thoreau purifies his desires by purifying *Walden*.

There is good reason for this purge. As Michael Warner observes, sexual desire is incompatible with Thoreau's idealization of independence. Desire for another marks his insufficiency, while desire for his own body or self marks his objecthood. In the latter case, Warner notes, "Self is an object to itself, even another self, rather than an experiential unity."[38] In other words, excessive narcissism threatens to imbricate Thoreau in a complex system of dependency. As possessor and possessed, he would no longer be free. Accordingly, he suppresses desire out of existence.

Thoreau's practice of suppression highlights his linguistic idealism—his belief in the influence of language use on perception. In *Nature* (1836),

Emerson claims, "The sensual man conforms thoughts to things; the poet conforms things to his thoughts."[39] Throughout *Walden*, Thoreau strives to attain the power of Emerson's poet. A belief in the power of language to restructure perception saturates the book. As Cavell argues, "writing [for Thoreau] is not a substitute for his life, but his way of prosecuting it."[40]

Thoreau's practice of receptivity and practice of suppression are not opposed—or even distinct. He learns to break out of the "the tyranny of egotistical self-enclosure" (to return to Cameron's definition of "self-reliance") by protecting himself from other tyrannies—persons, governments, his own desire. To see the world, Thoreau limits its influence on his life. He cultivates his vulnerability by ensuring his security.[41]

The intimacy between receptivity and suppression is evident in Thoreau's style. His prose reflects a commitment to minute observation and radical assimilation. A case in point: the "battle of ants" from "Brute Neighbors." As his description of the ants becomes increasingly detailed, it also becomes increasingly idiosyncratic:

> Looking farther, I was surprised to find that the chips were covered with such combatants, that it was not a *duellum*, but a *bellum*, a war between two races of ants, the red always pitted against the black, and frequently two red ones to one black. The legions of these Myrmidons covered all the hills and vales in my wood-yard, and the ground was already strewn with the dead and dying, both red and black. It was the only battle which I have ever witnessed, the only battle-field I ever trod while the battle was raging; internecine war; the red republicans on the one hand, and the black imperialists on the other. On every side they were engaged in deadly combat, yet without any noise that I could hear, and human soldiers never fought so resolutely. (228–29)

In the passage, Thoreau hones his perception of his environment by normativizing it. Eventually, the "battle of the ants" comes to resemble the Battle of Concord: "Why here every ant was a Buttrick,—'Fire! for God's sake fire!'—and thousands shared the fate of Davis and Hosmer" (230). "I was myself excited somewhat even as if they had been men," Thoreau declares; "The more you think of it, the less the difference" (230).

Later in the "battle," Thoreau actually domesticates the scene, literally bringing three ants into his house:

> I took up the chip on which the three I have particularly described were struggling, carried it into my house, and placed it under a tumbler on my window-sill, in order to see the issue. Holding a microscope to the first-mentioned red ant, I saw that, though he was assiduously gnawing at the near foreleg of his enemy, having severed his remaining feeler, his own breast was all torn away, exposing what vitals he had there to the

> jaws of the black warrior, whose breast-plate was apparently too thick for him to pierce; and the dark carbuncles of the sufferer's eyes shone with ferocity such as war only could excite. (230–31)

The scene exemplifies Kant's claim that the human is "the ultimate end of nature."[42] Thoreau is open to a world that caters to his openness. "You only need sit long enough in some attractive spot in the woods that all its inhabitants may exhibit themselves to you by turns," he writes (228). Things, here, conform to thoughts: Thoreau's dialectic of watching and writing generates a world subject to his control. "Nature is hard to overcome," he remarks in "Higher Laws, "but she must be overcome" (221).

At Walden and in *Walden*, Thoreau attempts to assimilate all the factors that limit his independence. In "Brute Neighbors," he attempts to assimilate nature itself. In the process, he mitigates his complicity in human violence. As he raises the "battle of the ants" to the level of an epic (or mock-epic), he reduces war (actual human war) to the level of the ants. His description of the battle concludes with the book's most explicit mention of contemporary politics: "The battle which I witnessed took place in the Presidency of Polk, five years before the passage of Webster's Fugitive-Slave Bill" (232). The mention minimizes the significance of the very contexts Thoreau aims to escape—Polk's imperialism, Webster's compromise. To put this point a different way: the identification of insect suffering and human suffering is an act of wish fulfillment. Ants and politicians represent extremes of intractability: our individual opinions rarely influence their behavior.[43] *Walden* changes that: the natural world and the world of high politics yield to the language of single individual—Thoreau himself.

This, I think, is what Thoreau learns at Walden and in *Walden*: how to create a utopia of one. The result may be temporary and maddeningly local, but it is significant nevertheless. Thoreau maximizes his independence by creating a world that is radically his own. In this world, there is little or no conflict between individual and collective interests because there is hardly any collective. And there is little or no conflict between Thoreau and his environment because *Walden* inhibits difference.

4

> *He is never speaking directly to us; he is speaking partly to himself and partly to something mystic beyond our sight.*
>
> —VIRGINIA WOOLF[44]

What is the relationship between Thoreau's *Walden* and our *Walden*? The book does not present a model we can follow. By imitating Thoreau's project we would contravene both his independence and our own. As his followers, we would distend his carefully tailored world, while assuming the nonsovereign position of dependents. To recreate Walden is to destroy it.

Is the book simply a record of a private project? Then why publish it? Satelmeyer suggests one answer. Thoreau's intentions for *Walden* changed during its composition:

> Thoreau conceived of his life at Walden at first as a kind of experimental community of one that could serve as a counter example not only to the unawakened among his townspeople but also to the false reforms and reformers of his age. [. . . But he] would develop the book as a whole along quite different lines, be less insistent upon addressing the outward condition of humanity, and come to regard his experience at Walden less as an example to misguided reformers and more as a personal quest involving doubt and uncertainty as well as discovery.[45]

As *Walden* developed, it became increasingly personal. But this fact only reinforces the question: Why publish the book?

One way to understand our role as readers might be to examine the role of Thoreau's friends and neighbors in the book. Do his relations with Therien (the Canadian woodchopper), Field, and Channing (his three most prominent interlocutors) illuminate his relation to his readers?

From its earliest drafts, the book forestalls what Walls calls "sympathy"—common feeling and mutual understanding between a "community's individual members." In "Visitors," Thoreau depicts Therien as alternately subhuman and superhuman:

> In him the animal man chiefly was developed. In physical endurance and contentment he was cousin to the pine and the rock. I asked him once if he was not sometimes tired at night, after working all day; and he answered, with a sincere and serious look, "Gorrappit, I never was tired in my life." But the intellectual and what is called spiritual man in him were slumbering as in an infant. . . . When Nature made him, she gave him a strong body and contentment for his portion, and propped him on every side with reverence and reliance, that he might live out his threescore years and ten a child. He was so genuine and unsophisticated that no introduction would serve to introduce him, more than if you introduced a woodchuck to your neighbor. (146–47)

The woodchopper is unknowable—like a pine or a rock or a woodchuck. (Thoreau never mentions his name—perhaps because our names mark our humanity.) Therien is outside Thoreau's sphere of influence—and vice versa. Thoreau's independence, as a result, is never threatened.

But Therien's role in *Walden* is not so simple. The woodchopper is also Thoreau's most conspicuously suppressed love interest in the book. In one passage, Therien holds a copy of the *Iliad*, while Thoreau translates over his shoulder. They focus on the line, "Why are you in tears, Patroclus, like a young girl?" to which Therien responds, "That's good" (144). The relationship illustrates what Warner, glossing Hegel, calls "possessive individualism."[46] Confronted by an insuppressible desire, Thoreau protects his independence by turning Therein into an object. Therien's nonhumanity allows him to be loved insofar as it allows him to be possessed.

Thoreau's relations with Field and Channing are disturbing in different ways. In the book's most explicitly pedagogical passage, Thoreau offers Field, a destitute Irish immigrant, a lesson on the benefits of simplicity:

> I tried to help him with my experience, telling him that he was one of my nearest neighbors, and that I too, who came a-fishing here, and looked like a loafer, was getting my living like himself; that I lived in a tight light and clean house, which hardly cost more than the annual rent of such a ruin as his commonly amounts to. (205)

This advice falls on deaf ears—a fact that does not surprise Thoreau: "For I purposely talked to him as if he were a philosopher, or desired to be one. . . . But alas! the culture of an Irishman is an enterprise to be undertaken with a sort of moral bog hoe" (205–6). Field's "inherited Irish poverty" (to quote Thoreau again) prevents his comprehension (209). The lesson, from the start, is less an intervention than an occasion for self-confirmation. There was never a chance for genuine interaction.

The scene with Channing is the most difficult to interpret. In "Brute Neighbors," it begins in medias res as a dialogue between a hermit and a poet. The poet intrudes on the hermit's meditation and invites him fishing. "Shall I go to heaven or a-fishing?" the hermit asks himself, before finally choosing the latter (224). The dialogue is riddled with references to Thoreau's idealization of independence—many of which are self-mocking. "Why will men worry themselves so?" the hermit asks. "He that does not eat need not work" (223). The scholarly consensus is that the dialogue represents a conversation between Thoreau (the hermit) and Channing (the poet). But their personalities are suppressed, and the prose is stilted and incongruous. This is the cost of meeting an equal at Walden: total depersonalization.[47]

Objectification and depersonalization: this is the fate of Thoreau's friends and neighbors in *Walden*. Could it be our fate as well? If so, the question remains, why publish the book?

One way to address this question would be to recall Deleuze and Guattari's account of aesthetic experience. We are not obliged to think of ourselves as individual readers tasked with delineating our relation to the experiences of the authors we read. Reading *Walden* could be different from reading Whitman's "Crossing Brooklyn Ferry" (1855), a poem that explicitly asks us to confirm its power. ("What I promis'd without mentioning it, have you not accepted?" Whitman asks us all individually.)[48] Virginia Woolf's description of *Walden*'s mode of address is, I think, correct. Thoreau, she writes, "is never speaking directly to us; he is speaking partly to himself and partly to something mystic beyond our sight." That "something" could be Emerson's Over-soul—a site of truth and collectivity. Or it could be normativity itself—the norms that govern our perception, behavior, and beliefs. Both readings suggest that Thoreau, in *Walden*, understands what Hegel and others make explicit: subjectivity is never autonomous. Physical independence is not the same as self-determination. Our understanding of the world and ourselves is inextricably social—even if we isolate ourselves from society.

This is why Thoreau locates Walden just one mile from Concord, and meets with but obscures his relations with Emerson (and his own mother, who did his laundry). This is also why he publishes *Walden*—and delivers a series of lectures about the book between 1845 and 1854. And this is why he *maximizes* his independence rather than simply establishing it. He must grapple with his imbrication in social life.

Language is the site of the book's most intense confrontation with sociality. As I suggested in section 3 of this chapter, Thoreau aims to inhabit the subject position of Emerson's poet. His goal is to identify world and word. Part of the challenge, of course, is that his words are not his own. As Cavell writes, "we have a choice over our words, but not over their meaning. Their meaning is in their language."[49] Every word refracts millennia of culture. Every sentence diffuses authority among a matrix of speakers and auditors—past, present, and future.[50] Mikhail Bakhtin's well-known claim makes the point: "Language is not a neutral medium that passes freely and easily into the private property of the speaker's intentions; it is populated—overpopulated—with the intentions of others."[51]

To augment his independence at Walden, Thoreau must manage the reception of *Walden*. To "win back . . . possession of our words" from a corrupt and corrupting culture, and from history itself (to quote Cavell again), he must maintain contact with the very thing he seeks to escape: us.[52] Readers confirm that his words have meaning, while his words prevent readers from violating his privacy—and from becoming dependents. (Thoreau, in this way, evades almost all forms of responsibility.) The book's inconsistency and banality, its beauty and brilliance, its offensiveness and integrity keep readers engaged, while keeping them at a distance. *Walden* wants and needs readers, but it does not want or need anything specific from you or from me.

It is tempting to argue that *Walden* represents an important event in literary history: the death of the reader.[53] The book does not treat readers as individuals. The personhood of only one person matters: Thoreau. But Roland Barthes's "The Death of the Author" (1967) already seems to understand the role of readers in *Walden*: "the unity of a text is not in its origin but in its destination, but this destination can no longer be personal: the reader is a man without history, without biography, without psychology; he is only that *someone* who holds collected into one and the same field all of the traces from which writing is constituted."[54] This is exactly the reader Thoreau envisions—a man without history, without biography, without psychology.[55] It would be misguided to ask whether such a reader learns anything at all.

5

> *If you're not familiar with* Walden, *to sum up: Thoreau, a nineteenth-century philosopher from Concord, Massachusetts, left town and built a shack next to Walden Pond where he lived for several years.* Walden *is a practical and philosophical guide to frugal living.*
>
> —KEN ILGUNAS[56]

If Thoreau did not want disciples, he failed. A few readers recognize his refusal of exemplarity. But most take him as a guide—despite the difficulty of doing so.[57]

Consider Ken Ilgunas, author of *Walden on Wheels* (2013), a book that began as a blog describing his experiences living in a van as a graduate student at Duke University. In one blog entry, titled "Thoreau's Disciple," he writes, "Thoreau extolled the virtues of voluntary poverty and the simple life. I, too, find something clean and healthy about spartan-living. Some of my finest moments have been spent alone in nature or traveling on hitchhikes." "*Walden*," he asserts, "is a practical and philosophical guide to frugal living."[58]

Reception histories of *Walden* testify to its influence—on American literature, but also on individuals, subcultures, and movements.[59] Lawrence Buell lists Thoreau's devotees:

> During one ten-year span from the mid-sixties through the mid-seventies . . . Thoreau was acclaimed as the first hippie by a nudist magazine, recommended as a model for disturbed teenagers, cited by the Viet Cong in broadcasts urging American GI's to desert, celebrated by environmental activists as "one of our first preservationists," and embraced by a contributor to the John Birch Society magazine as "our greatest reactionary."[60]

Buell is discussing Thoreau, not *Walden*, but the point stands—the book routinely fails to keep readers at a distance. Even those who do not attempt to recreate Thoreau's utopia remain certain of its pedagogical value. In their view, it is absurd to segregate *Walden* from "Resistance to Civil Government" (1849), "Slavery in Massachusetts" (1854), "A Plea for Captain John Brown" (1860), and other didactic essays.

Does this fact undermine my argument about the book's privacy and inimitability? How could so many readers be wrong? But how could so many readers be right? The aims of the Viet Cong and the John Birch Society are mutually exclusive. Could Thoreau be our "first hippie" and "our greatest reactionary"?

But one could also argue that Ilgunas is not a disciple at all. Thoreau does not teach him anything he does not already know. Instead, Thoreau confirms Ilgunas's view of the world, while validating his desire for authenticity. "When I read [*Walden*] for the first time years ago," Ilgunas writes, "it was one of those rare occasions when a book seemed to speak directly to my soul. Thoreau gave shape to some of my core beliefs that I, at that point, couldn't put into words."[61] For Ilgunas—and for many readers, myself included—this is what the book does: it articulates some of our core beliefs, and beautifully. But in this way, it is less a guide than a cliché. This is what clichés do: they help us live the lives we already know we want to live.[62]

Readers can learn many things from *Walden*. We can learn about American history and politics, and about the limit and cost of independence. We can learn about natural history, the depth of Walden Pond, and the value of careful, disciplined revision. But no matter how closely we look, we will not find "specific advice about ways in which [we] can achieve both microcosmic and macrocosmic fulfillment." Thoreau's own fulfillment depends on it.

Thoreau's utopia at Walden and in *Walden* is the first utopia of one I discuss in this book—and the most straightforward. On Independence Day, 1845, Thoreau moved to Walden to maximize his independence. He succeeded, creating a utopia of one to compensate for the utopia America had failed to be. The project fits my paradigm almost perfectly. As I wrote in the introduction, a writer responds to the failure of utopia by devising his or her own utopian project. The project is precarious. It risks solipsism at one extreme and mere critique at the other. Ultimately, its effects are asymmetrical and highly improbable: a perfect world that cannot be replicated or shared. This is the paradigm *Walden* represents, and the one I analyze throughout this book.

In chapter 2, on Du Bois, I identify a less straightforward utopia of one. Du Bois fits the paradigm—albeit uneasily. For the majority of his eighty-year writing career, he attempted to harmonize the individual and collective interests of the American public. His goal: racial equality. To achieve this goal, he wrote editorials and sociological papers, poems and stories, and personal narratives and revisionist histories. He did not retreat from the world—he engaged it, tenaciously. His writing was almost always pedagogical—designed to educate and inspire, and exemplify the potential of African American men and women. Yet at the end of his career, he adopted a different strategy—a strategy that led to a much more complicated relationship to his readers and, I believe, a utopia of one.

CHAPTER TWO

W.E.B. Du Bois's Hermeticism

1

On the eve of the March on Washington, on August 27, 1963, W.E.B. Du Bois died in Accra, Ghana. He was ninety-five. Roy Wilkins, executive secretary of the National Association for the Advancement of Colored People (NAACP), announced his death to the quarter-million men, women, and children gathered in the National Mall:

> Regardless of the fact that in his later years Dr. Du Bois chose another path, it is incontrovertible that at the dawn of the twentieth century his was the voice that was calling to you to gather here today in this cause. If you want to read something that applies to 1963 go back and get a volume of *The Souls of Black Folk* by Du Bois, published in 1903.[1]

The Souls of Black Folk did indeed anticipate the aims of the March on Washington—and the African American civil rights movement, more generally. "This, then, is the end of [the American Negro's] striving," Du Bois wrote in the book's opening chapter: "to be a co-worker in the kingdom of culture, to escape both death and isolation, to husband and use his best powers and his latent genius."[2] Sixty years later, Martin Luther King Jr. reaffirmed this vision of racial equality: "With this faith," he announced in "I Have a Dream" (1963), "we will be able to transform the jangling discords of our nation into a beautiful symphony of brotherhood."[3]

But what about Du Bois's "later years"? What does Wilkins mean by "another path"? The story will be familiar to Du Bois scholars. In 1948, Du Bois was fired from the NAACP, owing, in part, to his endorsement of Henry Wallace for president. (Wallace supported rapprochement with the Soviet Union.) In 1950, Du Bois completed *Russia and America: An Interpretation*, a passionate defense of Stalinism. (His publisher, Harcourt, Brace, rejected the book—and it remains unpublished.)[4] In 1951, he married the activist and Communist

Party member Shirley Graham (who became Shirley Graham Du Bois).[5] Later that year, he was indicted by the federal government as an "unregistered foreign agent" for his work with the Peace Information Center, an antiwar organization in New York. (He was acquitted after a five-day trial in November.) In 1955, he was refused a US passport to travel to Poland, and again, a year later, to travel to China. In 1958, after the Supreme Court, in *Dulles v. Kent*, voided a State Department policy denying passports to alleged communists, he traveled to Europe and the Soviet Union, and then, in 1959, to China, Ghana, and Nigeria. In 1961, he joined the US Communist Party and settled permanently in Ghana.[6] In 1963, he became a Ghanaian citizen—a decision that required him to give up his US citizenship. To Wilkins and others, Du Bois had abandoned the American dream at the moment King was revitalizing it.

What caused this change? Did Du Bois truly abandon the American dream? The development of Du Bois's thinking about race and politics has been well documented, especially by Du Bois himself.[7] Over his eighty-year writing career, he published almost 2,500 discrete items, including 4 autobiographies and 58 autobiographical essays. (He published his first article in 1883, when he was fifteen.) After his departure from the NAACP in 1948, he published more than 250 items, including his trilogy of novels, *The Black Flame* (1957, 1959, 1961), and his final autobiography, *The Autobiography of W.E.B. Du Bois: A Soliloquy on Viewing My Life from the Last Decade of Its First Century* (1962, 1968).[8] For Du Bois, writing about race and politics, and writing about his own life, were inextricably linked. As he argues in *Dusk of Dawn: An Essay toward an Autobiography of a Race Concept* (1940), "My life had its significance and its only deep significance because it was part of a Problem; but that problem was, as I continue to think, the central problem of the greatest of the world's democracies and so the Problem of the future world."[9]

What do these autobiographical texts reveal? For the vast majority of his career, Du Bois is both a pragmatist and a utopian—indeed, his pragmatism is an instrument of his utopianism.[10] In light of new evidence, he revises his tactics for achieving his ideal of racial equality. In "My Evolving Program for Negro Freedom" (1944), he divides his life into three overlapping phases. From 1885 to 1910, he addressed "the majority of white Americans" with "the assumption that once they realized the scientifically attested truth concerning Negros and race relations, they would take action to correct all wrong."[11] (His sociological studies represent this phase.) From 1900 to 1930, he addressed both white and black Americans, with the aim of showing how racism threatens democracy "not only for Negros but for whites; not only in America but in the world."[12] (Here, his work in the *Crisis* is representative.) From 1928 to 1944 (and after), he addressed black Americans with the aim of encouraging "*[s]cientific investigation and organized action . . . until the cultural development of America and the world is willing to recognize Negro freedom.*"[13] (*Phylon* at its founding is representative.)[14] For Du Bois, disappointment is an engine of innovation. When his tactics prove inadequate, he adopts a new approach to "the central problem of the greatest of the world's democracies."

Du Bois's pragmatism leads him to revise his conception of how to achieve racial equality. In *The Souls of Black Folk*, mutual understanding is key:

> And herein lies the tragedy of the age: not that men are poor,—all men know something of poverty; not that men are wicked,—who is good? not that men are ignorant,—what is Truth? Nay, but that men know so little of men.[15]

By *Darkwater* (1920), he is focused on economic issues:

> If the white workingmen of East St. Louis felt sure that Negro workers would not and could not take the bread and cake from their mouths, their race hatred would never have been translated into murder.[16]

This shift defines Du Bois's career after *Souls*, and eventually leads to his gradual rejection of liberalism and his embrace of socialism and, ultimately, communism.

In *Dusk of Dawn*, written at the end of the Great Depression, Du Bois criticizes the liberal policies of the NAACP:

> One thing, at any rate, was clear to me . . . continued agitation which had for its object simply free entrance into the present economy of the world, that looked at political rights as an end in itself rather than as a method of reorganizing the state; and that expected through civil rights and legal judgments to re-establish freedom on a broader and firmer basis, was not so much wrong as short-sighted.[17]

Later in *Dusk of Dawn*, Du Bois affirms his belief in economic determinism and praises the "miracle of Russia." But he stops short of endorsing communism. "I was not and am not a communist," he writes; "I do not believe in the dogma of inevitable revolution in order to right economic wrong."[18]

By *In Battle for Peace* (1952), Du Bois's criticism of liberalism is more virulent—and his praise of communism is more passionate. Efforts to end segregation, he argues, are not simply short-sighted, they are counterproductive:

> The very loosening of outer racial discriminatory pressures has not, as I had once believed, left Negros free to become a group cemented into a new cultural unity, capable of absorbing socialism, tolerance and democracy, and helping to lead America into a new heaven and new earth. But rather, partial emancipation is freeing some of them to ape the worst of American and Anglo-Saxon chauvinism, luxury, showing-off and "social climbing."[19]

Conspicuous consumption and "social climbing": this is the result of "partial emancipation" in America. In Du Bois's view, communism, and especially Soviet communism, is now the best model for achieving racial equality—"a new heaven and new earth." The Soviet Union, he concludes, is "the most hopeful nation on earth, not because of its theory, but because of what it has accomplished."[20]

In *Autobiography*, Du Bois's conversion is complete. American liberalism threatens the world:

> Today we are lying, stealing, and killing. We call all this by finer names: Advertising, Free Enterprise, and National Defense. But names in the end deceive no one; today we use science to help us deceive our fellows; we take wealth that we never earned and we are devoting all out energies to kill, maim and drive insane, men, women, and children who dare refuse to do what we want done. No nation threatens us. We threaten the world.[21]

In contrast, Soviet communism promises to save the world. In Du Bois's view, the Soviet Union supports anticolonialism, Pan-Africanism, and world revolution. It favors nuclear disarmament and centralized planning by an intellectual elite. It champions racial and gender equality, and secular education. It even promotes open, informed debate:

> Nowhere are public questions so thoroughly and exhaustively discussed. Russians sit and listen long to talks, lectures, expositions; they read books . . . not just picture books. Each problem of existence is discussed in village and factory. Comments, spoken and written, are welcomed, until every aspect, every opinion has been expressed and listened to, and the matter rises to higher echelons, and is discussed again. Gradually agreement is approached, until when the thrashed-out result reaches the All-Soviet height, there is usually but one opinion and decision. . . . This is a sifting of democracy which the West has lost.[22]

The Soviet Union, in other words, reflects Du Bois's own commitments—and, crucially, has the power to implement them. "I now state my conclusion frankly and clearly," he declares in *Autobiography*, "I believe in communism."

By the end of his long career, Du Bois had indeed abandoned the American dream. Wilkins was right. Future generations of Americans, Du Bois argues, must either begin again from scratch—"Our children must rebuild it"—or learn to tolerate injustice.[23] At his ninetieth birthday celebration, he addressed his speech to his two-month-old great-grandson, Arthur Edward McFarlane II. *Autobiography* includes an excerpt:

> You will find it the fashion in the America where eventually you will live and work to judge that life's work by the amount of money it brings you. This is a grave mistake. The return from your work must be the satisfaction which that work brings you and the world's need of that work. With this, life is heaven, or as near heaven as you can get.[24]

This is the best McFarlane can hope for in America: satisfying work.

Du Bois wrote *Autobiography* in 1958 and added a "postlude" a year later.[25] "[W]hen completed," Shirley Graham Du Bois recalls, "publishers in the United States would have none of it."[26] Harper and Brothers rejected it outright. Knopf asked for a rewrite. ("I urge you to give up the chronological form," Knopf's Angus Cameron wrote; "I know I ask a great deal, but it seems to me fitting that you should step into the present struggle with complete engagement.")[27] Du Bois even submitted chapters to academic journals, receiving rejections from the *Quarterly Journal of Economics* and the *Annals of the American Academy of Political and Social Science*, among others. (Only the *Massachusetts Review* accepted a chapter.)[28] In 1959, he sent the typescript to the Soviet Union. In 1962, after he had moved to Accra, *Autobiography* was published—in Russian translation—by the State Publishing House of Foreign Literature in Moscow.[29] In 1968, five years after his death, it was finally published in the United States—and in English—by International Publishers, a communist press in New York.

If *The Souls of Black Folk* was sixty years ahead of its time, one could argue that *Autobiography* was nine. By 1968, American audiences were finally ready to join Du Bois and reject American liberalism. (They remained skeptical of his valorization of Soviet communism—especially after the Warsaw Pact invasion of Czechoslovakia.) In a review of *Autobiography* for the *Saturday Review*, Gilbert Osofsky celebrates Du Bois as "a seer who sensed the future before most of his contemporaries were aware of the present."[30] In a review for the *New Republic*, Martin Duberman argues that "Du Bois prefigured by at least five years . . . the line of thought that has culminated in the philosophy of Black Power."[31] At the height of the Vietnam War, American liberalism was in crisis—and Du Bois was once again relevant.

In a speech commemorating Du Bois's centennial in 1968, King himself praised his intellectual forebear: "It is time to cease muting the fact that Dr. Du Bois was a genius and chose to be a Communist. Our irrational obsessive anti-communism has led us into too many quagmires to be retained as if it were a mode of scientific thinking."[32] The speech, delivered in the middle of King's Poor People's Campaign, celebrated Du Bois as a model for young African Americans. The "life style of Dr. Du Bois is the most important quality this generation of Negros needs to emulate," King argues. "He exemplified Black power in achievement and he organized Black power in action. It was no abstract slogan to him."[33] Du Bois, in this way, regained much of the status he had lost almost twenty years earlier.

2

This survey simplifies a long and complex life—and, more crucially for this chapter, obscures the difficulty and efficacy of *Autobiography*. In the book, Du Bois does more than document the development of his thinking about race and politics, and prefigure the "philosophy of Black Power"—he attempts to radically transform his life.

Autobiography is fundamentally different from Du Bois's earlier autobiographies. For example, it does not follow the template outlined in "My Evolving Program for Negro Freedom" and target a specific community of readers. Osofsky and Duberman argue that the book addresses the future—an American public (black and white) finally ready to hear the truth about liberalism and communism. The book's reception history indicates the "second world"—the Soviet Union and its socialist allies.[34] A typescript copy in the Du Bois Papers indicates the past—Du Bois dedicates a draft to "the Dead," naming his great-grandfather, grandfather, parents, first wife, and son and daughter, all of whom predeceased him.[35] The book's content corroborates all these scenarios. Du Bois includes speeches to his great-grandson and his fellow communists in Accra, Moscow, and Beijing, and he concludes the book with an apostrophe to the dead: "Suffer us not, Eternal Dead to stew in this Evil . . . Teach us, Forever Dead, there is no Dream but Deed, there is no Deed but Memory."[36]

Autobiography, in this way, addresses everyone and no one. Everyone because its address is universal: black and white Americans (past, present, and future), Soviet and Eastern Bloc workers, Chinese and Ghanaian revolutionaries, and Du Bois's family.[37] No one because its intended audience was not yet open to its message or no longer alive—or already convinced of its truth. Du Bois's few remaining supporters in the United States already endorsed his politics. Second-world communists already disapproved of American liberalism. At the moment of its composition and initial reception, *Autobiography* does not present a practical model for action. Du Bois is, at once, no longer and not yet relevant.

The book's content and form reflect (and exacerbate) this vexed relationship to audience. *Autobiography* opens with five chapters about Du Bois's travels after the Supreme Court decision in 1958. ("In the first paragraph he is literally escaping from the United States," observes Kenneth Mostern.)[38] Du Bois discusses his earlier autobiographies and autobiography as a genre, and then turns to politics. He celebrates the spread of communism to China and the suppression of the 1956 Hungarian uprising. He does not present reasoned, evidence-based arguments. His goal is not to persuade skeptics. ("It is hardly conceivable," writes James C. Hall, "that Du Bois is attempting any kind of seduction, or, less pejoratively, attempting to convince African-Americans of the necessity of joining the Communist Party U.S.A.")[39] "China is no utopia," he sardonically claims; "Fifth Avenue has better shops where the rich can buy and the whores parade." Defending the invasion of Tibet, he simply asserts, "The truth is there and I saw it."[40]

These five chapters lead to an interlude. "*I believe in communism*," Du Bois announces in italics:

> *I mean by communism, a planned way of life in the production of wealth and work designed for building a state whose object is the highest welfare of its people and not merely the profit of a part.*[41]

"*Who now am I to have come to these conclusions?*" he asks. "*This is the excuse for this writing which I call a Soliloquy.*"[42] Over the next nineteen chapters (including the postlude), he narrates his life up to his ninety-first year—ostensibly to justify his conversion to communism.

Most of this narrative, however, is taken, almost verbatim, from Du Bois's earlier autobiographies. "[S]ome two hundred pages are drawn from *Dusk of Dawn*," notes Nathan Huggins; "the account of the trial and acquittal comes from *In Battle for Peace*. . . ; and the Postlude chapter is taken from 'A Vista of Ninety Fruitful Years' in the *National Guardian*."[43] Much of the remaining material comes from *The Souls of Black Folk* and *Darkwater*. Chapter 6, for example, revises the opening of *Darkwater*, written forty years earlier: "I was born by a golden river and in the shadow of two great hills, five years after the Emancipation Proclamation, which began the freeing of American Negro slaves."[44] Only the final clause is new. (In *Darkwater*, the sentence ends after "Proclamation.")[45] What is the significance of this revision? Is Du Bois reminding us that the project of emancipation is still incomplete?

Other revisions are even more perplexing. For example, Du Bois makes subtle changes to his account from *Dusk of Dawn* of his life as a student at Harvard in the late nineteenth century. In *Dusk*, he writes:

> Something of a certain inferiority complex was possibly present: I was desperately afraid of not being wanted; of intruding without invitations; of appearing to desire the company of those who had no desire for me. I should have been pleased if most of my fellow students had desired to associate with me; if I had been popular and envied. But the absence of this made me neither unhappy nor morose. I had my "island within" and it was a fair country.[46]

In *Autobiography*, he ever so slightly revises the passage—I have marked the revisions:

> Something of a certain inferiority complex was possibly ~~present:~~ *a cause of this*. I was desperately afraid of ~~being~~ *intruding where I was* not wanted; ~~of intruding~~ *appearing* without invitations; of ~~appearing to~~ *showing a* desire *for* the company of those who had no desire for me. I should *in fact* have been pleased if most of my fellow students had ~~desired~~ *wanted* to associate with me; if I had been popular and envied. But the absence of this made me neither unhappy nor morose. I had my "island within" and it was a fair country.[47]

Why not simply replicate his earlier account? (Du Bois published the second, revised version of the chapter in the *Massachusetts Review* in 1960—but omitted this specific passage.) Is the revised passage clearer, or more concise or eloquent? I don't think so. Is Du Bois revising the story of his life to better justify his conversion to communism? I cannot find any evidence to support this claim. The import of the two passages is identical. Indeed, *Autobiography* seems disconnected from Du Bois's announcement in the interlude—perhaps because most of the book was written decades before the conversion described in the interlude took place.

Autobiography also replicates the plotting of the earlier autobiographies. Du Bois discusses his childhood and education at Fisk, Harvard, and Humboldt Universities; his sociological studies at Atlanta University and the University of Pennsylvania; his disagreement with Booker T. Washington; the Niagara Movement and the *Crisis*; his Pan-Africanism and Marxism; his disagreements with the NAACP and eventual resignation; his return to Atlanta University and his forced retirement; his return to the NAACP and dismissal; his peace activism; and his trial and acquittal. Following the model of the earlier autobiographies, he does not discuss the composition or reception of his major books—*The Souls of Black Folk* and *Black Reconstruction* (1935). He rarely mentions his family, his disagreements with Marcus Garvey, or his connection to the Harlem Renaissance. *Autobiography* adds plot points to Du Bois's life story—but does not alter the earlier ones.

The only entirely new material in *Autobiography* is the initial five chapters, the interlude, and chapter 16, "My Character," which includes a comparatively candid account of Du Bois's personal life—his finances, his sexuality, and his fifty-three-year marriage to his first wife, Nina Gomer.[48] The chapter's main concern, however, is his consistency. Du Bois describes various threats to his character (lust, greed, envy) and how he survives them (austerity, compunction, generosity). As Keith Byerman notes, "the Du Bois recreated in this chapter does not fundamentally change from childhood to old age."[49] This is surprising, considering Du Bois's obsession with his own development—and his earlier commitment to process, contingency, and change.

This consistency defines *Autobiography* as a whole. Arnold Rampersad laments the "sameness" of Du Bois's late writing.[50] Irving Howe claims that parts of the book "read as if they came from the very heart of a mimeograph machine."[51] Mostern describes the book as "theological": "the socialist political argument in *Dusk of Dawn* is sociological," he writes; "the Communist political argument in *Autobiography* is theological."[52] (Theological arguments, in Mostern's view, are nonempirical, even anti-empirical arguments.) Du Bois supplies his own metaphor in the book's title, "soliloquy," which Jodi Melamed glosses as "nondialogic discourse from the self to the self" and as a performance of "intimate self-revelation."[53] Together, these readings highlight the same fact: *Autobiography* is not only consistent, it is hermetic.

Indeed, the book is hermetic in two seemingly incompatible ways. First, it omits evidence that would undermine Du Bois's worldview—he unwaveringly maintains his optimism in communism and the Soviet Union. Second, the book replicates the receptivity of Du Bois's earlier autobiographies by literally replicating his earlier autobiographies. *Autobiography*, in this way, excludes differences of opinion and differences of identity—even when Du Bois is disagreeing with himself.

Cold War blacklisting, then, is not the only way to explain *Autobiography's* initial reception in the United States. Cameron's rejection of the book is a case in point. In many ways, Cameron was Du Bois's ideal reader. In 1951, he was blacklisted for his communist sympathies and forced to resign as editor in chief of Little, Brown. In 1958, he chaired Du Bois's ninetieth birthday celebration, where Du Bois addressed his two-month-old great-grandson. In 1959, Cameron was hired as a senior editor at Knopf. (The event marked the decline of McCarthyism.) When he asked Du Bois (in the letter quoted earlier in this chapter) to "step into the present struggle with complete engagement," he was asking for more politics, not less. He wanted to promote Du Bois as a model. "[T]he time is at hand," he writes in the same letter, "when a hip and thigh smiting book which forces everyone to see what you see, know what you know, suspect what you suspect, should be written." "I believe such a book," he adds, "could overthrow the convenient isolation so many think they have provided for you and which, in some ways, they have succeeded in doing."[54] For Cameron, *Autobiography*, as it was written, only reinforced Du Bois's isolation.

3

Du Bois was an old man when he began *Autobiography* in 1958. He was traveling constantly. He had just completed *The Black Flame*, the most ambitious creative project of his career. Is it any surprise that he recycled his earlier autobiographies and embraced Soviet cant? He must have been exhausted and unable to write a compelling new book.

Yet by most accounts, Du Bois was vibrant and lucid until at least the year before his death.[55] David Levering Lewis describes a meeting between the ninety-one-year-old Du Bois and Mao in Beijing in 1959:

> [W]hen the Chairman presumed to explain at some length the "diseased psychology" affecting the American Negro, Du Bois interjected to say that Negroes and the working people of his country were not afflicted by a psychological condition but by their lack of income, an observation that led Mao and Du Bois to debate the primacy of economics and psychology among evolving groups.[56]

Debating economics and psychology with Mao! This is not a sign of decrepitude. A few months after the meeting, according to Lewis, Du Bois vacationed in the Virgin Islands, where he "took high dives from the hotel diving board and swam across the lagoon."[57] From this perspective, *The Black Flame* does not mark the beginning of Du Bois's decline. It is evidence of his endurance.

Howe points to one danger of dismissing the elderly Du Bois: "precisely the sort of condescension he had always scorned."[58] In a review of *Autobiography*, Howe attempts to understand Du Bois's Stalinism:

> Du Bois suffered every defeat and humiliation of his people, and he kept changing his views because none seemed able to gain for American Negroes what should simply have been their birthright. Is it not entirely understandable, therefore, that in his ultimate despair he should have turned to the ideology of Stalinism? That he should have ignored its repressions and murders, so long as it seemed to champion the rights of black men? What is surprising is not that Du Bois turned toward a totalitarian outlook but that so few Negroes joined him.[59]

For Howe, this explanation does not excuse Du Bois's politics: "After all, there were other Negro leaders, equally militant, who found it possible to fight against Jim Crow in America without becoming apologists for dictatorship in Europe and Asia."[60] "Better to fight it out," Howe argues, "than 'make allowances.'" Howe thus approaches *Autobiography* by reestablishing a debate that Du Bois attempts to transcend. As I mentioned in my earlier survey of Du Bois's career, *Autobiography* does not try to persuade skeptics or even provide evidence for its claims.

Melamed adopts a different approach. In her view, the book is an "oppositional practice" that decouples Du Bois's "life story" from narratives of American exceptionalism:

> Rather than reading here a dogmatic pledge of allegiance to the Soviet Union, I contend that if we situate these lines within the geopolitics of blackness as a global symbol during the era of decolonization, then we can read them to be a rhetorically, politically, and theoretically sophisticated attempt by Du Bois to re-fashion his life story as a countersymbol that might rupture American exceptionalist representations of African American racial formation as a symbol for the probity of US-led global capitalism.[61]

This link between "representations of African American racial formation" and American power is long-standing. (In the preface to *Narrative of the Life of Frederick Douglass* (1845), for example, William Lloyd Garrison links Douglass's freedom to the freedom of America's "Pilgrim fathers" and "revolutionary sires.")[62] According to Melamed, *Autobiography* refuses to participate in this tradition and, as a result, memorializes what she calls "the negative history of race in the development of capitalism."[63]

Kate Baldwin goes further than Melamed. *Autobiography*, she suggests, is wholly oppositional. Du Bois violates "expectations for originality and newness"; manipulates "sites of overlap, contradiction, and/or emptiness"; and rejects "the authority conventionally appointed the author."[64] The result: a book that "demonstrates how a disarticulation of continuity—that is, a breakdown in signification; a failure—presents a condition of possibility."[65] In this reading, *Autobiography* is an avant-garde provocation—an attempt to alert readers that the status quo is neither acceptable nor inevitable.

Are these approaches convincing? Howe confronts the book's politics but refuses to respect its hermeticism—its resistance to debate. Melamed and Baldwin, in contrast, respect the book's hermeticism but refuse to confront its politics.[66] For them, *Autobiography* rejects American liberalism but does not truly endorse Soviet communism.

Is there a way to approach *Autobiography* that avoids these pitfalls, that recognizes the book's hermeticism without excusing its politics? One way to avoid these pitfalls might be to ask what Du Bois himself gained by writing the book.[67] As Peter Shaw remarks in a review of *Autobiography*, "what is useful to the author may not coincide with what is useful for the reader."[68] For Du Bois, writing was a way of life—and a way to remain alive. "[T]he novelty of Du Bois's place in the black tradition," argues Henry Louis Gates Jr., "is that he wrote himself to . . . power, rather than spoke himself to power."[69] Perhaps *Autobiography* represents an attempt to augment and conserve that power?

But there is, I think, a much more specific way to describe the book's value for Du Bois. *Autobiography* should be read as an attempt to resolve a contradiction at the heart of his career—a contradiction between two conceptions of freedom and, ultimately, between pragmatism and utopianism. The first conception of freedom, derived from William James, defined Du Bois's sociological research. "Sociology," he writes in "The Atlanta Conferences" (1904), "is the science that seeks to measure the limits of chance in human action, or if you will excuse the paradox, it is the science of free will."[70] Freedom, here, is a synonym for chance. "Indeterminate future volitions *do* mean chance," James argues in "The Dilemma of Determinism" (1894): "Let us not fear to shout it from the house-tops if need be; for we now know that the idea of chance is, at bottom, exactly the same thing as the idea of gift."[71]

The second conception of freedom, derived from Marx, defined Du Bois's political activism. "By 'Freedom' for Negroes," he writes in "My Evolving Program for Negro Freedom," "I meant and still mean, *full economic, political and social equality with American citizens*."[72] Freedom, here, is a synonym for equality—specifically, equality as imagined in the *Manifesto of the Communist Party* (1848). "In place of the old bourgeois society, with its classes and class antagonisms," Marx and Engels write, "we shall have an association, in which the free development of each is the condition for the free development of all."[73]

At first glance, these two conceptions of freedom seem compatible. Du Bois can be a Jamesian and a historical materialist.[74] He can valorize chance and combat the class antagonisms that promote racism. But upon closer examination, the two are mutually exclusive. For orthodox Marxists—or at least a specific tradition of orthodox Marxists—necessity is the guarantor of freedom, not its opposite. As Engels argues in *Anti-Dühring* (1887), "Freedom does not consist in any dreamt-of independence from natural laws, but in the knowledge of these laws, and in the possibility this gives of systematically making them work towards definite ends."[75] Indeed, it is this knowledge that allows Marx and Engels to maintain their utopianism, and to promise readers of the *Manifesto* that the "fall [of the bourgeoisie] and the victory of the proletariat are equally inevitable."[76]

In an exchange with Herbert Aptheker in 1956, Du Bois confronts the incompatibility of these two conceptions of freedom. (Aptheker was Du Bois's literary executor. In 1955, he published *History and Reality*, a collection of essays defending historical materialism.) When "I finished reading your 'History and Reality,'" Du Bois writes, "I was not certain of your attitude or how far [historical] materialism agreed with my formulation [of pragmatism]. A second reading reassured me somewhat."[77] Aptheker, in response, demurred: "I do not think, as you appear to say . . . that the power of mankind to better human conditions is ensconced within the control of chance rather than law."[78] The discussion ends there. Their next exchange focuses on *The Black Flame*, which Aptheker was editing for an imprint of New Century Publishers.

This is my hypothesis—and, ultimately, my argument: In *Autobiography*, Du Bois resolves the contradiction by abandoning the first conception of freedom and embracing the second. His aim is not merely to disavow pragmatism—or link pragmatism and liberalism. (Rampersad correctly notes that Du Bois's later work rejects "the accoutrements of liberal pragmatism.")[79] His aim is to maintain his utopianism by discovering freedom in necessity. This is the real significance of the book's hermeticism: by rewriting and synthesizing his earlier autobiographies, he learns to freely inhabit the events that determined his life, including his own descriptions of those events. (Hence his rewriting of the passage from *Dusk of Dawn* about his life as a student at Harvard in the late nineteenth century.) The book's hermeticism and politics are not distinct—they are a means and an end. *Autobiography* is an exercise in historical materialism.

Why is this "exercise" necessary? There is a difference between endorsing historical materialism as a theory and living as a historical materialist. The former requires accepting certain propositions: for example, that "the mode of production of a society" determines "its ideas and theories"—to quote Stalin's *Dialectical and Historical Materialism* (1938).[80] The latter, in contrast, requires accepting a counterintuitive account of one's own agency in the world. In this counterintuitive account, one's interests are not one's own—they reflect one's class position. The future is not open to chance—it obeys specific laws. As Stalin asserts, "the connection and interdependence of the phenomena of social life are laws of the development of society, and not something accidental."[81] To coordinate these third- and first-person perspectives is a challenge—although not an unhappy one: Du Bois must learn to live with the knowledge that world revolution is inevitable, but that he as a particular person (with a rich and complex interior life, and specific desires) is superfluous.

In *History and Reality*, Aptheker cites a well-known letter from Engels that discusses the relative unimportance of particular people in history:

> That Napoleon, this particular Corsican, was the military dictator rendered necessary by a French Republic bled white by her own wars, was fortuitous; but that, in the absence of Napoleon, someone else would have taken his place is proved by the fact that the moment someone becomes necessary—Caesar, Augustus, Cromwell, etc.—he invariably turns up. If it was Marx who discovered the materialist view of history, the work of Thierry, Mignett[,] Guizot, and every English historiographer prior to 1850 goes to show that efforts were being made in that direction, while the discovery of the same view by Morgan shows that the time was ripe for it and that it was *bound* to be discovered.[82]

To apply this extraordinarily counterintuitive theory to Du Bois's own life, if a particular man named William Edward Burghardt Du Bois had not been born in Great Barrington, Massachusetts, in 1868, someone else would have "turned up" to oppose the policies of Booker T. Washington, contribute to the development of sociology as an academic discipline, propose an influential account of double consciousness, establish the NAACP, edit the *Crisis*, fight for the inclusion of black officers in World War I, write one of the most important revisionist histories of Reconstruction, and so on.[83]

Does Du Bois's exercise succeed? I think it does. He commits to a conception of freedom as equality and, in the process, commits to a radically attenuated conception of his own freedom. The book's hermeticism trains him to accept—even be grateful for—his determination. Or to be more precise, the book's hermeticism trains him to recognize his determination as freedom—freedom to be on the right side of history, freedom to think structurally, freedom to purge himself of an inflated sense of his own agency.

(I am wary of overpsychologizing, but this conception of freedom must have been consoling to Du Bois at the end of his life. Early in life, one might benefit from an inflated sense of agency: it can be empowering and life-sustaining. There is time to change the world. Late in life, however, one might want to minimize one's agency and cultivate one's faith in the inevitable.)

The exercise has ancillary benefits. For example, it offers Du Bois a greater understanding of his own life. In the book's opening chapter, he writes:

> Who and what is this I, which in the last year looked on a torn world and tried to judge it? Prejudiced I certainly am by my twisted life; by the way in which I have been treated by my fellows; by what I myself have thought and done. I have passed through changes by reason of my growth and willing; by my surroundings without; by knowledge and ignorance. What I think of myself, now and in the past, furnishes no certain document proving what I really am.[84]

Autobiography provided that "certain document." By rewriting and synthesizing his earlier autobiographies, Du Bois was able to reassess the impact of his "growth and willing," his "surroundings," and his "knowledge and ignorance." Chapter 16, "My Character," which I discussed in section 2 in this chapter, reflects this assessment. Du Bois's affirmation of his consistency in the chapter is not an affirmation of his freedom from social and historical reality but rather an affirmation of his ability to respond rationally to social and historical reality—to the challenges of a life lived between the ratification of the Fourteenth Amendment and the end of Jim Crow.

The book thus remains faithful to one aspect of Du Bois's career: the pursuit of self-knowledge. The pursuit predates *The Souls of Black Folk* and connects all the autobiographies. It even motivates Du Bois's fiction. In *The Black Flame*, for example, he reexamines his life by dividing it among three characters—James Burghardt, Jean Du Bignon, and Manuel Mansart. Du Bois then tracks how these characters respond to a series of historical events. If *Autobiography* is an exercise in historical materialism, *The Black Flame* is (like much fiction) an experiment in scientific modeling.

Self-knowledge is a way to advance the revolution and abide in advance of the revolution. "Freedom of the will," argues Engels in *Anti-Dühring*, "means nothing but the capacity to make decisions with knowledge of the subject."[85] (Aptheker quotes this exact line in *History and Reality*.)[86] But a few sentences later, Engels notes that "talk of real human freedom" is impossible in a society with "class distinctions" and "anxiety over the means of subsistence."[87] In response to this impasse, Du Bois embraces his freedom to know as he prepares to live in a world that is truly free.

Autobiography has no single precedent. Du Bois draws from various genres to invent his own. Autobiography is relevant, of course—from Rousseau to Adams. ("[T]he original sin of autobiography," writes Georges Gusdorf, is "logical coherence and rationalization.")[88] African American autobiography is especially relevant—from Douglass to Washington to Du Bois himself. (Paul Gilroy traces how African American autobiography became "an act or process of simultaneous self-creation and self-emancipation.")[89] Finally, socialist realism is relevant. As Katerina Clark writes in *The Soviet Novel* (1981): "[T]he master plot personalizes the general processes outlined in Marxist-Leninist historiography by encoding them in biographical terms: the positive hero passes in stages from a state of relative 'spontaneity' to a higher degree of 'consciousness,' which he attains by some individual revolution."[90] Du Bois is that positive hero. His shift from pragmatism to historical materialism is a shift from "spontaneity" (actions not guided by an awareness of historical necessity) to "consciousness" (actions guided by awareness of historical necessity). By joining the Communist Party in 1961, he announces the outcome of his individual revolution.

Although *Autobiography*'s hermeticism might frustrate readers and fail to adequately justify Du Bois's conversion to communism, it makes that conversion possible. The book allows him to preserve his utopianism, purge himself of pragmatism, and become the person he wants to be.

4

In 1958, the year Du Bois began to write *Autobiography*, the writer and activist Truman Nelson published "W.E.B. DuBois: Prophet in Limbo" in the *Nation*. "DuBois has been rewarded as this country nearly always rewards its prophets," Nelson declares; "He was arrested—as Thoreau was arrested."[91]

The analogy is illuminating. Both Thoreau and Du Bois were arrested for acts of civil disobedience. Both devoted their lives to writing. Both ostracized their readers. Both created utopias of one in response to America's failure to realize its own utopian ideals.

The analogy points toward a disconcerting conclusion. Utopias of one might not be an alternative to American liberalism or even an escape from it. They might be a symptom. Indeed, utopias of one might correspond to the "privatopias" David Harvey deplores in *Spaces of Hope* (2000). (Harvey's examples are Baltimore's suburban homes and gated communities.)[92] An ideal life in an unjust world—this might be what America has to offer.

But the analogy also obscures important differences between the two writers—most significantly, the effects of white privilege. For Thoreau, exemplarity is a given: he automatically speaks to and for readers, and for humanity itself. *Walden* is an attempt to inhibit his exemplarity—and thus his complicity. For Du Bois, in contrast, exemplarity is never a real possibility. (The forced exemplarity of African Americans under Jim Crow is not exemplarity at all: it applies only to African Americans and is damaged by double consciousness.) Complicity is rarely a concern.[93] Du Bois's career is defined by a series of ill-fated attempts to speak to and for readers.[94] *Autobiography* adopts a radically different strategy: the book addresses everyone and no one, but its true audience is Du Bois alone.

This difference between the two writers illuminates another. Thoreau's utopia of one is nonmimetic, logically inimitable. Du Bois's utopia is imitable. In principle, we could all become historical materialists. Yet it is worth asking: Does the book actually help us become historical materialists? Does it present a practical model for remaking our lives? My answer to these questions is no. Du Bois's commitment to the Communist Party might be a commitment to community, but his exercise in historical materialism is singular and specific. As *Autobiography* fails to create an ideal community devoted to Stalinism, it creates a utopia of one.

In part 2, I examine Du Bois's Stalinism in a different context: the Soviet Union. Chapter 3 is a reminder that the United States is not the only country that arrests its prophets. In 1934, the Russian poet, Osip Mandel'shtam, was arrested for performing a poem critical of Stalin.

PART II

The Soviet Union

CHAPTER THREE

Osip and Nadezhda Mandel'shtam's Utopian Anti-Utopianism

1

Du Bois first visited the Soviet Union in 1926, two years before the beginning of Stalin's first five-year plan—a period of rapid industrialization and forced collectivization. One of the most well-known achievements of this plan was the construction of a canal to link the White and Baltic Seas in northern Russia. Built between 1931 and 1933, the White Sea–Baltic Canal involved the labor of approximately 150,000 criminal and political prisoners, and the relocation of nearly 4,000 peasants.[1] Historians estimate that 25,000 prisoners died during its construction.[2] Once operational, it served as a transportation route for timber, coal, and other materials from the Far North.

The canal quickly became a fixture in Soviet propaganda. In August 1933, two months after its completion, Maksim Gor'kii organized a tour for 120 writers from the newly formed Writers' Union. In January 1934, a six-hundred-page book appeared, *The White Sea-Baltic Canal in the Name of Stalin*, collecting collaboratively written contributions from thirty-five of these writers, including Viktor Shklovskii, Aleksei Tolstoi, and Mikhail Zoshchenko—"almost all the best of Soviet literature and criticism," according to Nikita Struve.[3] (That same year, Du Bois resigned from the NAACP over disagreements about segregation.) The book celebrates the canal's grandeur, and economic and moral significance, while promoting a new form of collective authorship.[4] One section begins, "[the canal] is one of the most dazzling victories of the collective organization of people over the harsh, elemental nature of the north. At the same time, it has successfully transformed former enemies of the dictatorship of the proletariat and the Soviet public into qualified

Изменяя природу, человек изменяет самого себя

(К. Маркс)

FIG. 3.1 Photograph of a woman with a jackhammer

members of the working class."[5] A photograph of a female prisoner with a jackhammer, possibly by Aleksandr Rodchenko, has the caption, adapted from Marx, "Changing nature, man changes himself."[6]

The canal and propaganda campaign exemplify the two goals of Soviet utopianism: to harmonize individual interests under a single authority (the

Communist Party) and remake individuals into ideal Soviet subjects (the Soviet New Man). These goals affected nearly every aspect of life in the Soviet Union during the early Stalinist period. As the historian Jochen Hellbeck writes, "individuals were expected to refashion their very selves, by enacting revolutions of their souls, paralleling the revolutions of the social and political landscape."[7] In autobiographies and diaries, Soviet citizens recorded how they "*made* the Revolution, *constructed* a factory, *built* the Metro, and so on, and at the same time, how they themselves *were made* by the Revolution and how they *were forged* as subjects in the course of the Stalinist industrialization drive."[8] The female prisoner with the jackhammer represented a mass project in which every person was supposed to perfect his or her self by perfecting the state.

2

> *But there is always the drop that fills the cup to overflowing. By 1933 we had made great progress in our understanding of what was going on. Stalinism had shown its colors in one large-scale undertaking—the mass deportation of the peasants, and in the lesser one of bringing the writers to heel.*
>
> —NADEZHDA MANDEL'SHTAM[9]

Disgust for the White Sea–Baltic Canal—and for Gor'kii and his collaborators—may have been the specific "drop" that caused Osip Mandel'shtam to compose and perform the Stalin epigram.[10] For the poet, the canal was not simply a construction project that cost thousands of lives but a testament to the immorality of Soviet utopianism as an idea. The use of prison labor was wrong; the forced relocation of peasants was wrong; and the attempt to unify the interests of artists and the state was wrong. In his essay "Fourth Prose" (1931), Mandel'shtam declares, "I divide all of world literature into authorized and unauthorized works. The former are all trash; the latter—stolen air. I want to spit in the face of every writer who first obtains permission and then writes. I want to beat such writers over the head with a stick."[11]

This, in brief, is the story of the epigram's performance and its aftermath. In November 1933, Mandel'shtam composed and performed a short poem (quoted in full below) for his friends and neighbors that criticized Stalin. In May 1934, Mandel'shtam was arrested, interrogated, and found guilty of counterrevolutionary activity. To his surprise, he was sentenced to three years in exile rather than forced labor or death. Stalin had issued an order to "isolate, but preserve." The poet was sent to Cherdyn, a town in the northern Urals, and then allowed to move to Voronezh, a small city in southwest Russia.[12] In 1937, after three years of forced unemployment and near-starvation, he was permitted to return to Moscow. He was rearrested in May 1938, again for counterrevolutionary activity. In December 1938, he died in a Gulag transit camp at the age of forty-seven. His widow, Nadezhda Mandel'shtam, shared his exile in Cherdyn and Voronezh, and their experiences are the subject of her influential memoirs.

Seamus Heaney has described Mandel'shtam's performance in this way: "David had faced Goliath with eight stony couplets in his sling."[13] The analogy seems misguided—David did not die in a prison camp as Goliath terrorized his imagined rivals—until one realizes that, for Heaney, Mandel'shtam triumphed over Stalin because the epigram caused Mandel'shtam's death and by causing his death, vindicated his account of Stalin's cruelty. The epigram, in other words, not only outlasted Stalin and Stalinism, it confirmed Stalin's guilt. "[T]he death of an artist should not be excluded from the chain of his creative achievements, but should be viewed as its final, closing link."[14] This sentence, from Mandel'shtam's "Pushkin and Skriabin" (1915–20), anticipates Heaney's perspective almost perfectly: Mandel'shtam's death was a creative act that defeated Stalin by transforming a man into a martyr.

This view of the epigram has helped canonize Mandel'shtam inside and outside Russia. In addition to Heaney, the epigram's non-Russian commentators alone include Robert Alter, Isaiah Berlin, Bruce Chatwin, J. M. Coetzee, Guy Davenport, Wai Chee Dimock, Robert Littell, Czesław Miłosz, Jose Manuel Prieto, Adrienne Rich, Salman Rushdie, George Steiner, and Susan Stewart.[15] For most of these commentators, Mandel'shtam's triumph is a triumph for poetry—evidence for Shelley's claim that "poets are the unacknowledged legislators of the world."[16] ("Poetic legislation thus trumps the murderous official variety," Clare Cavanagh declares.)[17] Today, the epigram is a touchstone for a tradition of world literature, and especially Nobel-worthy world literature: daring acts of witness and resistance that promote liberal values—free expression, mutual understanding, and universal human rights.

Here is the Stalin epigram, followed by my literal prose translation:

Мы живем, под собою не чуя страны,
Наши речи за десять шагов не слышны,
А где хватит на полразговорца,
Там припомнят кремлевского горца.
Его толстые пальцы, как черви, жирны,
А слова, как пудовые гири, верны,
Тараканьи смеются усища
И сияют его голенища.

А вокруг него сброд тонкошеих вождей,
Он играет услугами полулюдей.
Кто свистит, кто мяучит, кто хнычет,
Он один лишь бабачит и тычет,
Как подкову, кует за указом указ:
Кому в пах, кому в лоб, кому в бровь, кому в глаз.

Что ни казнь у него—то малина,
И широкая грудь осетина.

ноябрь 1933[18]

[We live, not sensing the country beneath us, / our speeches are not audible ten steps away, / but where there's enough for half a conversation, / we commemorate the Kremlin highlander. / His fat, greasy fingers like worms, / his words true as thirty-six-pound weights, / His cockroach mustache laughs / and his boot-tops shine. // And with a rabble of thin-necked chiefs around him, / he plays with the services of half-men. / Some whistle, some meow, some whimper, / he alone babbles and prods. / He forges decree after decree like horseshoes: / one gets it in the groin, one in the head, one in the brow, one in the eye. / His every execution—a raspberry / and the broad chest of the Ossetian. // November 1933]

How does the poem achieve its transformative effects? Primarily by not being a poem at all. A Russian version of my prose translation would have ensured Mandel'shtam's arrest and martyrdom just as effectively as the lineated, rhyming original.[19]

What is the Stalin epigram then, if not simply a poem? It is an act of civil disobedience and a test. About twenty people heard the epigram before Mandel'shtam's arrest, including Shklovskii, Anna Akhmatova, and Boris Pasternak. The epigram tested their convictions as it demonstrated Mandel'shtam's own. It was an invitation to join in protest or report the poet to the authorities. (At least one person did the latter.) The epigram, in this way, highlighted each individual's complicity in the Soviet regime and called on him or her to do something about it. Indeed, it forced the matter: after hearing the epigram, auditors were implicated in its message. They had to choose sides, for they would have been punished for remaining silent—a fact Pasternak recognized immediately. "What you have read me has nothing to do with literature, with poetry," he proclaimed. "It is . . . an act of suicide, which I do not accept and in which I do not want to participate. You have not read me anything, I have not heard anything, and I ask you not to read it to anyone else."[20]

At the same time, the epigram was also a test of poetry. In her memoirs, Nadezhda Mandel'shtam writes, "In choosing his manner of death, M. was counting on one remarkable feature of our leaders: their boundless, almost superstitious respect for poetry. 'Why do you complain?' M. used to ask. 'Poetry is respected only in this country—people are killed for it. There's no place where more people are killed for it.'"[21] The epigram tested the validity of this claim: Would Mandel'shtam's speech be audible ten steps away?[22] The irony is obvious: as a test for poetry, the epigram did not rely on the features that made it a poem, save one—that it was written by a poet.

But the Stalin epigram is also a poem, of course. Its sonic and semantic complexity cannot be captured in paraphrase (or translation). The rhyme that links "верны" (the true) with "жирны" (greasy) lampoons Soviet morality. The syllable-rhyme linking "*пол*разговорца" (half-conversation) with "*гол*енища" (boot-tops) and "*пол*улюдей" (half-men) creates a sound pattern that unifies the poem as a whole. The neologism "бабачит," which takes the form of a third-person, singular, present-tense verb, works to suggest something like "babble" and the sound of a heavy blow ("бабахнуть" [to bang]).[23] The pun on "малина"—literally "raspberry" and figuratively "a thieves' den"—recreates Stalin's point of view: every victim is a treat and an easily neutralized threat.

As the epigram exploits these formal devices, it improves its efficacy as propaganda. It delights as it teaches. Rhyme is an aid to memory: the poem does not need to be written down because it will be remembered.[24] As a result, it is able to address audiences outside Mandel'shtam's immediate circle. It can be passed from friend to friend; no one need fear being caught with incriminating evidence. It can survive even the most censorious environments.

The epigram is a poem in yet another sense as well: it is an instrument of discovery. Its opening lines present a dysfunctional public sphere, an insensate, anonymous "we" lost in endless commemoration of its leader. This public catches glimpses of Stalin's immense body—his fingers, boot-tops, mustache, chest—as his physique literally overwhelms the poem. Each glimpse is met with a corresponding blow—to the head, brow, eye, and groin. Taken together, these body parts compose a single body, which is also a body politic—powerful and ignorant, decorative and emasculated. (Stalin's greasy, prodding fingers and shiny boots substitute for the public's injured eye and groin.) This is the Soviet Union: a picture of immense and ongoing self-harm, a body destroying itself.

There are thus two "versions" of the same text: non-poem and poem, civic test and aesthetic instrument. There is an act of "pedagogical clarity" and an act of "genuine poetry"—to borrow two phrases from Mandel'shtam's essay "Conversation about Dante" (1933).[25] What unites these two versions? One answer might be genre. An epigram is a poem that deploys a statement in verse. But the Stalin epigram's generic features only supplement its efficacy—they do not constitute it. As I have been arguing, Mandel'shtam could have performed any anti-Stalin text to ensure his death—and without his death, Heaney would not be reading the epigram, let alone describing it as "eight stony couplets."[26]

For Mandel'shtam something else unites these two versions: a conception of purity. As a non-poem, the epigram displays the moral purity of a would-be martyr. Its dissent is direct and concise. The poet's willingness to sacrifice himself for justice is unmistakable. As a poem, the epigram displays the aesthetic purity one would expect from a former Acmeist. Its imagery is direct and concise. Its craftsmanship and musicality are unmistakable.[27] But what unites these instances of purity? The idea of purity itself. To be pure, everything must submit to a single organizing principle—in this case, the will of the artist.

This idea of purity is best understood in relation to Mandel'shtam's reading of Dante's *Divine Comedy*. "The structure of the Dantean monologue," he writes in "Conversation about Dante," "can be well understood by making use of an analogy with rock strata whose purity has been destroyed by the intrusion of foreign bodies."[28] The *Divine Comedy*, he argues, unifies this rock without, paradoxically, removing these "foreign bodies." "Imagine a granite monument erected in honor of granite, as if to reveal its very idea. Having grasped this, you will then be able to understand quite clearly just how form and content are related in Dante's work."[29] Despite the presence of old substrates and the constant absorption of new ones—new readers, new readings—the *Divine Comedy* remains pure: self-contained, self-sufficient, self-referential. "Examining the structure of the *Divina Commedia* as best I can," he adds, "I come to the conclusion that the entire poem is but one unified and indivisible stanza. Rather, it is not a stanza, but a crystallographic figure, that is, a body."[30] This last metaphor is especially revealing: the *Divine Comedy* is a body, purifying all it ingests. Likewise, the epigram: it is a body, Mandel'shtam's body, purifying itself as it purifies the body politic it simultaneously represents and opposes.

But perhaps "purity" is not the best word to choose—with its connection to racial hygiene, on the one hand, and abstract art, on the other.[31] "Aesthetic unity" or simply "form" might be better—insofar as both describe art's power to assimilate and redeem previously disparate ideas and aims, and persons and communities. Ultimately, the reason why Mandel'shtam's civic test must also be an aesthetic instrument is that they are both products of a great artist. This is what great artists do—at least in Mandel'shtam's view: unify the ununifiable and, in the process, make the contingent necessary.

In a 1934 speech on poetry to the first Soviet writers' congress, Nikolai Bukharin proposed that "The forms of poetic creation should be the most diverse, unified by the one great style or method of socialist realism." As Bukharin explained:

> Unity does not mean that we must all sing the same song at the same time—now about sugar beets, now about the "live man," now about the class struggle in the countryside, now about a Party membership card. Unity does not mean the presentation of the same ideal types and the same "villains," nor the abolition—on paper—of all contradictions and evils. Unity consists in a single *aspect*—that of building socialism.[32]

Bukharin's definition of socialist realism would prove optimistic. Yet its logic captures a central feature of official Soviet ideology in the period: the belief that socialism would simultaneously preserve and purify the diverse interests of Soviet citizens. This logic parallels the logic of Mandel'shtam's reading of

Divine Comedy—indeed, Dante's granite monument represents the Soviet conception of pluralism in miniature. This is not pluralism at all but the subordination of difference to a single unifying principle. Bukharin admits as much; where heterogeneity exists, it exists "on paper"—that is, it does not really exist at all.

This correspondence suggests a need to reevaluate the epigram's relation to a tradition of world literature that promotes (or seems to promote) liberalism and human rights. The epigram does not fight Stalinism with liberal values but with its own competing conception of purity. "The central impulse behind the domestication of literature [under Stalin] was to preserve its crucial function as generator and repository of myth," writes Katerina Clark. "Consequently both intellectualist tendencies among writers, on the one hand, and the production of countervailing myths, on the other, were equally anathema to those watchmen (both within and without literature) who would guard its purity."[33] The Stalin epigram presents such a countervailing myth—a myth in which Mandel'shtam becomes a martyr and thus defeats Stalin, his Goliath.

The epigram replicates other aspects of Soviet utopianism as well. "The hallmark of the new man was the *extra*ordinary—not to say superhuman—feat," Clark writes. "The secret of his success lay in his *daring* to discount established empirical norms," rather than his "sheer human strength."[34] Mandel'shtam represents a *détournement* of this ideal—Soviet in method, anti-Soviet in form and content. (He did not physically resemble the ultra-masculine Soviet archetype of the New Man.)[35] Performing the epigram, he becomes a superhuman man of daring, violating established norms of behavior and modeling new norms for his community.

But these correspondences are just that—correspondences. They are not equivalences. I am wary of making a category mistake. Mandel'shtam was a poet. Stalin was a dictator. I do not mean to suggest that Mandel'shtam's performance was unjust or unwarranted or unheroic. Stripped of his independence, he reasserted it. Yet the fact remains: the epigram promoted (or at least exploited) the specific conditions responsible for the oppression it opposed—a commitment to purity combined with a pedagogy of perfectionism. The epigram, in other words, did not tackle Stalinism as an idea but as a cult of personality—as a cult of the wrong personality.[36] For Mandel'shtam, the problem was not unanimity but state-sponsored unanimity.

I do not think Mandel'shtam would have disagreed with this argument. When asked during his interrogation by the state police about Akhmatova's response to the epigram, he declared:

> With her customary laconicism and poetic acuity, Anna Akhmatova pointed out the "monumental, rough-hewed, broad-sheet character of the piece." This was a correct assessment. For while an enormous force of social poison, political hatred and even contempt for the person depicted has been concentrated in this foul, counter-revolutionary,

> libellous lampoon, she recognized its great power and that it possesses the qualities of a propaganda poster of great effective force.[37]

Mandel'shtam was under duress when he made this statement.[38] He wanted to protect Akhmatova. Yet he does not apologize or express remorse. Instead, he describes a dialectic of complicity and dissent. Protest, he acknowledges, is never ahistorical.[39] The epigram assimilated the power it opposed: it is a "propaganda poster" suffused with "an enormous force of social poison."

Heaney's reading of the epigram might thus be more insightful than it first seemed. The epigram marks a confrontation between two men rather than two forms of governance: a ruined utopianism and a practical liberalism. The epigram demands that its auditors submit to the poet and his art rather than Stalin and his decrees. It is as utopian as the utopianism it was designed to undermine. Perhaps even more utopian. During the six months between Mandel'shtam's initial performance and his arrest, he was free. By inviting his own death, he took control of his life, robbing Stalin of one of his most powerful means of oppression.[40] The performance, in this way, was an instrument of self-determination. Mandel'shtam's utopianism resulted briefly, but genuinely, in a utopia of one.

"The logical culmination of the process of destroying everything through which I can possibly be wounded is suicide," writes Isaiah Berlin in a passage I quote in my introduction.[41] "Total liberation," he concludes, "is conferred only by death."[42] Mandel'shtam's performance fits this paradigm. The performance also fits the paradigm that connects the central chapters of this book: a writer responds to the failure of utopia by devising his or her own utopian project. Its effects are asymmetrical and highly improbable: a perfect world that cannot be shared. Like Du Bois's utopia of one, Mandel'shtam's is practically inimitable, but not logically inimitable. But unlike Du Bois's utopia (and, for that matter, Thoreau's), Mandel'shtam's utopia does not simply ostracize readers—it endangers them.

If I have a target in this chapter, it is not Mandel'shtam but the critics who view the epigram as a triumph for poetry. Not all the epigram's commentators endorse this view. But those who do endorse Mandel'shtam's aestheticization of politics. To put this point another way, investment in this view of the epigram is an investment in the hierarchies the epigram reproduces. It is an investment in a specific kind of utopianism, the repercussions of which are evident in Mandel'shtam's performance and the context that provoked it.

3

> *The arts only ever lend to projects of domination and emancipation what they are able to lend them, that is to say, quite simply, what they have in common with them: bodily positions and movements, functions of speech, the parcelling out of the visible and the invisible.*
>
> —JACQUES RANCIÈRE[43]

Rancière's description of the connection between aesthetics and politics (and especially between art and "bodily positions and movements") suggests a counterfactual reading of Mandel'shtam's performance. When Mandel'shtam performed the epigram, he not only tested his auditors' allegiance, he made them complicit in a conspiracy. Everyone who heard the epigram was responsible for *not* informing on Mandel'shtam. Anyone who chose to inform was responsible for informing on everyone who did not. The epigram, in this way, had the potential to create a network bound by love and fear in which everyone was responsible for everyone else—a network in which care for family and friends had to become care for a wider community.

Latent in the performance were the conditions for the network's infinite expansion. Had this counterfactual been realized, auditors who recited the epigram would have created their own networks, their own conspiracies. The epigram would have spread like a virus from one reading to another, in apartments across Moscow and the Soviet Union. The scenario suggests one reason why the epigram could not have been written down. The anonymity of a physical text would have threatened the network by weakening the bonds holding it together. Every expression of dissent had to have a human face. Intellectual affiliation had to be supplemented by emotional investment, empathy. The epigram's character as a poem would have facilitated this investment. Its depth of feeling and semantic complexity, its musicality and wit would have humanized and popularized its message, helping to spread the contagion.[44]

This counterfactual and Mandel'shtam's actual performance are mutually exclusive. One promotes the expansion of a rhizomatic community of coconspirators, the other the heroism and independence of a single actor. One requires the poet's obscurity, the other his arrest and martyrdom. In the counterfactual, Mandel'shtam would have been no more important than any other node in the network. Arresting him alone would have been as pointless as quarantining one sick person during an epidemic.

Nadezhda Mandel'shtam's memoirs, I believe, realized a version of this counterfactual by, paradoxically, valorizing her husband's sacrifice. She began to write her memoirs in the late 1950s, during the Khrushchev-era reform period known as the Thaw. By the early 1960s, the first volume was in circulation in the Soviet Union in samizdat, and, in 1970, it was published in English as *Hope against Hope*, translated by Max Hayward.[45] (Despite changes in the political climate in the Soviet Union, state-sanctioned publication remained impossible until 1989.)[46] The book describes the Mandel'shtams' married life and combines a detailed account of her husband's arrest, exile, and death with commentaries on his poems and poetics, the Soviet intelligentsia, and Stalinism. It is an act of witness and testimony: "[T]he champions of terror invariably leave one thing out of account," she writes, "namely, that they can't kill everyone, and among their cowed, half-demented subjects there are always witnesses who survive to tell the tale."[47]

The second volume, written in the mid-1960s, after the first had earned her a position of "unofficial prominence" in the Soviet Union, opens with a promise to tell her own story but soon refocuses on her life with her husband.[48] (Guy Davenport describes the book, published in English in 1974 as *Hope Abandoned*, as a "sustained digression [621 pages] to the first volume.")[49] The book devotes substantial space to politics and cultural criticism, and to descriptions of Akhmatova's relationship with Mandel'shtam. A third volume, published posthumously in France in 1987, continues in this vein, collecting miscellaneous criticism and memories.[50]

The memoirs—especially the first volume—are masterly: suspenseful, witty, novelistic, terrifying. Davenport argues that they are "designed as a Formalist novel, its components arranged according to a sense of kinship amongst its subjects rather than according to chronology."[51] Short chapters are the main units of action: each focuses on a theme or problem, combining dramatic descriptions of people and events with incisive commentary. Each chapter is self-contained and easily excerpted from the whole. This is witness literature as a series of adventure stories. The first volume opens:

> After slapping Alexei Tolstoi in the face, M. immediately returned to Moscow. From there he rang Akhmatova every day, begging her to come. She was hesitant and he was angry. When she packed and bought her ticket, her brilliant, irritable husband Punin asked her, as she stood in thought by a window: "Are you praying that this cup should pass from you?" It was he who had once said to her when they were walking through the Tretiakov Gallery: "Now let's go and see how they'll take you to your execution." . . . But in the end they overlooked her and didn't arrest her. Instead, she was always seeing others off to their last journey.[52]

The passage establishes the memoirs' central themes and actors. Mandel'shtam's slap foreshadows his performance of the epigram; Punin's prediction anticipates the poet's fate.[53] Akhmatova and Nadezhda Mandel'shtam are, from the start, survivors. The atmosphere is tense. The passage sets up the chapter's main action: Akhmatova's arrival (from Leningrad, where she lived), Mandel'shtam's first arrest, and the police search of the Mandel'shtams' apartment.

This passage also introduces an important typology. Gregory Freidin notes that Mandel'shtam's "scandalous slap belongs to the Dostoevskian tradition of unmasking an antichrist in a sudden breakdown of social conventions . . . As befits an imitator of the one who prayed at Gethsemane, Mandelstam pleads with his friend Akhmatova to come and keep vigil with him; and as befits one assigned the role of the poet's apostle, she delays."[54] The scene assigns roles of Messiah, apostle, and gospel writer to the memoirs' characters. Readers are set up to expect Mandel'shtam's sacrifice and to recognize its magnitude.

This typology effectively binds the validity of Nadezhda Mandel'shtam's testimony about the horrors of Stalinism to her account of her husband's martyrdom. To accept one is to accept the other. Conversely, to deny Mandel'shtam's martyrdom (or to criticize his poetry) is to endorse Stalinism. Consider, for example, the depiction of the scholar Emma Gershtein, one of the epigram's first auditors:

> Emma Gerstein . . . looked on our apartment as a place where she met "interesting people" and unsuccessfully pursued her amorous designs on Lev Gumilev, Narbut, and whoever else happened to be there, but she paid little attention to M. and never understood his poetry. Needless to say, these were not favorable times for M.—his ideas, the brilliance of his conversation, his humor, could not be appreciated without equipment of a different order than anything produced in the first half of the century. We were surrounded by swarms of people who saw everything in another light from M., and they were always trying to turn me against him, tempting me with the thought of a more ordered and sensible existence, and the good things that would go with it: common sense, Marxism, innovation, an easy life, theaters and bars, a proper home, and all the latest trends.[55]

The scene quickly moves from gossip about Gershtein to her intellectual failings, and from these failings to the failings of the Soviet intelligentsia as a whole. Gershtein-as-intelligentsia then becomes a representative of the Soviet government as it tempts artists with "theaters and bars," "a proper home," "common sense," and "Marxism." (Marxism, here, is equivalent to the "easy life.") The Mandel'shtams' apartment becomes a Garden of Eden, with Gershtein as a less-than-cunning Satan, tempting the memoirist to abandon her husband and his values. Gershtein's mundane self-interest, in this way, comes to represent the origin of Mandel'shtam's persecution.[56]

As a genre, witness literature challenges readers to disseminate its testimony.[57] Nadezhda Mandel'shtam addressed this challenge to two sets of readers in particular: a younger generation of intelligentsia in the Soviet Union, who came of age after Stalinism, and readers in the West. Joseph Brodsky, one of the most prominent members of the former set of readers, accepted the challenge without reserve. In a review of the second volume of memoirs, he proclaims:

> I don't think any other poet has been as fortunate in his widow: Mandelstam is resurrected. But not only Mandelstam—that which killed him, outlived him, and continues to exist and gain popularity is also reincarnated. . . . Her book is relentless, it breathes typical Judaic devotion to justice. What Mme Mandelstam does in its 621 pages is nothing other than hold a Day of Judgment on earth for her age and its

> literature—a judgment administered all the more rightfully since it was this age that had undertaken the construction of paradise on earth.[58]

Note the passive voice ("Mandelstam is resurrected"), which implies Mandel'shtam's divinity (he resurrects himself). Note, too, the identification of "that which killed him" with poetry instead of the secret police. In this way, the epigram's aims are realized: Mandel'shtam overcomes his Goliath.

In the West, the challenge was also effective. Consider two episodes in the history of the memoirs' circulation—one involving Clarence Brown and the other Carl R. Proffer. In 1965, Brown, a Russian literature professor at Princeton and a recent Harvard PhD, traveled to Moscow "ostensibly to study the problems of translation."[59] On the recommendation of the scholar and translator Ryszard Przybylski, he visited Nadezhda Mandel'shtam and read the first volume of her memoirs. "I had little need to leave Nadezhda Iakovlevna's apartment," he writes, "to be in the mainstream of what liberal thought there was in the Brezhnev ice age. The kitchen table was the forum for an education that not even Harvard could have provided."[60] Brown was soon asked to smuggle the memoirs to the United States, which he did successfully.[61] Back at Princeton, he organized a translation project:

> Nadezhda is to blame for my first and only deliberate deception of the dean of the Graduate School at Princeton. I invented a seminar with some such phony name as "Studies in Twentieth-Century Russian Literature." I recruited a group of graduate students. I swore them to secrecy. Then we set about translating the memoirs of Nadezhda Mandel'shtam. It just might have been the most personally gratifying (for me) and useful (for the students) of any graduate seminar I ever offered. As I sat with each student, revising his or her translation, we necessarily dealt with topics in twentieth-century Russian literature. What is more, the urgency, to say nothing of the secrecy, made this seminar, I hope, a memorable experience for my students.[62]

"Our translation," he concludes, was "doomed to remain an academic exercise"; Max Hayward had already agreed to translate another smuggled copy "with all possible speed."[63] Brown remained devoted to Mandel'shtam. In 1973, he published the first biography of the poet and cotranslated (with W. S. Merwin) the first edition of Mandel'shtam's poems in English.

In 1973, Carl R. Proffer, copublisher of Ardis Publishing, traveled to Moscow and reported on the reception of the memoirs for the *New York Review of Books*. "Everywhere I went," he writes, "I was given examples of what various people considered slander of other people—usually friends or relatives. 'X is not mentally unbalanced,' 'Y was never an informer,' 'Z did not destroy Mandelstam's poem.'" Proffer continues, "Almost everyone seems to have a friend, favorite, or relative whom they think she slanders—and for that matter, many of the victims themselves are still alive and kicking. The chorus of complaint began with the circulation of her memoirs in manuscript, intensified each time one was published in Russian abroad, and has reached its peak with the publication of the translation of *Hope Abandoned*."[64] Proffer then quotes from an open letter from the writer Veniamin Kaverin to Nadezhda Mandel'shtam about her portrayal of Iurii Tynianov, the formalist critic (and Kaverin's brother-in-law).[65] "Spite drips from every line of your book," Kaverin writes. "Those who have long ago evaluated Tynyanov's works as a new stage in the history of world literary scholarship will also know how to evaluate the self-satisfied helplessness with which you have written about them."[66] Proffer defends Nadezhda Mandel'shtam and refutes Kaverin's central claims, noting that "For the non-Russian reader the specific individuals and names are not especially important—the Western reader cannot pronounce them and does not know who they are anyway. The larger picture and moral viewpoint of Mme Mandelstam are much more important to us."[67]

What do these two episodes reveal about the memoirs' efficacy in the West? The episode involving Brown highlights the memoirs' geopolitical influence. (He involved his students in an act of espionage!) The episode involving Proffer, in turn, highlights the significance of the memoirs' circulation between Moscow and New York. Kaverin's final claim is revealing—for if it is true, so is its opposite: those who have *not* "long ago evaluated" Tynianov's work will not know how to evaluate the memoirs' accuracy. They will not, in other words, be able to extract Tynianov from Nadezhda Mandel'shtam's characterization. This is why Kaverin is so furious: he recognizes that Tynianov's legacy (and his own) will be determined, in part, by the memoirs' readers in the West (including Brown's students). Nadezhda Mandel'shtam's "moral viewpoint" will determine the legacy of Russian literature and the history of Stalinism.[68]

These two episodes are, of course, part of the history of the Cold War. (The *New York Review of Books* was a front in this war.)[69] Beginning in the late 1940s, the United States Central Intelligence Agency (CIA) funded a range of cultural institutions to counter the Soviet Union's own robust program of "cultural diplomacy," and to promote democracy to the noncommunist left in Western Europe and to émigré communities in the United States. Through the Ford Foundation, for example, the CIA funded the Congress for Cultural Freedom, the Institute of Contemporary Arts, James Laughlin's *Perspectives* magazine, and Melvin Lasky's *Der Monat*, as well as a host of individual artists and intellectuals. In 1951, on a recommendation from the diplomat and historian George Kennan, Brown's friend and neighbor in Princeton, the Ford Foundation gave $523,000 to the Chekhov Publishing House to publish proscribed works of Russian literature and translations of Western classics. "[F]or the first time," Kennan writes, "[we] broke the monopoly of the Soviet government on current literary publication in the Russian language."[70] One of the most important books published by the Chekhov Publishing House was the first collected edition of Mandel'shtam's poems, which appeared in 1955.[71]

"[I]n reconstructing the past," writes Irina Paperno, "survivors of the Soviet regime started a new utopian project: to inhabit the future."[72] This is what Nadezhda Mandel'shtam does in her memoirs: she reconstructs her past and, in the process, constructs a real community defined by its anti-Stalinism and its devotion to her late husband. She defines what it means to support or resist Soviet power, and then compels readers to act out these definitions. Brodsky worships Mandel'shtam. Brown promotes Mandel'shtam's liberalism. Proffer publicizes (and refutes) Kaverin's denunciation. Kaverin's denunciation, in turn, corroborates the memoirs' Manichaeism. (Kaverin's own liberalism is lost.)[73] As the memoirs gain readers in the West, they attract a younger generation of readers in the Soviet Union—readers disgusted by the state-sanctioned literary establishment and attracted to Western culture and politics.

This community benefits from (but does not require) the constant circulation of new material. New memoirs lead to new translators, new smugglers, new letters of protest, new controversies, new readers, new disciples. These disciples, in turn, motivate new letters, new readers, new translations. The memoirs' two main volumes (digressions and all), plus the essays that would eventually compose the third posthumous volume, facilitate this process, as does the memoirs' form: short, discrete, nonchronological chapters—portable, accessible, memorable. Once released into their target communities, they assume a life of their own. Arresting their author would, at best, only slow their dissemination. The memoirs, in this way, realize the potential of the epigram as described in my counterfactual: they create a nonhierarchical, viral community with Mandel'shtam as its absent center.

In her second volume of memoirs, Nadezhda Mandel'shtam describes two responses to Soviet utopianism. In our age, she observes, people either embrace "blatant individualism" and treat life as "an accidental and fleeting windfall to be exploited for every drop of pleasure it can give" or they "sink into a torpor and think only of how to 'shed the burden of time.'"[74] This latter group "often cherish the mad hope of surviving to a future in which they will recover their lost selves. . . . Their whole life thus consists of waiting for the first glimpse of a promised land, like a radiant shoreline on the horizon."[75] This "mad hope" for survival is encoded in the memoirs as a genre; witness literature, by definition, assumes a future that will confirm its testimony. But the memoirs take this one step further, actively fashioning their own promised land. They turn waiting—or writing about waiting—into praxis. They realize a dream of independence—the recovery of one's lost self—by assuming control over others. This is the significance of their characterizations. As the memoirs recover lost selves, they make sure others remain lost. This may be what all forms of memorialization do. Nadezhda Mandel'shtam's memoirs do it incredibly well, turning a purge on paper into a purified community.

This, then, is Nadezhda Mandel'shtam's utopia of one: an experience of the "promised land" she would not live to see. In 1987, seven years after her death, Mandel'shtam was officially rehabilitated by the Soviet Union, and Brodsky, now living in the United States, won the Nobel Prize in Literature. In 1991, the Soviet Union collapsed—and Brodsky became the United States Poet Laureate. Nadezhda Mandel'shtam, by writing her memoirs, lived these events as she worked toward their realization.

4

Those myths that combine to form "culture"! Barely a half dozen or a dozen years pass, and people are already spinning threads and entangling a man, events, in a cocoon for their own benefit.

I have read many poems in several languages about Osip Mandelstam as a martyr for freedom. I have also heard the tapes of a Polish theatrical montage in his honor. All this has very little in common with the real Mandelstam.

A question: Is distortion, banalization, inescapable? Is it true that the wider the range—of fame, for example—the smaller the number of complications that are permitted to survive? And what is our role, we who already belong to the past, in inciting the myth? Which of our features, in other words, promotes it?

—CZESŁAW MIŁOSZ[76]

In January 1937, Mandel'shtam, exiled and destitute in Voronezh, wrote a letter to his friend, the writer Kornei Chukovskii:

> What is happening to me cannot go on any longer. Neither my wife nor I have the strength to prolong this nightmare. . . . I said those who condemned me were right. I have found historical meaning in everything. . . . [A]lthough I had done nothing else wrong, everything was taken away from me: my right to life, to work, to treatment. I was put in the position of a dog, a cur . . . I am a shadow. . . . There is only one person in the whole world to whom I can and must turn for help in this matter.[77]

That "one person" was, of course, Stalin. Later that month, Mandel'shtam wrote an ode to the Soviet leader.

The eighty-four-line "Stalin ode" (as it has come to be known) combines the rhetoric of Stalin's cult of personality with the features of a classical ode.[78] Mandel'shtam portrays himself as an artist trying to depict his inimitable leader. Stalin is a Georgian revolutionary, a warrior, an orator, a friendly harvester, and a Greek god. The poet-as-artist fixates on the leader's face—the shape of his brow, mouth, and eyes—but cannot fully capture his greatness. The conditional mood marks Mandel'shtam's modesty:

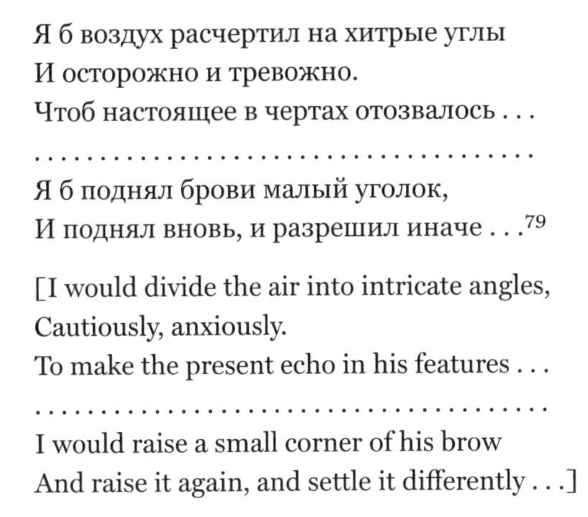

Я б воздух расчертил на хитрые углы
И осторожно и тревожно.
Чтоб настоящее в чертах отозвалось . . .
. . . .
Я б поднял брови малый уголок,
И поднял вновь, и разрешил иначе . . .[79]

[I would divide the air into intricate angles,
Cautiously, anxiously.
To make the present echo in his features . . .
. . . .
I would raise a small corner of his brow
And raise it again, and settle it differently . . .]

In the fifth stanza, the difficulty of representing Stalin becomes an opportunity for self-criticism:

Я у него учусь—не для себя учась,
Я у него учусь—к себе не знать пощады.[80]

[I am learning from him—not learning for my own sake,
I am learning from him—to be merciless to myself.]

In the seventh and final stanza, the poet-as-artist vanishes into a crowd assembled around the Soviet leader:

Я уменьшаюсь там. Меня уж не заметят.
Но в книгах ласковых и в играх детворы
Воскресну я сказать, как солнце светит.[81]

[There I recede. They will not even notice me.
But in tender books and in children's games
I will be resurrected to say how the sun shines.]

In these lines, Mandel'shtam denigrates his own work, reducing it to a celebration of the obvious and the inevitable. The shining sun is a figure for Soviet power.

The ode circulated widely. After Mandel'shtam's exile ended in May 1937, he performed it on numerous occasions in Moscow.[82] In March 1938, Vladimir Stavskii, the head of the Writers' Union, wrote Nikolai Yezhov, head of the NKVD (precursor of the KGB), about Mandel'shtam and the ode:

> [H]e quite often visits his friends, primarily among the writers, in Moscow. They support him, collect money for him, treat him as a "martyr"—genius poet, unacknowledged by anyone. Valentin Kataev, I. Prut, and other writers spoke openly in his defense. . . .
>
> Recently [he] wrote a series of poems. But they are not of exceptionally high value, according to the opinion of those comrades whom I

> have asked to look at them (including comrade Pavlenko, whose opinion is attached).
>
> Once again I beseech you to help resolve the issue of O. Mandelstam.[83]

Petr Pavlenko, in his attached opinion, notes that the ode is undeniably Soviet but also flawed. It is "filled with strong feeling," he writes, but contains "a great deal of clumsy phrasing which is inappropriate to the theme of Stalin." It "is worse than its individual stanzas."[84] No one knows whether the ode ever reached Stalin. In May 1938, at the end of the Great Purge, Mandel'shtam was rearrested for counterrevolutionary activity (likely on Yezhov's order). In December, he died in a Gulag transit camp near Vladivostok.

What should readers make of the ode? Is it a sincere celebration of Stalin's power? An Aesopian act of subversion? An act of madness? As J. M. Coetzee observes, the question is important, not only for "those concerned with the integrity of Mandelstam's reputation" but also for the "honor of poetry in general."[85] Does the Stalin ode neutralize or counteract the Stalin epigram?

Most accounts of the ode try to justify or excuse its "tone of profound sincerity" and "consummate skill."[86] Nadezhda Mandel'shtam claims that her husband had to enter a trance to compose the poem: "To write an ode to Stalin it was necessary to get in tune, like a musical instrument, by deliberately giving way to the general hypnosis and putting oneself under the spell of the liturgy which in those days blotted out all human voices."[87] Freidin suggests that the poet's own messianism facilitated his conversion to Stalinism: his own cult of personality set the terms for accommodating Stalin's. (Freidin also notes that it is not "unusual for a victim to identify with his tormentor, especially if the tormentor happens to be exalted and the victim either physically or psychologically isolated." The ode's composition, he concludes, "appears overdetermined.")[88] M. L. Gasparov claims that Mandel'shtam used the poem to realize a long-held ambition: to become one with the Soviet people.[89] Coetzee reads the ode as an attempt to force a stalemate with the Soviet leader—to write a poem that would neutralize Stalin's anger.[90] Matthew McGarry argues that Mandel'shtam's descriptions are "laden with examples of Aesopian language" that caricature Stalin.[91]

Despite the range of these interpretations, they share an aim: to preserve Mandel'shtam's purity. The poet is a lyre, a victim of ideology, a populist, a brilliant tactician, a satirist-hero. He is true to his beliefs or devoid of beliefs altogether. In these readings, the ode does not undermine the epigram's legacy—it consolidates it. Indeed, one could argue that the ode simply replaces one act of self-destruction with another.

But these readings all neglect the most obvious interpretation of the poem: the ode is an apology. Mandel'shtam, worn out by his slow death in exile, wrote the poem to save his life. He disavowed the epigram and decided to submit to Soviet utopianism. The ode, in this interpretation, is neither sincere nor insincere—or, more accurately, it is both. It represents Mandel'shtam's sincere desire to live, but not his true feelings about Stalin. Like most apologies, it is a compromise—and as a compromise it is impure. Yet, as a compromise, it is also an act of self-determination—a way to establish a modicum of autonomy in the face of inescapable power.

Evidence for this interpretation may be drawn from the ode itself. The poem revises many of the epigram's central images. For example, it celebrates the integrity of the Soviet Union by reassembling Stalin's body: the head, brow, and eye in the ode belong to the Soviet leader, not his injured apparatchiks. Georgia, Stalin's birthplace, is no longer a site of ridicule but an occasion for intimacy. Quoting Stalin's birth name (Dzhugashvili), Mandel'shtam proclaims:

> Он родился в горах и горечь знал тюрьмы.
> Хочу его назвать—не Сталин,—Джугашвили![92]

> [He was born in the mountains and knew the bitterness of jail.
> I want to call him—not Stalin,—Dzhugashvili!]

The ode also revises the terms of the poet's sacrifice: Mandel'shtam disappears in a crowd rather than at the hands of a joyous executioner.

When read as an apology, the ode is a human act in the face of inhuman conditions. It does not represent the triumph or failure of Mandel'shtam's integrity, or the triumph or failure of poetry, but Mandel'shtam's humanity, and the human cost of totalitarianism.

The ode was not Mandel'shtam's only attempt to write a pro-Stalin poem. After his exile ended, he went on a tour of the White Sea–Baltic Canal—the canal that Gor'kii and his collaborators had celebrated four years earlier, and that might have influenced Mandel'shtam's decision to perform the epigram in the first place. An official from the Writers' Union had organized the trip with the hope that Mandel'shtam would write a poem that would facilitate his reintegration into Soviet society—by affirming his commitment to Soviet utopianism. The poem "describing the beauties of the Canal" was never published. Nadezhda Mandel'shtam and Akhmatova burned it after Mandel'shtam's death. "If anybody happens to have kept a stray copy of this poem," Nadezhda Mandel'shtam writes in her memoirs, "I beg and pray [he] set aside his love of original manuscripts and throw it in the fire."[93]

Miłosz asks, "Is distortion, banalization, inescapable? Is it true that the wider the range—of fame, for example—the smaller the number of complications that are permitted to survive?" The answer to these questions seems to be yes, at least in the case of the Mandel'shtams. To read Mandel'shtam as "a martyr for freedom" (or even as a David facing Goliath) is to simplify the complex efficacy of his poetry and Nadezhda Mandel'shtam's memoirs—and, perhaps more importantly, the complexity of his poetry as poetry. The Mandel'shtams may have engineered their reception, but they do not need to be defined by it.

But the answer might also be yes *and* no—for the banal is the very thing that Mandel'shtam's martyrdom distorts. The most important lesson of the three central texts in this chapter might not concern their complexity and efficacy—that is, their relation to the argument of *Utopias of One*. The lesson might, instead, concern the banality of violence, and the basic, unquantifiable value of human life.

CHAPTER FOUR

Anna Akhmatova's Complicity

1

In 1965, Soviet authorities permitted Anna Akhmatova to travel to the University of Oxford to receive an honorary degree. Once there, she met Isaiah Berlin, and they discussed their meetings in Leningrad twenty years earlier. In an essay for the *New York Review of Books*, Berlin recalls the discussion:

> In Oxford she told me that she was convinced that Stalin's fury, which we had caused, had unleashed the cold war—that she and I had changed the history of mankind. She meant this quite literally and insisted on its truth. She saw herself and me as world-historical personages chosen by destiny to play our fateful part in a cosmic conflict, and this is reflected in her poems of this time.[1]

In any context, such a conviction would be immoderate. But if any poet had reason to believe that he or she had contributed to the central geopolitical event of the second half of the twentieth century, it was Akhmatova.

In prerevolutionary Russia, Akhmatova had been a famous poet—her second book, *Четки* (1914) (*Rosary*), went through eleven printings.[2] After the revolution, she became a symbol of the czarist past: in 1920, Kornei Chukovskii delivered an influential lecture, "Akhmatova or Maiakovskii: Two Russias," that identified her as the "Old Russia."[3] (Maiakovskii was the new Russia.) In 1921, her ex-husband, the poet Nikolai Gumilev, was executed for participating in a monarchist conspiracy. By the mid-1920s, she was prohibited from publishing her poems and mocked in the press. A series of articles in *Pravda*, the official newspaper of the Communist Party, portrayed her as "an internal émigré" and "Yesterday's 'Today.'"[4]

In the 1930s, Akhmatova became further enmeshed in Soviet politics, despite her disappearance from public view. Her third husband, Nikolai Punin, and son, Lev Gumilev, were arrested on trumped-up charges of counterrevolutionary activity. She appealed directly to Stalin and they were released.[5] (Both were eventually rearrested: Punin died in the Gulag in 1953, and Gumilev spent more than twelve years in the prison system. Scholars suspect that the arrests were used to control the poet.)[6] During the buildup to World War II, her political status slowly started to improve. In 1940, she was allowed to publish a selection of poems, *Из шести книг* (*From Six Books*), but the book was immediately suppressed. In an internal government memo, the secretariat of the Central Committee called its publication a "crude mistake" and the editors were reprimanded.[7] After the German attack on the Soviet Union in June 1941, she was invited to make patriotic radio broadcasts and was among the elite evacuated to Tashkent. Her poem "Мужество" ("Courage") appeared in *Pravda* in 1942 in support of the war effort.[8]

During this period, she also became a central figure in "unofficial" Soviet culture. From 1938 through 1942, her everyday life was secretly chronicled by Lidiia Chukovskaia, Chukovskii's daughter.[9] Chukovskaia's diary depicts Akhmatova in the constant company of admirers, who ensure her well-being and memorize her poetry. "Everyone is happy to provide food, supply tobacco, stoke the stove, fetch water," Chukovskaia observes. "This is the genuine 'common cause.'"[10] These admirers memorized her *Реквием* (1935–62) (*Requiem*), her masterpiece about the Great Purges, because it was not safe to keep a written copy. As Irina Paperno notes, "Akhmatova's symbolic status in the community—her historic role as the great Russian poet in distress, which she played with relish—made her an object of general attention and common care."[11]

Her first meeting with Berlin only heightened her sense of her world-historical significance. In November 1945, the philosopher, who was working at the British Embassy in Moscow, visited Leningrad. At a bookstore, he ran into the scholar Vladimir Orlov, who offered to take Berlin to Akhmatova's apartment.[12] Soon after he was introduced to Akhmatova, he heard his name shouted from the courtyard. He rushed outside to find Randolph Churchill—the son of Winston Churchill. (Randolph, who was working as a journalist in Leningrad, needed an interpreter and had heard that Berlin, a native Russian speaker, was in the city.) "I have no notion whether I was followed by agents of the secret police," Berlin recalls, "but there could be no doubt that Randolph Churchill was. It was this untoward event that caused absurd rumors to circulate in Leningrad that a foreign delegation had arrived to persuade Akhmatova to leave Russia; that Winston Churchill, a lifelong admirer of the poet, was sending a special aircraft to take Akhmatova to England."[13]

A second meeting later that night between Akhmatova and Berlin was less dramatic and more substantive. They met in the evening and talked until the following afternoon. She recited her poetry (including *Requiem* and the unfinished *Поэма без героя* [1940–65] [*Poem without a Hero*]) and gave her views on world literature. ("She worshipped Dostoevsky and, like him, despised Turgenev.") She told Berlin about her childhood and marriages, and her confrontations with the state. "She showed no sign of wishing me to leave, and I was far too moved and absorbed to stir," Berlin recalls. "She had, she said, met only one foreigner—a Pole—since the First World War."

The meeting was symbolic for both participants. For Berlin, Akhmatova personified the effects of Soviet oppression. ("The account of the unrelieved tragedy of her life went beyond anything which anyone had ever described to me in spoken words.")[14] For Akhmatova, Berlin personified the West—liberty, but also literary recognition and canonization.

In 1946, thirteen months after the meeting, Andrei Zhdanov, the director of the Soviet Union's cultural policy, issued his famous report on the "thick" literary journals, *Звезда* (*Star*) and *Ленинград* (*Leningrad*). The resulting doctrine, known as the Zhdanovshchina, singled out Akhmatova and the writer Mikhail Zoshchenko, and reemphasized the party's commitment to socialist realism as the only valid style of art in the Soviet Union. Literature has one goal, writes Zhdanov, "to bring up the new generation to be alert, believing in its work, fearless of any obstacles and ready to overcome them." Consequently, "any preaching, which lacks ideas, and is apolitical, such as 'art for art's sake,' is alien to Soviet literature, is harmful to the interests of the Soviet people and the state, and must not be allowed to have any space in our journals."[15] "Akhmatova's poetry," he adds, "is remote from the people. It is the poetry of the ten thousand members of the upper class, the condemned ones who had nothing else left but to sigh. . . . She is neither a nun nor a fornicator, but really both of them, mixing fornication and prayer. . . . What can the work of Akhmatova give our youth? Nothing but harm."[16] News of the report appeared in *Pravda* in August 1946, and in September, Stalin sent Zhdanov a congratulatory letter: "Com. Zhdanov! I've read your report. I think the report came out superbly."[17] In the years following the report, Akhmatova witnessed her son's third arrest, wrote pro-Stalin poems in an unsuccessful attempt to secure his release, and remained under the watchful eyes of the state and her community of admirers. Some admirers, she suspected, were informers.

In 1956, three years after Stalin's death, Berlin again visited the Soviet Union. He learned from Boris Pasternak that Akhmatova was nervous about receiving foreign visitors and preferred to be telephoned instead. ("[T]his was far safer, for all her telephone conversations were monitored.") When they spoke, they discussed her "experiences as a condemned writer" and her translations of classical Korean poetry. "There is no need for you to read [them]," she admitted.[18]

In the late 1950s and early 1960s, during the Thaw, Akhmatova's status in the Soviet Union improved. She started to publish sporadically in journals, and in 1958, a short volume of her selected poems appeared in Moscow.[19] She was permitted to travel abroad, and in 1964 she went to Italy to accept the Taormina poetry prize. She remained under surveillance but became a symbol of the state's new openness and respect for its cultural heritage.[20] (This respect was inconsistent; Pasternak, for example, was not allowed to accept the Nobel Prize in 1958.) In 1965, one year before her death, she traveled to Oxford to receive her honorary degree, met Berlin, and expressed her conviction about their role in starting the Cold War.

2

In *Requiem*, Akhmatova embraces her role as a "world-historical personage." In a sequence of ten lyrics and various supplementary texts, she challenges Soviet historiography and, as a result, the Soviet Union itself. Her anguish during the Great Purge or Terror of the late 1930s represents the anguish of all the women who lost their husbands, sons, and friends to mass arrests and executions. The anguish of these women, in turn, represents the Terror's impact on the nation as a whole. The poem is an act of witness—but it is also a testament to poetry's power to transform subjective experience into collective event.

The sequence opens with a set piece. Akhmatova waits outside a Leningrad prison to see her son. It is cold. The chance of seeing him is slim. Someone identifies her as a poet. Then, the wife or mother of another prisoner asks if Akhmatova can describe their experience. Akhmatova replies, "I can":

> В страшные годы ежовщины я провела семнадцать месяцев в тюремных очередях в Ленинграде. Как-то раз кто-то «опознал» меня. Тогда стоящая за мной женщина с голубыми губами, которая, конечно, никогда в жизни не слыхала моего имени, очнулась от свойственного нам всем оцепенения и спросила меня на ухо (там все говорили шепотом):
>
> —А это вы можете описать?
>
> И я сказала:
>
> —Могу.
>
> Тогда что-то вроде улыбки скользнуло по тому, что некогда было ее лицом.
>
> *1 апреля 1957*
> *Ленинград*[21]

> [In the terrible years of the Yezhovshchina (Great Purge) I spent seventeen months waiting in prison lines in Leningrad. One day, someone "identified" me. Then, a woman with blue lips, who was standing behind me, and who, of course, had never heard my name, woke from the stupor that beset us all, and asked in my ear (everyone spoke in whispers):
>
> —Can you describe this?
>
> And I said:

—I can.

Then something like a smile passed over what had once been her face.

1 April 1957
Leningrad]

The woman who poses this question is presumably not a member of the intelligentsia. She approaches Akhmatova only after learning that she is a poet. What matters is the abstract concept "poet"—that poets speak for the oppressed and challenge state power. This is Akhmatova's "destiny"—"her fateful part" in world history.

To fulfill this destiny, Akhmatova constructs a voice that alternately dissolves and reconstitutes her identity.[22] In the poem's second lyric, she concentrates a range of personal stories in a single plea for deliverance. The "me" that concludes the lyric represents every woman waiting in line and, by extension, every person (man and woman) harmed by Soviet utopianism:

Эта женщина больна,
Эта женщина одна,

Муж в могиле, сын в тюрьме,
Помолитесь обо мне. (24)

[This woman is sick,
This woman is alone,

Husband in the grave, son in prison,
Pray for me.]

As the sequence develops, the arrest of Akhmatova's son becomes the story of every arrest. The speaker's torment and disorientation are all-encompassing. As Robert Bird notes, the "first person is no longer specific, but, having incorporated the voices of friends and listeners, having wrested itself free of the cacophony of the world, it has become anyone's voice."[23]

But elsewhere in the sequence, Akhmatova's suffering is specifically her own. In the fourth lyric, she uses the second person to address her younger self:

Показать бы тебе, насмешнице
И любимице всех друзей,
Царскосельской веселой грешнице,
Что случилось с жизнью твоей. (24)

[If you could have been shown, jester
And darling of all your friends,
The cheerful sinner of Tsarskoe Selo,
What would happen to your life.]

She reflects on the incommensurability of life in prerevolutionary Russia (when she lived in Tsarskoe Selo, a town outside Saint Petersburg) and life during the Terror. The disparity testifies to the efficacy of Soviet utopianism: her former self is barely recognizable.

The poem's constant dissolution and reconstitution of identity is both evidence of trauma and a rhetorical strategy. As Akhmatova loses herself, she exemplifies the impact of Stalinism. As she finds herself, she fashions a new identity: survivor, witness, hero. The process is therapeutic and open to everyone damaged by the regime. Indeed, assent is unnecessary: *Requiem* already speaks for its target audience. As Clare Cavanagh argues, "Akhmatova counters the Soviet's 'state hymn' of enforced collectivity with her own collective voice made up of the shattered selves and unheard words of the nation's tormented mothers and wives."[24] This is *Requiem*'s aim: to reconstitute and represent an anti-Soviet counterpublic.

Requiem, in this way, is continuous with both the Stalin epigram and Nadezhda Mandel'shtam's memoirs. All three texts divide the just and unjust, the pure and the impure. As a result, they replicate the rigid dichotomies of the regime they oppose. Their war on complicity becomes a form of complicity.

"Strictly speaking, *Requiem* is the ideal embodiment of Soviet poetry," writes the poet Anatolii Naiman. This is not an indictment. Naiman was closer to Akhmatova than almost anyone in the 1960s. He was her secretary and one of her "orphans," a community of young poets devoted to her work. (Joseph Brodsky, Dmitrii Bobyshev, and Evgenii Rein were the other core members.) For Naiman, *Requiem*'s divisive populism is its defining feature. "This is poetry which speaks on behalf of the people," he writes. "Not a larger or smaller plurality of individuals called 'the people' . . . but the whole people, every single one of whom participates in what is happening on one side or the other."[25] "One side or the other": these are the "two Russias" that Akhmatova would describe to Chukovskaia in 1956—"the one that pronounced sentences, and the one that served them."[26]

Requiem's afterlife confirmed the poet's "fateful part" in world history. In the 1960s, the poem circulated in samizdat along with the transcript of Joseph Brodsky's trial for "social parasitism."[27] According to Naiman, the poem came to symbolize the stakes of the trial and the significance of poetry itself. He recalls:

> *Requiem* began to circulate clandestinely . . . in the same circles and in the same number of copies as Vigdorova's transcript of Brodsky's trial. Public opinion unconsciously made a link between these two things, though not one which could be named openly: the poet defends the right to be a poet and not to have any other occupation so that he or she should be able when necessary to speak on everyone's behalf.[28]

To these readers, *Requiem* "sounded like a transcript of the repressions, a kind of martyrology, a record of acts of self-sacrifice and martyrdom."[29] Brodsky himself confirms Naiman's account. Discussing the poem, he writes:

> At certain periods of history, it is only poetry that is capable of dealing with reality by condensing it into something graspable, something that otherwise couldn't be retained in the mind. In that sense, the whole nation took up . . . the name Akhmatova—which explains her popularity and which, more importantly, enabled her to speak for the nation as well as to tell it something it didn't know.[30]

From this perspective, Akhmatova's conception of her own significance was not inappropriate. *Requiem* did represent the nation.

The poem's significance was recognized in the West. In 1963, it was published in Munich, and in 1964, Robert Lowell published a translation in the *Atlantic Monthly*.[31] By the end of the Cold War, at least nine other English translations had appeared in print. In 1987, when the poem was first published in the Soviet Union, Western media outlets, including the *New York Times*, the *Washington Post*, the *Christian Science Monitor*, and the BBC, covered the event. The "Akhmatova poem," the *New York Times* reported, "is in tune with the times of Mikhail S. Gorbachev and his campaign for openness."[32] The anachronism is telling: by representing the Soviet past, the poem also comes to represent the Soviet present and future.

In 1988, Ronald Reagan visited Moscow and delivered a speech to the country's "artists and cultural leaders":

> And let me . . . refer to a Soviet artist, a poet— . . . one of the world's greatest. At the beginning of "Requiem," Anna Akhmatova writes of standing in a line outside a prison when someone in the crowd recognizes her as a well-known poet.

Reagan then read a passage from the opening of the poem, and presented his own interpretation, which connected his experience as an actor to Akhmatova's experience as a poet:

> That exchange—"Can you describe this?" "I can"—is at the heart of acting as it is of poetry and of so many of the arts. You get inside a character, a place, and a moment. You come to know the character in that instant not as an abstraction, one of the people, one of the masses, but as a particular person—yearning, hoping, fearing, loving—a face, even what had once been a face, apart from all others; and you convey that knowledge. You describe it, you describe the face. Pretty soon, at least for me, it becomes harder and harder to force any member of humanity into a straitjacket, into some rigid form in which you all expect to fit. In acting, even as you develop an appreciation for what we call the dramatic, you become in a more intimate way less taken with superficial pomp and circumstance, more attentive to the core of the soul—that part of each of us that God holds in the hollow of his hand and into which he breathes the breath of life.[33]

In Reagan's interpretation, *Requiem* represents a mix of American values: humanism, individualism, religious fundamentalism. Akhmatova-the-poet is a harbinger of Reagan-the-actor-politician. For Reagan, there is no better testament to the "evil empire" than *Requiem.*

3

> *In* Poem without a Hero *Akhmatova is throughout evasive and equivocal—quite the opposite of her usual manner, whose strength lay in forthrightness, the head-on attack.*
>
> —NADEZHDA MANDEL'SHTAM[34]

"[P]oetry makes nothing happen"—W. H. Auden's provocation is made ridiculous by Akhmatova's career.[35] Her poetry made too much happen—that was the problem. Her confrontation with the Soviet state made her a dissident hero and an accessory. Her testimony perpetuated the state's valorization of purity as it confirmed its status as an evil empire—much like Mandel'shtam's epigram and Nadezhda Mandel'shtam's memoirs.

Is complicity always a condition of dissent? Is there a way to oppose totalitarianism without replicating its worldview? These are the questions that motivate *Poem without a Hero.* The poem attempts to realize a different kind of dissent—one that does not promote Soviet utopianism or the Mandel'shtams' utopian anti-utopianism. How? By inhibiting its own influence and universality. "What comes under siege in the *Poem,*" argues Cavanagh, "[is] precisely the choral 'we' of . . . *Requiem,* the 'we' that triumphally asserts the speaker's right and obligation to speak for all the suffering women of her tormented nation."[36]

At the time of Akhmatova's death, in 1966, *Poem without a Hero* included two opening notes, three page-length dedications, an introduction, three main sections, editor's annotations by the poet herself, and an appendix with eighteen stanzas not included in the main structure of the poem. These "three main parts," in turn, included four separate chapters, an intermission, an afterword, an "intermezzo," and an epilogue. Akhmatova began the poem in 1940 and worked on it for twenty-five years. ("Worked" is not quite sufficient: during the course of the poem's construction, she constantly tweaked, expanded, discussed, promoted, obsessed over, and listened to the poem.)[37] In her collected works, the poem appears with four earlier versions, including a facsimile of an early manuscript. These five iterations take up 171 pages and solicit 138 pages of commentary. The final version is 47 pages. The first 18.

These 309 pages of poetry and commentary are not merely a scholarly extravagance. The apparatus literalizes two themes that permeate the poem: the construction of the poem itself and how the poem represents and constructs a life. The final version is final only because of Akhmatova's death, not because it is in any other way complete. (Cavanagh compares the poem to the Winchester Mystery House.)[38] *Poem without a Hero*, in other words, is no granite monument. It is a sprawling collection of memories, fantasies, voices, accidents, influences, revisions, and forms. Purity is out of the question.

The poem begins with a fantasia of prerevolutionary Saint Petersburg, entitled "Девятьсот тринадцатый год: Петербургская повесть" ("1913: A Petersburg Tale"). The main action is a masquerade. The guests are artists and literary characters—Dorian Gray, Don Juan, and Faust. Akhmatova is their anxious host. Mandel'shtam makes an appearance in the form of the minor silver-age poet and twenty-year-old suicide Vsevolod Kniazev, and announces, "Я к смерти готов" ("I am ready to die" [176]).[39] (According to Akhmatova, Mandel'shtam uttered these exact words in February 1934, just before his first arrest.[40] The conflation of Kniazev and Mandel'shtam is one node in a maddeningly complex typology that saturates "1913."[41]) The next section, "Решка" ("Tails"—as in the side of a coin), focuses on the poem's composition and the poet's dealings with Soviet bureaucracy and the "official" Soviet intelligentsia. The poem ends with an epilogue—an apostrophe to Leningrad—that details the poet's real and imagined experiences in the city, in Tashkent, and in Siberia, before, during, and after the war. Embedded in these sections is a history of Russian literature and art—with a special focus on the role of Russian poets—and a commentary on the origins of the Revolution and the Cold War.[42]

In the two opening notes, Akhmatova first rejects and then accepts responsibility for her poem. Unlike *Requiem*, however, her identity remains constant. In the first note, dated April 8, 1943, in Tashkent, she describes "receiving" the poem during the siege of Leningrad:

> Я не звала ее. Я даже не ждала ее в тот холодный и темный день моей последней ленинградрадской зимы. (165)
>
> [I did not invite it. I did not even expect it on that cold and dark day during my last Leningrad winter.]

She dedicates the poem to its "первых слушателей" (first auditors) and suggests that they are its true authors:

> Их голоса я слышу и вспоминаю их, когда читаю поэму вслух, и этот тайный хор стал для меня навсегда оправданием этой вещи. (165)
>
> [I hear their voices and remember them when I read the poem aloud, and this secret choir has for me become the lasting justification for this work.]

Akhmatova, here, does not speak for her contemporaries; her contemporaries speak through her. She is their reluctant medium and this is their poem.

But in the second note, dated November 1944, in Leningrad, she asserts her authority. The poem has one meaning, she insists, which she refuses to clarify:

> До меня часто доходят слухи о превратных и нелепых толкованиях «Поэмы без героя». И кто-то даже советует мне сделать поэму более понятной.
>
> Я воздержусь от этого.
>
> Никаких третьих, седьмых и двадцать девятых смыслов поэма не содержит.
>
> Ни изменять, ни объяснять ее я не буду.
>
> «Еже писахъ—писахъ». (166)

> [False and absurd interpretations of *Poem without a Hero* have often reached my ears. And someone even advised me to make the poem more comprehensible.
>
> I will refrain from this.
>
> The poem does not have any third, seventh, or twenty-ninth meaning.
>
> I am not going to change or explain it.
>
> "What I have written—I have written."]

The poem does not have any "third, seventh, or twenty-ninth meaning" because it has one meaning. Akhmatova could make it more comprehensible, but she refrains from doing so. The poem's difficulty is deliberate. If she is its reluctant medium, she is also its privileged interpreter.

As the poem continues, so does Akhmatova's assertion and subversion of her own authority. In the first dedication, she delicately takes control of her palimpsest:

> . . . .
> . . . а так как мне бумаги не хватило,
> Я на твоем пишу черновике.
> И вот чужое слово проступает,
> И, как тогда снежинка на руке,
> Доверчиво и без упрека тает. (167)

> [. . . . .
> . . . and because my paper has run out,
> I am writing on your rough draft.
> And there an alien word shows through,
> And like a snowflake in my hand,
> Melts, trustingly and without reproach.]

The "alien word" melts into her manuscript. The source text becomes her own.[43] Yet in the second dedication, a different voice appears, which she struggles to silence:

Не диктуй мне, сама я слышу:
Теплый ливень уперся в крышу,
Шепоточек слышу в плюще. (168)

[Don't dictate to me, I hear it myself:
A warm downpour presses on the roof,
I hear whispers in the ivy.]

Is Akhmatova suppressing one voice to attend to another? Or does "whispers" merely refer to the sound of the rain? Whatever the answer, the import of the lines is clear: this is not a bard appealing to her muse but a poet fighting to maintain her independence.

By the epilogue to the first section, she has lost the fight. Four distinct voices intermingle: a "theme," its response, the poem, and Akhmatova herself:

ВСЕ В ПОРЯДКЕ: ЛЕЖИТ ПОЭМА
И, КАК СВОЙСТВЕННО ЕЙ, МОЛЧИТ.
НУ, А ВДРУГ КАК ВЫРВЕТСЯ ТЕМА,
КУЛАКОМ В ОКНО ЗАСТУЧИТ,—
И ОТКЛИКНЕТСЯ ИЗДАЛЕКА
НА ПРИЗЫВ ЭТОТ СТРАШНЫЙ ЗВУК—
КЛОКОТАНЬЕ, СТОН И КЛЕКОТ—
И ВИДЕНЬЕ СКРЕЩЕННЫХ РУК?.. (189)

[ALL IS IN ORDER: HERE LIES THE POEM
WHICH, CHARACTERISTICALLY, IS SILENT.
BUT WHAT IF SUDDENLY A THEME BREAKS OUT,
KNOCKS ON THE WINDOW WITH ITS FIST,—
AND FROM AFAR, RESPONDING
TO THIS CALL AN AWFUL SOUND—
GURGLING, GROANS AND SCREECHES—
AND A VISION OF CROSSED ARMS?..]

There is no one to take responsibility for the violence that invades the scene. The poem is silent, Akhmatova is reading its epitaph. A "theme" appears and knocks on the window, and an "awful sound" responds "from afar." The "what if" indicates a counterfactual; it is unclear whether this "break" has in fact occurred. The final question-mark-double-period suggests that Akhmatova is as surprised by the intrusion as her readers are.

In notebooks written during the poem's composition, Akhmatova revels in this cacophony of voices and events. In an entry from 1962, she sounds Nabokovian, outlining her plans for the poem's metacommentary:

> In contrast to the editor's commentary, wh‹‹ich›› will be correct to the point of absurdity, the author's commentary won't contain a single true word, it will have jokes, both witty and stupid, hints, both

> comprehensible and incomprehensible, irrelevant references to great figures (Pushkin) and in general everything one finds in life.[44]

In a later entry she adds, "I've noticed that the more I explain [the poem], the more enigmatic and incomprehensible it is."[45] Here and elsewhere, Akhmatova celebrates and promotes the poem's difficulty. Authorial intention is intentionally obscured; chaos is cultivated.

In the poem's second section, Akhmatova introduces a proxy for the reader, a bewildered editor, who complains about the poem's obscurity:

1

Мой редактор был недоволен,
Клялся мне, что занят и болен,
Засекретил свой телефон
И ворчал: «Там три темы сразу!
Дочитав последнюю фразу,
Не поймешь, кто в кого влюблен,

2

Кто, когда и зачем встречался,
Кто погиб, и кто жив остался,
И кто автор, и кто герой,—
И к чему нам сегодня эти
Рассуждения о поэте
И каких-то призраков рой?» (191)

[1

My editor was dissatisfied,
Swearing to me that he was busy and sick,
He restricted access to his telephone number
And grumbled: "There's three themes at once!
Having read the last phrase,
You do not know who is in love with whom,

2

Who met whom, and when and why,
Who died, and who was left alive,
And who is the author, and who the hero,—
And what to us today are these
Stories about a poet
And a swarm of ghosts?"]

According to most critics, this editor is a parody of the "official" Soviet intelligentsia. Nancy K. Anderson, for example, argues:

> Akhmatova displays a grim flash of humor in her depiction of this figure's bewilderment at the work that does not fit the Socialist Realist pigeonhole: he tries to avoid dealing with it by claiming he is "busy and sick" (one excuse wasn't enough!) and ensuring that he can't be reached on the phone. When his evasions fail, his uncomprehending response to "The Year 1913" echoes standard Soviet literary criticism: it's much too complex.[46]

Anderson is correct up to a point: the poem does not fit the "Socialist Realist pigeonhole." But it does not fit any pigeonhole—including ones established by *Requiem* and other anti-Soviet texts. The editor's objections may be crude, but they are accurate: there are (at least) "three themes at once!"[47]

"It seems different to everyone," Akhmatova writes with obvious pleasure in her notebooks. She even provides a list of interpretations and interpreters:

> A poem of conscience (Shklovsk‹‹y››)
> A dance (Berkovsky)
> Music (almost everyone)
> The Symbolists' dream realiz‹‹ed›› (Zh‹‹irmunsky››)
> A poem of the eve, the holy night (B. Filippov)
> The poem as my biography
> A historical picture, the chronicle of an epoch (Chukovsk‹‹y››)
> Why the Revolution occurred (Shtok)
> One of the figures of Russian folk dance (hands outspread and forward) (Past‹‹ernak››).
> (Lyrics, stepping away and covered with a kerchief.)
> The way magic arises (Nayman)[48]

Chukovskii, Pasternak, Naiman: these are not party hacks. The best minds of the period seem to disagree about the poem's import. Berlin recalls hearing Akhmatova read a draft of the poem in Leningrad in 1945: "I realized even then that I was listening to a work of genius," he writes. "I do not suppose that I understood that many-faceted and most magical poem and its deeply personal allusions any better than when I read it now."[49]

The poem communicates a series of incompatible intentions: to be bewildering, to be precise, to be orphic, to be an act of witness, to have no intentions at all. It also presents a series of obscure allusions, many seemingly private. How should we, as readers, respond? We might follow Berlin and simply enjoy the poem's magic. Or we might read the poem as an open text.[50] In this latter scenario, the poem would be beyond the control of any particular reader (Akhmatova included) and yet responsive to each reader's particular experience.[51]

Alternatively, we could read the poem as a puzzle. In her monograph on Akhmatova's late poetry, Susan Amert concludes that the "constant emphasis on the role of concealment and secrets in the later metapoetry challenges the reader to decipher those texts, to uncover their deeper levels of meaning, to recognize literary references and come to terms with their significance." Amert accepts the challenge, coordinating hints from Akhmatova's notebooks, glosses from earlier studies, and readings of the poem's source texts. She identifies the masquerade's guests and Akhmatova's personal allusions. Readers develop a sense of the poem's import: "Tails," writes Amert, concerns "the persecution of Russian poets by the state after the revolution." The conclusion predicts "a highly ambiguous vengeance, surely to be wrought not only against the invaders who destroyed Peter's city but also against those responsible for the camps of Siberia."[52]

Amert's approach is reasonable: the more we learn about Akhmatova's references, the better we should expect to understand the poem. But the results are unimpressive. We already know that Russian poets were persecuted after the revolution. The prediction of Russia's eventual liberation is no surprise. By reading Amert and similar studies, one gains insight into the poem's composition history, but not the poem's significance. Berlin warns, "a tumulus of learned commentary is inexorably rising over [the poem]. Soon it may be buried under its weight."[53]

But there is another option: bracket Akhmatova's metacommentary and read the poem. If we refuse to submit to the poem's promotion of its own difficulty, we discover a coherent set of themes, supported by accessible, public allusions. Indeed, if we then return to the responses cataloged in Akhmatova's notebook, we find a plausible summary of the poem, not a list of mutually exclusive interpretations: a poem of conscience, a dance, a biography, a chronicle of an epoch, a story of why the revolution occurred, the symbolists' dream realized, and so on.

In "1913," Akhmatova mocks the hedonism and self-importance of her guests while reveling in memories of prerevolutionary Saint Petersburg. The scene is one of excess—a world populated by Don Juan, E.T.A. Hoffman's Dappertutto, and Jokanaan from Oscar Wilde's *Salomé*. Parodying Shelley's famous declaration, she tells one guest:

> Ты железные пишешь законы,
> Хаммураби, ликурги, солоны
> У тебя поучиться должны. (175)

> [You write iron laws,
> Hammurabi, Lycurgus, Solon
> Must learn from you.]

Decadence—especially artistic decadence—is Akhmatova's target. Akhmatova asks herself:

Веселиться—так веселиться,
Только как же могло случиться,
что одна я из них жива?" (173)

[To cheer myself—to cheer myself like this,
Only how was it able to happen,
That I alone of all of them am alive?]

The stanza recalls the fourth lyric of *Requiem*, which I discussed in section 2 in this chapter. In that poem, Akhmatova uses her life in Tsarskoe Selo to emphasize her suffering during the Terror. In "1913," in contrast, her memories of her life before the revolution occasion survivor's guilt. The poem is a record of her complicity in events she simultaneously relishes and condemns. She reprimands herself:

С той, какою была когда-то
В ожерелье черных агатов
до долины Иосафата
Снова встретиться не хочу . . . (174)

[That woman I was once
Wearing a necklace of black agate
Before the valley of Jehoshaphat
I do not want to meet again . . .]

The import is obvious: Akhmatova is standing in judgment of herself and her age.

As Galina Rylkova argues, "Akhmatova was the first to verbalize the link between two seemingly disconnected phenomena—the Silver Age and the Soviet Age."[54] This is the link that Nadezhda Mandel'shtam, in her memoirs, calls the poem's "hidden theme":

> In *Poem Without a Hero* [Akhmatova] talks about sin in those years when the awareness of it had been lost by everybody, particularly by those who regarded themselves as the elite. It took courage to look back on her youth and judge it by the standards of the "valley of Jehoshaphat," when everybody else is so lenient on the pre-revolutionary years and the twenties. . . . This indeed is the hidden theme of the *Poem*, which she tried to conceal . . . Overlaid by a frenetic rhythm, the *Poem* tells of retribution for a heedless youth spent among people who reckoned themselves part of the elite, and speaks volumes on the "Silver Age."[55]

To identify this "theme," readers do not need to arbitrate between the poem's orphic and civic poetics, or to learn that Dappertutto was also Vsevolod Meierkhol'd's pseudonym and the name of a puppet given to Akhmatova by Ol'ga Glebova-Sudeikina in 1924. The theme is hidden in plain view.

Why then go to such lengths to distract readers from such a clearly delineated theme? An answer emerges from what Nadezhda Mandel'shtam herself misses in her reading of the poem. She praises the poem's story of "retribution" but objects to its representation of her husband. "[F]or the sake of a literary game," she writes, "Akhmatova evidently decided to 'blend' Kniazev and M., after passing them through a literary meat grinder."[56] But this is not a game; it is a critique. Every mention of Kniazev suggests a moral equivalence between the actions of the young suicide and the author of the Stalin epigram. For Nadezhda Mandel'shtam, this is unthinkable. Akhmatova writes:

(Столько гибелей шло к поэту,
Глупый мальчик: он выбрал эту,—
Первых он не стерпел обид. (188)

[*(So many disasters went to the poet,*
Stupid boy: he chose this,—
He could not bear the first insults.]

David Wells argues that the identification of the two poets lends Kniazev's suicide "a clear political meaning"—that his "death both prefigures the breakdown of civilisation that came with war and revolution after 1913, and foreshadows the deaths of individuals during the Terror of the 1930s."[57] But the identification works the other way as well, establishing a link between Kniazev's romanticism and Mandel'shtam's martyrdom.

Reading *Poem without a Hero*, Nadezhda Mandel'shtam accepts a version of the poem's testimony but avoids its censure. The silver age is condemned; her husband remains beyond reproach. She sees what she wants to see—or, more accurately, she sees what she is prepared to see. The poem's "hidden theme" remains partially hidden.

This is how Akhmatova resolves her complicity: she dissociates truth and power. Rather than attempt to change minds, she creates a space for truth devoid of rhetorical force. *Poem without a Hero* defers its demand for justice indefinitely. Readers determine their relationship to its testimony. Shklovskii discovers a "poem of conscience"; Naum Berkovskii, a "dance"; Nadezhda Mandel'shtam, a critique of the silver age. The poem's distractions encourage partial access. Its extravagant form protects readers from harm. Paradoxically, the readers most likely to recognize the poem's full import are the least likely to be implicated by its testimony. Disinterestedness facilitates perspicacity.

For more than twenty-five years, Akhmatova lived this poem. Revisions, readings, debates—these were all occasions for her to experience the poem's truth and its innocuousness. This was her utopia of one: a poem that resolved her complicity in world historical events. *Poem without a Hero* speaks truth to power—without attempting to seize that power.

4

They leave themselves dismissible, protecting society from wrong access to them, if they can, as when the writer of Walden *successively identifies himself with the bird of awakening (the rooster), the bird of prophecy (the owl), and the bird of madness (the loon): you may take him or leave him alone, which is where and what he is.*

—STANLEY CAVELL[58]

"They leave themselves dismissible"—Cavell is describing Emerson and Thoreau, but the phrase also applies to Akhmatova in *Poem without a Hero*. The poem protects readers from her influence—and, as a result, protects her as well. This is the poem's power: its capacity for powerlessness.

But this conclusion is perhaps too sanguine. Does *Poem without a Hero* truly evade its contexts? After Stalin's death in 1953, mass violence was no longer used to regulate life in the Soviet Union. A massive bureaucracy assumed control and new cultural practices took hold. The state no longer required ideological purity. Outward compliance was sufficient. As Alexei Yurchak argues, "the performative dimension of ideological texts" displaced "their constative dimension."[59] Citizens could now live the truth if they lived it privately. *Poem without a Hero* exploited this change in Soviet culture. Its capacity for powerlessness did not interfere with state power. To put the point cynically: like *Requiem*, it was of its time.

Must all utopias of one reflect their contexts? Yes. But a better question to ask might be: What do utopias of one reveal about their contexts? The most obvious answer: the relation between writing and independence at specific moments in history. Thoreau's pursuit of independence in 1845 was necessarily different than Du Bois's in 1958—and Mandel'shtam's in 1933, Nadezhda Mandel'shtam's in 1956, and Akhmatova's in 1965. Every utopia of one is a negative index of oppression, and a positive index of artistic vision and ingenuity. Thoreau maximized his independence by moving to Walden and writing *Walden*. Mandel'shtam maximized his independence by ridiculing Stalin. These facts illuminate the radical differences between America in the mid-nineteenth century and the Soviet Union in the mid-1930s.

Yet utopias of one also reveal the insignificance of context. As strange as it may sound, Du Bois's exercise in historical materialism has the same source as Nadezhda Mandel'shtam's efforts to canonize her husband. The desire for freedom is nonnational and transhistorical. From this perspective, *Poem without a Hero* is of its time—and outside it.

All the writers I have discussed in this book thus far have had nonnational, transhistorical aims and transnational audiences, yet have created utopias of one in response to the politics and policies of their respective nation-states:

the United States of America and the Soviet Union. Their utopias of one are all deeply connected to problems of national citizenship.

In part 3 of the book, I depart from this focus on national citizenship. The next three writers I discuss respond to the failures of modernity: humanism, rationalization, global capitalism. These writers write as citizens of specific nations, of course, but their concerns are, at once, more local and more global. National politics and policies matter less than abstract ideas about value, education, labor, language, and justice.

Indeed, the writer I discuss in chapter 5 seems wholly uninterested in politics. Wallace Stevens's concerns are metaphysical: how to discover value in a world of fact, how to self-regulate. Ultimately, these concerns are not apolitical at all—they are prepolitical. Stevens's desire to write a poem that would dissolve the threat of nihilism is a desire to make politics meaningful.

PART III

The World

CHAPTER FIVE

Wallace Stevens's Point of View

1

In November 1929, in Cambridge, England, Ludwig Wittgenstein gave his first and only public lecture.[1] "A Lecture on Ethics" (as it came to be known) presents the following thought experiment:

> Suppose one of you were an omniscient person and therefore knew all the movements of all the bodies in the world dead or alive and that he also knew all the states of mind of all the human beings that ever lived, and suppose this man wrote all he knew in a big book, then this book would contain the whole description of the world; and what I want to say is, that book would contain nothing that we would call an *ethical* judgment or anything that would logically imply such a judgment. It would of course contain all relative judgments of value and all true scientific propositions and in fact all true propositions that can be made. But all the facts described would, as it were, stand on the same level and in the same way all propositions stand on the same level. There are no propositions which, in any absolute sense, are sublime, important, or trivial.[2]

Wittgenstein then provides an example:

> If for instance in our world-book we read the description of a murder with all its details physical and psychological, the mere description of these facts will contain nothing which we could call an *ethical* proposition. The murder will be on exactly the same level as any other event, for instance the falling of a stone. Certainly the reading of this description might cause us pain or rage or any other emotion, or we might read about the pain or rage caused by this murder in other people when they heard of it, but there will simply be facts, facts, facts, but no Ethics.[3]

The implications of this version of the fact-ethics dichotomy (known more generally as the fact/value dichotomy) resonate across Wallace Stevens's poetry.[4] Indeed, the dichotomy captures the metaphysical foundations of Stevens's work. It is the source of his anxieties about nihilism and relativism—about living in a world without God.

Translated into Stevensese, "facts, facts, facts, but no Ethics" becomes, in a line from the first version of "Owl's Clover" (1936), "Fromage and coffee and cognac and no gods" (579).[5] The "falling of a stone" becomes Stevens's rocks, which mark the same absence of value, and "mere description" resounds as "Mere blusteriness," "mere delight," "mere sound," "mere example," "mere weather," "mere air," "Mere repetitions," "mere desire," "mere brown clods," "mere catching weeds of talk," "mere savage presence," "mere objectiveness of things," "mere flowing of the water," "Mere Being" (36, 110, 116, 117, 333, 333, 350, 396, 415, 415, 442, 449, 451, 476). In all these cases, "mere" marks the same deficiency: things (stones, cognac) and psychological states (pain, rage, pleasure) without absolute or intrinsic value.

The fact/value dichotomy thus grounds the two commonplaces of Stevens's poetry: his desire for absolute value in a world of fact (what Schopenhauer would call his "metaphysical need") and his belief in poetry's ability to satisfy that desire.[6] (This is the condition of possibility for Stevens's utopia: a world without metaphysical need.) "The earth, for us, is flat and bare," he writes in "The Man with the Blue Guitar" (1937); "Poetry // Exceeding music must take the place / Of empty heaven and its hymns" (136–37). In his lecture "Two or Three Ideas" (1951), he asserts, "In an age of disbelief, or, what is the same thing, in a time that is largely humanistic, in one sense or another, it is for the poet to supply the satisfactions of belief, in his measure and in his style" (841). Stevens's *Collected Poetry and Prose* is replete with such statements—statements that point to the absence of absolute value and maintain poetry's compensatory power.

Is there anything left to say about Stevens's pursuit of value? The pursuit connects almost all Stevens scholarship. Arguments for his aestheticism or existentialism, pragmatism or skepticism, or realism or idealism are arguments for how best to describe his response to his metaphysical need. Kant, Hegel, Emerson, James, Nietzsche, Husserl, Heidegger, Derrida, Rorty—these names, in Stevens scholarship, represent ways of addressing the fact/value dichotomy.[7] Is the only option for scholars to continue to pair poet and philosophy, or poet and philosopher—or to ignore the problem of value altogether?

In this chapter, I try to describe Stevens's pursuit of value from his point of view—especially during the act of writing. I begin with an account of his attitude toward his metaphysical need and then examine how three poems fail to satisfy it: "Sunday Morning" (1915, 1923), "The Idea of Order at Key West" (1934), and "Credences of Summer" (1947). Each poem, I argue, approaches the problem of value as a problem of community formation. Each poem is an experiment—an attempt to coordinate a collective solution to the fact/value dichotomy that avoids both nihilism and what Wittgenstein, later in his lecture, calls the "supernatural."[8] Ultimately, I detail how a fourth poem, "The Auroras of Autumn" (1948), solves the problem of value (for Stevens) by abandoning the idea of community altogether. The poem's success hinges on its inaccessibility—how it prevents readers from sharing Stevens's point of view.

2

In "Exoticism and Structuralism in Wallace Stevens" (1984), Fredric Jameson identifies Stevens's belief in poetry's power to generate value in a world of fact as his "ideology." Jameson describes this ideology—"systematically elaborated and produced in the poems on death and the religion of art, from the early 'Sunday Morning' on"—as "the least interesting [part] of the Stevens canon." Citing "Notes toward a Supreme Fiction" (1942), he adds that "as soon as we come to be convinced of the fictionality of meaning, the whole operation loses its interest; philosophies of 'as if' are notoriously unsatisfying and self-unravelling."[9] For Jameson, Stevens's ideology is not just banal—it is self-defeating.

One could compound this critique by objecting to Jameson's "and produced"—for Stevens's engagement with value never seems to move beyond elaboration. The poetry is obsessed with its own aims and resources. As A. Alvarez writes in *Stewards of Excellence* (1958), "many of the long poems [are] almost unreadable: . . . you work down to what he is saying on *this* topic only to find that it is much the same as he has always said about everything else."[10] From this perspective, Jameson's claim that Stevens's ideology is the "least interesting" part of his canon is a wry joke. Stevens repeats himself endlessly: his ideology is his canon. "He might have taken to drink," J. V. Cunningham suggests; "he took to poems, instead, to too many rot-gut poems."[11]

Scholars with disparate critical commitments present similar objections to Stevens's poetry. Randall Jarrell argues, "The habit of philosophizing in poetry—or of seeming to philosophize, of using a philosophical tone, images, constructions, of having quasi-philosophic daydreams—has been unfortunate for Stevens."[12] Hugh Kenner calls the content of the poems "discursive variations on the familiar theme of a first-generation agnostic."[13] Camille Paglia complains that in the late work, "Gorgeous images or lines still abound, but pompous, big-think gestures have become a crutch."[14] For these scholars, Stevens is his own worst enemy: his endless metacommentary compromises his art.

Stevens, I think, would have sympathized with these views. Indeed, these scholars get right something that Stevens's less critical readers miss—readers who endorse his ideology and accept his poems as consolatory. The poems are repetitive. Philosophies of "as if" are unsatisfying. Yet Stevens's recognition of these facts does not diminish his ideology. He remains committed to providing an account of poetry's metaphysical efficacy in his poetry. Why? What explains his career-long attachment to an ideology he recognizes as frustrating, even impractical?[15] Are his poems symptoms of akrasia or cruel optimism?[16] Is he perverse? Is he addicted to poetry?

In poem after poem and across sequences of poems, Stevens asserts the efficacy of his poetry and then laments its inadequacy. A central claim of this chapter is that this process is repetitive, but not in Cunningham's specific sense. Writing a poem, for Stevens, is not like tossing back one more drink, each the same as the last, save for its diminishing marginal utility. Rather, writing a poem is repetitive in the way experiments are repetitive: iterations that seek closer approximations to the solution of a problem. This is why his ideology survives his dissatisfaction: his poems are not discrete events but elements in series. Every failure to "supply the satisfactions of belief" warrants yet another attempt. *Collected Poetry and Prose* is a progressive—although not always unilinear—metaphysical project.

3

In "Sunday Morning," Stevens attempts to ameliorate the implications of the fact/value dichotomy by convincing himself and his readers of the adequacy of relative judgments of value.

The poem opens with a woman at home, enjoying her breakfast on a Sunday morning. Her experience of pleasure catalyzes rather than satisfies her metaphysical need:

> Complacencies of the peignoir, and late
> Coffee and oranges in a sunny chair,
> And the green freedom of a cockatoo
> Upon a rug mingle to dissipate
> The holy hush of ancient sacrifice.
> She dreams a little, and she feels the dark
> Encroachment of that old catastrophe,
> As a calm darkens among water-lights. (53)

"Complacencies" (a general sense of satisfaction) combine with specific pleasures (the heat from the sun, the taste and smell of coffee and oranges, the images on a rug) to first "dissipate" and then spur "the dark / Encroachment of that old catastrophe." This catastrophe, as the poem's title suggests and the poem will recount, is Jesus's crucifixion. The recognition of beauty, here, leads to metaphysical need. In the fifth canto, the woman declares, "in contentment I still feel / The need of some imperishable bliss" (55).

In response to this predicament, Stevens famously claims, "Death is the mother of beauty; hence from her, / Alone, shall come fulfilment to our dreams / And our desires" (55). In other words, "imperishable bliss" is a contradiction in terms: the experience of beauty (and of value, generally) requires the apprehension of loss. To adapt the claim to the framework of the fact/value dichotomy: all judgments of value are necessarily relative—relative to every individual's experience of the world, to every individual's sense of mortality. Accordingly, the absence of absolute judgments of value is not a cause for anxiety—such judgments do not exist and cannot exist.

For the remainder of the poem, Stevens tests the adequacy of this claim. In the penultimate canto, he imagines its social implications, depicting a community of men, "Supple and turbulent," offering "boisterous devotion to the sun, / Not as a god, but as a god might be" (55, 56). The acknowledgment of their authority—that their "chant of paradise" comes "Out of their blood" rather than from a supernatural source—enables their communion (56). Stevens writes, "They shall know well the heavenly fellowship / Of men that perish and of the summer morn" (56). Enjambment, here, makes the point: heavenly fellowship results from a fellowship "of men that perish"—not men enjoying eternal life in heaven.

In the final canto, Stevens returns to the woman's point of view and offers a portrait of a fully secular world:

> She hears, upon that water without sound,
> A voice that cries, "The tomb in Palestine
> Is not the porch of spirits lingering.
> It is the grave of Jesus, where he lay."
> We live in an old chaos of the sun,
> Or old dependency of day and night,
> Or island solitude, unsponsored, free,
> Of that wide water, inescapable.
> Deer walk upon our mountains, and the quail
> Whistle about us their spontaneous cries;
> Sweet berries ripen in the wilderness;
> And, in the isolation of the sky,
> At evening, casual flocks of pigeons make
> Ambiguous undulations as they sink,
> Downward to darkness, on extended wings. (56)

In a still influential reading, J. Hillis Miller claims that "the lady's experience of the dissolution of the gods leaves her living in a world of exquisite particulars." This world is compensatory: its "endless round of birth, death, and the seasons" inspires and sustains individual and collective acts of valorization. Stevens's humanism resolves the woman's metaphysical need and his own. Quoting from "Esthétique du Mal," Miller writes, "'Sunday Morning' is Stevens's most eloquent description of the moment when the gods dissolve. Bereft of the supernatural, man does not lie down paralyzed in despair. He sings the creative hymns of a new culture, the culture of those who are 'wholly human' and know themselves." For Miller, "Sunday Morning" is a "creative hymn" that evades both nihilism and the supernatural. It makes a virtue of necessity. The discovery that "there never has been any celestial world is a joyful liberation."[17]

This is wishful thinking. "We live in the old chaos of the sun," Stevens writes—not a world of cyclical change. The canto's repeated use of "or" links, but does not arbitrate between, competing descriptions of emptiness. Our freedom is inescapable—and thus is no freedom at all. To put this point another way, the poem describes a world without positive liberty and replete with negative liberty (to return to Isaiah Berlin's terms). There is no constraint on action, but also no reason to act—an inauspicious setting for Miller's "new culture."

The canto's final seven lines confirm this emptiness by animating a process of deanthropomorphization: *our* mountains devolve into the quail's indefinite, spontaneous whistles *about us*. The pun is caustic in its obviousness: it exists to mark our insignificance, the impossibility of the cries' actually concerning us. "[A]bout us" only indicates the fact of spatial relations. The pun introduces the poem's final image: the descent of the pigeons, which, despite their natural markings, are an undifferentiated flock. This is not a world of "exquisite particulars" at all. Stevens emphasizes the pigeons' fall four times with "sink," "Downward," "evening" (the setting sun), and "casual" (from *casus*, "fall" and also "death").

If the "extended wings" in the poem's final line provide solace, it is at the expense of Stevens's ideology, and the efforts of the poem up to this point. Although the wings remain visible despite the darkness, they do so in an atmosphere of religious imagery (the Fall, angel's wings, wings forming an image of the cross) that troubles the stanza's assertion that "The tomb in Palestine / Is not the porch of spirits lingering. / It is the grave of Jesus, where he lay." If we refuse this form of consolation, the "extended wings" simply reaffirm our one bastion of certainty: perception of physical extension in space. The poem, in this way, ends irresolutely between two incompatible, unsatisfactory alternatives: Christianity and bald materialism.[18]

"Sunday Morning," for Stevens, is a failure. The poem represents a community that he cannot persuade himself to join. Its solution to the fact/value dichotomy is, ultimately, no solution at all. But a failure? This sounds ridiculous. The poem is beautiful and persuasive. Its pleasures exceed the pleasures it describes. It convinces Miller, who lionizes its "ring of men" (55). It convinces me.[19] It is Stevens's most anthologized long poem—surpassing even "Thirteen Ways of Looking at a Blackbird" (1917).[20] Yet Stevens remains unsatisfied—a fact that forces the question: If "Sunday Morning" cannot resolve his metaphysical need, can any poem?[21]

Stevens's subsequent poetry can be read as a response to this question. In "The Idea of Order at Key West" (1934), he tests a different approach to the problem of value. Instead of defending the adequacy of relative judgments of value, he constructs a counterfactual world in which judgments of value are necessarily unanimous, and thus absolute. In this world, dissent is impossible: I cannot disagree with Miller, we cannot disagree with Stevens, and (most importantly), Stevens cannot disagree with himself.

The poem opens with a woman singing by the shore of Key West. Stevens and a companion, the critic Ramon Fernandez, marvel at the efficacy of her song: "And when she sang, the sea, / Whatever self it had, became the self / That was her song, for she was the maker." As the song absorbs the sea, the world becomes her world: "there never was a world for her / Except the one she sang and, singing, made" (106). Making, here, is an aesthetic and political act. The song is an exercise in sovereignty.

Yet this account is imprecise. The woman may be the song's maker, but she is not the sole source of its power. As Stevens and Fernandez describe the song's efficacy, they speculate about its etiology: "Whose spirit is this? we said, because we knew / It was the spirit that we sought and knew / That we should ask this often as she sang" (105). Stevens and Fernandez then claim that the spirit that composes the song is "more" than "the dark voice of the sea / That rose" and the "the outer voice of the sky / And cloud." It is "More even than her voice, and ours" (105). The spirit ultimately is indistinguishable from the world it creates. It is at once human and nonhuman, artifact and event.

What is the significance of this etiology? A radical monism. The song assimilates its maker. Stevens and Fernandez speak with a single voice. This is why both men appear in the poem: their duet exemplifies the song's efficacy, its power to dissolve difference.[22]

A world without difference—this is the poem's response to the problem of value. As Wittgenstein notes in his lecture, "the *absolute good*, if it is a describable state of affairs, would be one which everybody, independent of his tastes and inclinations, would *necessarily* bring about."[23] "The Idea of Order" represents just such a state of affairs—or, more accurately, it represents a state of affairs without individual tastes and inclinations.[24] Judgments of value are unanimous because everything is unanimous.

Unsurprisingly, this solution also proves unsatisfactory. In the poem's penultimate stanza, Stevens addresses Fernandez by name—an act that dissolves their union. In the final stanza, he revises his account of the song's etiology:

> Oh! Blessed rage for order, pale Ramon,
> The maker's rage to order words of the sea,
> Words of the fragrant portals, dimly-starred,
> And of ourselves and of our origins,
> In ghostlier demarcations, keener sounds. (106)

A "rage for order": this is the song's true source—not an amalgam of mind and world but an affective response to chaos. To emphasize this point, Stevens ends the poem with an image of discord. The maker's rage cannot reconcile the "words of the sea" and the words "of ourselves and of our origins." The seascape resists assimilation: "ghostlier demarcations, keener sounds" describe a world beyond comprehension.

What prompts this reversal? One answer is the end of the song itself. In the diegesis of the poem, Stevens abandons his description of unanimity as soon as the song ends. The message: in the face of metaphysical need, art provides respite, not permanent satisfaction. To put this point another way, art helps us temporarily forget inconvenient truths—in this case, that judgments require volition, that unanimity without individual agency is not unanimity at all.

The skyscapes and seascapes, the solitary woman, the community of men—"The Idea of Order" recasts the central tropes of "Sunday Morning" to imagine a world without the possibility of dissent. Instead of trying to justify the adequacy of relative judgments of value, the poem eliminates the need for justification. But the outcome of the two poems is the same: metaphysical need and failure.

Yet this account is still imprecise. Stevens, the poem's speaker, is seduced by the woman's song and temporarily forgets his metaphysical need. From his point of view, the song fails because its effects are at once chimerical and fleeting. But what about Stevens, the poem's author? From his point of view, the song's failure is an occasion to investigate art's etiology and efficacy. The poem, in this way, does not simply reject a fantastic counterfactual; it uses a fantastic counterfactual to test art's instrumentality.

Results from this test are on display in "Credences of Summer." The poem's second canto presents a series of instructions:

> Postpone the anatomy of summer, as
> The physical pine, the metaphysical pine.
> Let's see the very thing and nothing else.
> Let's see it with the hottest fire of sight.
> Burn everything not part of it to ash. (322)

The first two lines ask us to bracket the fact/value dichotomy. The next three, to concentrate our gaze on an unspecified object. Together, the lines describe a point of view—a line of vision and a mental attitude. The canto concludes:

> Trace the gold sun about the whitened sky
> Without evasion by a single metaphor.
> Look at it in its essential barrenness
> And say this, this is the centre that I seek.
> Fix it in an eternal foliage
>
> And fill the foliage with arrested peace,
> Joy of such permanence, right ignorance
> Of change still possible. Exile desire
> For what is not. This is the barrenness
> Of the fertile thing that can attain no more. (322–23)

These instructions have two aims. First, to imprint a scene on the mind's eye—the sun shining through a canopy of leaves. (The word "foliage" denotes the leaves of the trees and the leaves of the book we hold in our hands. We literally see through the pages of *Collected Poetry and Prose*.) Second, to preempt personal associations that might splinter our collective gaze. "[A]rrested peace" and "right ignorance" are occasions for synchrony—states of mind that we can all share. "Exile desire / For what is not" is a demand for presentness. This is Stevens's latest experiment: to coordinate a new form of unanimity—a real, empirical unanimity. His hypothesis: if we adopt a common point of view—a point of view defined by the canto's viewing instructions—we will develop a common set of values.

The experiment, at its core, implies a critique of Wittgenstein's version of the fact/value dichotomy. This is the significance of "Let's see it with the hottest fire of sight": the recognition that no person could present a "mere description" of anything. The line fuses subject and object, the act of perception and the thing perceived. The message is that we are integral to what we see. We do not have unmediated access to facts as such. Our perspective influences our perception of the world. Wittgenstein's omniscient world-book author is a fallacy.

This account of perception is by no means exceptional. Sebastian Gardner, Simon Critchley, and Charles Altieri all describe how Stevens rejects what Richard Rorty calls "sense-data empiricism"—the idea that sense perception provides unmediated access to a world of fact.[25] Gardner details Stevens's affinity to Kant and transcendental idealism.[26] Critchley links Stevens to Heidegger, among others.[27] Altieri offers a powerful account of Stevens and phenomenology.[28] Together, these scholars provide a framework for understanding how Stevens rejects naive forms of empiricism without embracing equally naive forms of idealism.[29]

But what does this account of perception have to do with Stevens's experiment in "Credences of Summer" and his pursuit of value more generally? The account grounds his hypothesis that a common point of view will generate a common set of values. How? By illuminating a connection between our perception of facts and our judgments of value. Both activities are in some sense relative. Both reflect a frame of reference. For Stevens this connection (however vague) motivates another attempt to coordinate an alternative to nihilism.

One way to begin to explicate this connection and its significance for Stevens is to invoke Wilfrid Sellars's distinction between epistemic and nonepistemic facts in *Empiricism and the Philosophy of Mind* (1956). According to Sellars, epistemic facts are normative. "[T]he ability to recognize that something *looks green*," he writes, "presupposes the concept of *being green*." This concept, in turn, presupposes a "long process of publicly reinforced responses to public objects . . . in public situations."[30] In contrast, nonepistemic facts are not normative: they do not rely on concepts and a history of "public situations." Such facts are the exclusive domain of the natural sciences and Wittgenstein's world-book author.

For Sellars, epistemic facts are all we know. More than that: they are how we assimilate sense data.[31] As John McDowell explains, "'epistemic,' in Sellars's usage, acquires a sense that cuts loose from its etymological connection with knowledge. In the wider sense epistemic facts relate to world-directed thought as such, whether knowledge-involving or not."[32] To put this point another way, all our intentional acts rely on socially mediated concepts. Our engagement with norms is all-encompassing. To notice a falling rock or to condemn a murder is to rely on a complex history of social relations.

Does the hegemony of epistemic facts deny us access to the natural world? One aim of McDowell's reading of Sellars is to "exorcize" (rather than answer) anxieties about the relation between epistemic and nonepistemic facts. "In receiving impressions," McDowell claims, "a subject can be open to the way things manifestly are. This yields a satisfying interpretation for the image of postures that are answerable to the world through being answerable to experience."[33] Perception is both normative and responsive to the world as it is. Our minds do not deny us reality but allow us to access it through concepts. As a result, we can endorse a minimal empiricism without accepting the implications of Wittgenstein's version of the fact/value dichotomy.

Does this description of epistemic facts justify Stevens's experiment? Is perception a viable site for value formation? In "Credences of Summer," Stevens does not give himself an opportunity to find out. Halfway through the poem, he retracts his call for unanimity. "The rock cannot be broken," he writes. "It is the truth" (324). In the final canto, he depicts an "inhuman author" who "does not hear his characters talk." In the final line, he laments the characters' "youthful happiness"—a happiness that fades with experience (326). The poem retreats from its experiment. Philosophical speculation cedes, yet again, to metaphysical need. This is ultimately one source of the poem's power: Stevens's inability to fully grapple with his recognition that our engagement with facts involves the stuff of value. Stevens, here, cannot accept his own insights.

Yet the retreat does not mark the end of this particular experiment: Stevens's hypothesis in "Credences of Summer" returns in the poem's sequel, "The Auroras of Autumn" (1948).

4

In "The Auroras of Autumn," Stevens tries to focus our collective gaze on yet another skyscape—the aurora borealis. This time, however, he does not present a set of viewing instructions (as in "Credences of Summer"). Instead, he attempts to establish a common ground—a ground expansive enough to accommodate our disparate subject positions.

The canto opens in a nonplace that recalls both the Garden of Eden and Plato's cave:

> This is where the serpent lives, the bodiless.
> His head is air. Beneath his tip at night
> Eyes open and fix on us in every sky.
>
> Or is this another wriggling out of the egg,
> Another image at the end of the cave,
> Another bodiless for the body's slough? (355)

The deictics work like puns: pointing to the sky and the auroras, to the poem and a canon of poetry, to the book in our hands. The nouns work in a similar way. The serpent is Satan in the garden, and the knowledge and danger he represents. The serpent is also the serpentine designs in the sky and their green, serpentine color. The cave is Plato's cave of refracted images as well as an image of the night sky. The puns even thematize themselves: Eden's serpent and Plato's cave are sites of duplicity. If one attempts to catalog all these combinations, one ends up describing the act of interpretation—an effect that the poem seems to anticipate. The serpent's eyes "fix on us in every sky," which presumably includes our own.

Stevens seems overwhelmed by this proliferation of perspectives. Is this "another wriggling out of the egg," he asks, "Another image at the end of the cave, / Another bodiless for the body's slough?" The lines conflate images of rebirth and misapprehension, freedom and constraint. "Slough" (if pronounced "*slou*") suggests the Slough of Despond in *The Pilgrim's Progress*. In this reading, our bodies block any attempt to collectivize. But if pronounced "*sləf*," slough suggests a radical transformation: an act of abandoning our bodies for a collective "bodilessness." (Stevens pronounces the word "*sləf*" on a recording of the poem.)[34] As we confront these images, we might remind ourselves that we are still reading a description of the auroras, which resemble a serpent shedding its serpentine slough.

This is how Stevens intends to establish a common ground: by offering a surplus of perspectives on the auroras. As David Wiggins notes, "Perspective is not a form of illusion, distortion, or delusion. All the different perspectives of a single array of objects are perfectly consistent with one another. Given a set of perspectives, we can recover, if only they be reliably collected, a unified true account of the shape, spatial relations, and relative dimensions of the objects in the array."[35] Do the perspectives in the canto provide a "unified true account" of the auroras? The canto continues:

> This is where the serpent lives. This is his nest,
> These fields, these hills, these tinted distances,
> And the pines above and along and beside the sea. (355)

The view is cinematic: an aerial shot sweeps across the landscape, capturing the pines from above and then beside the sea. The perspectives are consistent: they seem to compose a plausible portrait of the auroras' compass.

The auroras are particularly well suited to sustain this proliferation of perspectives. As natural phenomena, they support empirical description. Fleeting and sublime, they license puns and other figures. Unlike earthquakes, they are intangible and unindexed by the landscape. (They do not leave evidence directly available to human perception in their wake.) And unlike eclipses and clouds, they are unpredictable, rare, and geographically circumscribed.[36] As a result, they justify a written record—insofar as a written record provides access to the event, after the event. Even more importantly, they bind percept with perceiver—descriptions of the auroras are descriptions of perceiving the auroras.[37]

Yet Stevens quickly recognizes two threats to the experiment. First, there is the danger that the poem's descriptions will not be expansive enough. Second, there is the danger that they will be too expansive, and dissolve our common ground and common object. Stevens thematizes these threats as he continues to describe the auroras:

> This is form gulping after formlessness,
> Skin flashing to wished-for disappearances
> And the serpent body flashing without the skin.
>
> This is the height emerging and its base
> These lights may finally attain a pole
> In the midmost midnight and find the serpent there,
>
> In another nest, the master of the maze
> Of body and air and forms and images,
> Relentlessly in possession of happiness. (355)

The lines describe an asymptote: the poem "gulping after formlessness." Stevens wants the act of reading the poem to be identical to the act of looking at the inconstant auroras. The problem, of course, is the materiality of the poem. For us the very thing that facilitates representation obstructs identity. "This" for Stevens, designates the auroras and "The Auroras of Autumn." For us, "This" designates the poem only. He is the poem's maker: master and occupant of the "maze / Of body and air and forms and images." We are its occupants only. The difference establishes a hierarchy that makes developing a common ground difficult, if not impossible.

Perhaps unsurprisingly, the poem's proliferation of perspectives falters as soon as Stevens confronts this impasse:

> This is his poison: that we should disbelieve
> Even that. His meditations in the ferns,
> When he moved so slightly to make sure of sun,
>
> Made us no less as sure.

As the serpent tests the sun by shifting under its rays, he makes "us no less as sure." The statement tells us nothing about our certainty. The serpent's poison is not disbelief but our awareness that his knowledge has no bearing on our own. The canto ends ambiguously: "We saw in his head, / Black beaded on the rock, the flecked animal, / The moving grass, the Indian in his glade" (355). Does the sentence present the auroras ranging over and patterning the rock, the grass, the "Indian in his glade"? Does it depict the serpent's thoughts—Stevens's thoughts? Does it picture a post-aurora landscape with a black beaded serpent weaving its way through the grass? Does it describe the auroras? Does Stevens's "we" include us? We cannot be certain.

The next three cantos all begin, "Farewell to an idea . . ." as though Stevens were saying farewell to his latest experiment (355–57). This is farewell to the idea of common ground and to ideas as such—for ideas unite us despite our different contexts. Stevens no longer looks to readers to resolve his metaphysical need. Instead, he looks inward and at the auroras. This is his next experiment: to give a comprehensive account of his personal experience. In the language of the poem, he aims to get to the "midmost midnight" of the auroras and find himself there: to describe the world so perfectly that he describes himself as well. This is happiness: union between mind and world—union that identifies his values as values in the world.

To delimit his experience of the auroras, Stevens no longer attempts to share his point of view. Solipsism becomes a strategy. But if this strategy is successful, how can we evaluate his experiment or even identify it as such? The answer is we cannot. All we can do is test my argument against other arguments about the poem, and against the poem's metacommentary. What follows is necessarily speculative.

A survey of Stevens scholarship reveals two standard responses to the poem: scholars miss its import or concede its impenetrability—sometimes both. Harold Bloom presents an uncharacteristically evasive account of the third canto and then admits that it "demonstrates so oddly original a mode of writing as to make critical description very difficult."[38] Frank Doggett and Dorothy Emerson note the poem's "inner secrecy."[39] Joseph Riddel calls parts "bafflingly obscure."[40] Paraphrase is not the problem: the poem does not communicate a particular feeling that resists conceptualization. Kenner describes Ezra Pound's *Cantos* as "apprehensible, not explicable"; "The Auroras of Autumn" is the opposite: explicable, but seldom apprehensible.[41] One may identify references, but they rarely disclose their significance.

"The Auroras of Autumn" offers an account of its own difficulty when the "we" first returns in the fifth canto. The canto completes a suite of domestic scenes: the second presents a cabin on an isolated beach; the third, a mother figure; the fourth, variations on a regal, conflicted father. In the fifth, the mother and father orchestrate a festival. Stevens writes, "This then is Chatillon or as you please. / We stand in the tumult of a festival" (358). As Eleanor Cook notes, Chatillon is Stevens's "possible ancestor."[42] For Stevens, this is a domestic scene. For us it is simply as we please. Like the love of one family member for another, the scene's significance is unavailable to outsiders. Stevens and his readers both stand in "tumult of a festival," but the festivals are different. He stands in tumult of his auroras and self-descriptions; we stand in tumult of the poem. The poem's import is private—in the same way that love (erotic, familial) is private. Personal identity is a condition of meaning.[43]

The best evidence for this argument is ultimately your own experience of the poem. Yet one reading provides an especially helpful picture of the poem's difficulty.[44] In "Wallace Stevens and the King James Bible" (1991), Cook reads the poem's seventh canto, which begins:

> Is there an imagination that sits enthroned
> As grim as it is benevolent, the just
> And the unjust, which in the midst of summer stops
>
> To imagine winter? When the leaves are dead,
> Does it take its place in the north and enfold itself,
> Goat-leaper, crystalled and luminous, sitting
>
> In highest night? (360)

Cook examines how the image of the goat-leaper-as-auroras coordinates a series of references. She cites the book of Ezekiel, Revelation, the bombing of Hiroshima, Shelley's preface to *Hellas*, *Brewer's Dictionary*, Matthew, *As You Like It*, *As You Like It*'s Ovid, Joyce, Milton, classical pastoral, and Hazlitt.[45] The gloss depicts a lifetime of reading spurred into description by the auroras. I cannot imagine a better illustration of how description bifurcates to represent an act of perception and a percept.

Cook tells us almost everything we could possibly know about the image and its construction. We only miss extratextual elements—the feel of Stevens's chair, the typography of his *Hellas*. Yet despite this knowledge, my experience of the canto departs radically from my experience of the poem's first canto—and "Sunday Morning," "The Idea of Order at Key West," and "Credences of Summer." I marvel at the canto's beauty, but I cannot empathize with Stevens—I cannot imaginatively recreate his point of view. (I expect your experience is similar.) Cook's conclusions are ultimately mundane: "A whole series of associations . . . works retrospectively to undo the jetted tragedy of goats, their black destiny." Stevens is "separating out New Testament pastoral from classical pastoral, where goats enjoy life. He is moving against the entire great force of Christian pastoral tradition."[46] This reading may be accurate (it reconfirms Stevens's view of Christianity), but it does not begin to make sense of the care and skill that seems to have gone into the poem's composition.

Does "The Auroras of Autumn" resolve Stevens's metaphysical need? Does it represent his utopia? I do not know. But my uncertainty is revealing: unlike Stevens's previous experiments, the poem does not announce its own inadequacy. Instead, it maintains its investment in the auroras as a medium for union between mind and world. One could argue that the poem is meaningless for all involved or a puzzle still waiting to be solved. But such arguments do not account for the poem's strange difficulty or its relation to Stevens's earlier work—how it translates an insight into normativity into an experiment in description. This is my argument: if the poem makes something happen, it happens for Stevens alone. Its efficacy is asymmetrical.

What can readers learn from such an inaccessible poem? "The Auroras of Autumn" (like the other utopian projects discussed in this book) suggests a way to understand aesthetic difficulty and literary efficacy, and their interrelation. Standard explanations for aesthetic difficulty are inapplicable or insufficient—political resistance, defamiliarization, elitism, prophecy. Likewise, standard conceptions of literary efficacy—symbolic action, negative critique, sympathetic identification. The poem is not (or not only) a reaction against reification or an instrument of provocation or persuasion. It is an attempt to construct a utopia in which an individual's relative judgments of value are absolute judgments of value. The poem's success hinges on its inaccessibility.

The poem also offers a way to understand what we mean when we describe a poem as experimental or a poet as thinking in verse. The transition between the first and second cantos reveals a mind in action. Stevens is learning from his poem as he shapes it. Failure is a form of inspiration—an opportunity to renegotiate his approach to the problem of value. The process defines Stevens's career as a whole. From *Harmonium* (1923) to the poems collected in *Opus Posthumous* (1957), he tests and retests how the best words in the best order might resolve his metaphysical need. Poetry is at once a means and an end—a way to identify value and a value in itself.

But the poem does not offer any practical lessons to readers. It does not even teach us how to resolve our own metaphysical need. Its response to the fact/value dichotomy is not pedagogical or redemptive. It is not even philosophical. After the first canto, Stevens constructs a world beyond justification, reciprocity, ideas. His response to the problem of value is thoroughly singular, idiosyncratic.

So why publish the poem? The most banal response is that is what poets do—they publish. But another response is possible: the poem exploits its audience as it alienates it. By recognizing Stevens's descriptions of the auroras as descriptions of the auroras, we tacitly confirm his values (without understanding their specific content). The poem establishes a transitive relation between the value of the auroras and Stevens's values in the world. To marvel bewildered at his goat-leaper is to partially verify the efficacy of his experiment.

5

Tracking Stevens's pursuit of value reveals a series of increasingly extravagant experiments. An attempt to confirm the sufficiency of relative judgments of value in "Sunday Morning" leads to a fantastic counterfactual in "The Idea of Order at Key West." An insight into normativity in "Credences of Summer" leads to the strategic solipsism of "The Auroras of Autumn." Ultimately, this is the result (and cost) of Stevens's experimentation: a hermetic poem and a hermetic world. "The Auroras of Autumn" succeeds (possibly!) because it sacrifices the thing "Sunday Morning" and his other poems hold dear: community. Self-making becomes a form of world-making and vice versa—and readers lose access to Stevens's point of view.

This chapter thus presents two narratives. The first tells a story about Stevens's experience of his own poetry—how he attempts to create a livable form of secularism. The second tells a story about the limits of this approach—how his attempts lead (or seem to lead) to a utopia of one. The chapter, in this way, presents a variation on the book's basic paradigm. Stevens responds to the failure of utopia—but that failure is, at least in part, his own: he cannot convince himself of the adequacy of humanism as a system of thought. (He also reads about the failure of humanism every day in the *New York Times* and *Hartford Courant*. Between "Sunday Morning" and "The Auroras of Autumn," he witnessed the horrors of two world wars and the advent of the Cold War.) This failure leads to a new utopian project that risks solipsism by embracing it. (True and complete solipsism is difficult, even impossible to achieve.)[47] The result is asymmetrical and highly improbable: a union of mind and world that resolves Stevens's metaphysical need and severs him almost completely from the world of his readers.

But there are other narratives one could present about Stevens's career. In his final poems, he embraces a pragmatic approach to the problem of value—an approach that rejects the extravagance of "The Auroras of Autumn." In the fifteen-line poem "The Course of a Particular" (1951), he realizes McDowell's desired "exorcism." Stevens, instead of attempting to satisfy his metaphysical need, exorcises it.

"The Course of a Particular" is a poem about receptivity, and the nature and adequacy of human perception. It opens with a description of leaves on a cold and windy day:

> Today the leaves cry, hanging on branches swept by wind,
> Yet the nothingness of winter becomes a little less.
> It is still full of icy shades and shapen snow.
>
> The leaves cry . . . One holds off and merely hears the cry.
> It is a busy cry, concerning someone else.
> And though one says that one is part of everything,
>
> There is a conflict, there is a resistance involved;
> And being part is an exertion that declines:
> One feels the life of that which gives life as it is. (460)

"And though one says that one is part of everything": Stevens cannot accept this platitude. "There is a conflict." (His use of "one" exemplifies the conflict.

The pronoun is personal and impersonal, singular and plural: he knows what he should believe, what a reasonable person would believe, but cannot find a way to believe it.) Yet the conflict subsides: "And being part is an exertion that declines." Stevens yields to his experience and begins to feel "the life of that which gives life as it is." Mind and world, here, are neither distinct nor indistinguishable: Stevens recognizes (and *feels*) his connection to the world he describes.

This paraphrase may seem too optimistic. "One holds off and merely hears the cry"—this is not a happy description of receptivity. Indeed, "merely" seems to mark the same lack of absolute or intrinsic value. But here that lack is not an occasion for regret. It is an occasion for acceptance. The poem concludes:

> The leaves cry. It is not a cry of divine attention,
> Nor the smoke-drift of puffed-out heroes, nor human cry.
> It is the cry of leaves that do not transcend themselves,
>
> In the absence of fantasia, without meaning more
> Than they are in the final finding of the ear, in the thing
> Itself, until, at last, the cry concerns no one at all. (460)

The leaves, Stevens asserts, "do not transcend themselves." Yet they are meaningful, nevertheless. Stevens's own experience is proof. He is the recipient of their sad music. To recognize this fact, he does not have to isolate himself—he has to maintain his receptivity.

"The Course of a Particular" is a pedagogical poem. Stevens models a practice of receptivity and acceptance for readers. Transcendence, he tells us, is unnecessary. Indeed, the desire for transcendence inhibits receptivity. What matters is our experience of value and our ability to share it. The poem thus revives the experiment of "Sunday Morning." This time, however, relative judgments of value are sufficient. The poem's austere beauty is enough.

Stevens's practice of receptivity and acceptance in "The Course of a Particular" recalls a passage in the *Philosophical Investigations* (1953)—Wittgenstein's own revision of his earlier commitment to the fact/value dichotomy. Wittgenstein writes:

> 105. When we believe that we have to find that order, the ideal, in our actual language, we become dissatisfied with what are ordinarily called "sentences," "words," "signs . . ."
>
> 106. Here it is difficult to keep our heads above water, as it were, to see that we must stick to matters of everyday thought, and not to get on the wrong track where it seems that we have to describe extreme subtleties, which again we are quite unable to describe with the means at our disposal. We feel as if we had to repair a torn spider's web with our fingers.[48]

To mix metaphors, I would say that "The Auroras of Autumn" comes as close as possible to repairing that spider's web. The wisdom of "The Course of a Particular" is that such an effort is impractical and, possibly, harmful.

Which poem one prefers depends, I think, on something more than the poems themselves. Yvor Winters, who objected to Stevens's self-indulgence, called "The Course of a Particular" "one of the greatest of [his] poems, and perhaps the greatest."[49] But for readers who identify with Stevens's need—or who, like me, relish its extravagance—"The Auroras of Autumn" is a better poem. (It is Helen Vendler's favorite Stevens poem.)[50] "The Auroras of Autumn" gets close to confirming poetry's power to satisfy our most quixotic desires, whatever the cost.

CHAPTER SIX

Reading Ezra Pound and J. H. Prynne in Chinese

1

In 1992, the Cambridge-based poet J. H. Prynne wrote a poem in Chinese for a predominantly English-speaking audience. The poem was published as a four-page pamphlet (on a single sheet of paper, folded once) in Peter Riley's pamphlet series, Poetical Histories, and distributed by Riley's bookshop in Cambridge, England.[1] The only English text appears on the cover and colophon. (The latter includes Prynne's copyright.) In 1999, 2005, and 2015, the poem was reprinted in the second, third, and fourth editions of Prynne's collected poems with the transliterated title, "Jie ban mi Shi Hu."[2] A second printing of the pamphlet appeared in 2004. None of these versions included an English translation. As Riley recalls, Prynne "preferred not to have a translation included. 'No explanations,' he said."[3] Riley adds that "Some clandestine photocopied translations were floated around Cambridge at the time (not by me)."[4]

What should Prynne's readers—or at least those of us who do not read Chinese—do with this pamphlet? We could take it as an exercise by a longtime student of Chinese or as a joke on Prynne's notoriously devoted readers—or we could follow these readers and surreptitiously seek out a translation. Alternatively, we could take the pamphlet as a comment on artistic invention and influence. If, as T. S. Eliot claimed, Ezra Pound "invented" Chinese poetry for the West, perhaps the poem represents the absurd, postmodern conclusion of that invention—not a poem from Chinese or including Chinese but actually in Chinese.[5] Or we could take the pamphlet as an attempt to revitalize Pound's commitment to Chinese art and philosophy—or as a critique of Pound's orientalism—or as a Rorschach test of our own critical priorities. Finally, we could reject the question as academic and dismiss the pamphlet as a minor work by a minor poet.

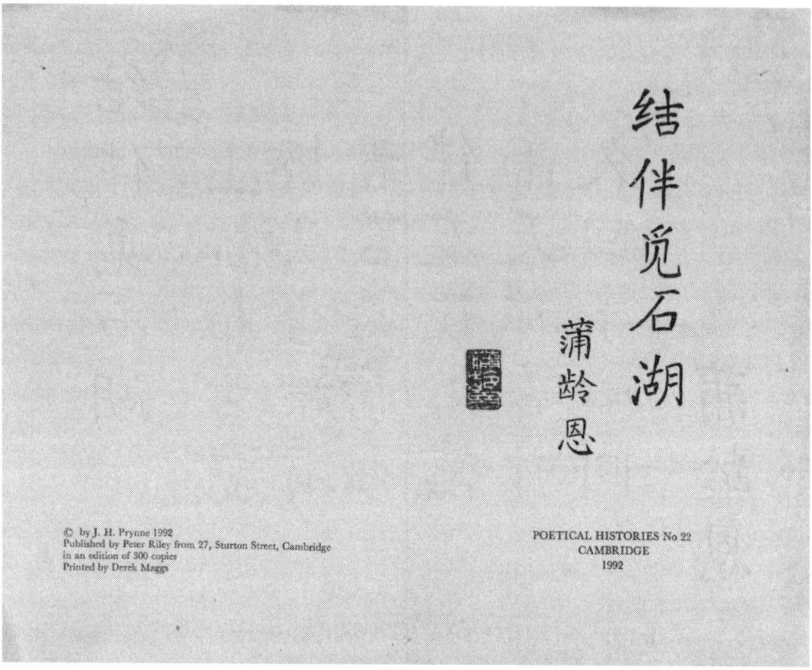

结伴觅石湖

蒲龄恩

© by J. H. Prynne 1992
Published by Peter Riley from 27, Sturton Street, Cambridge
in an edition of 300 copies
Printed by Derek Maggs

POETICAL HISTORIES No 22
CAMBRIDGE
1992

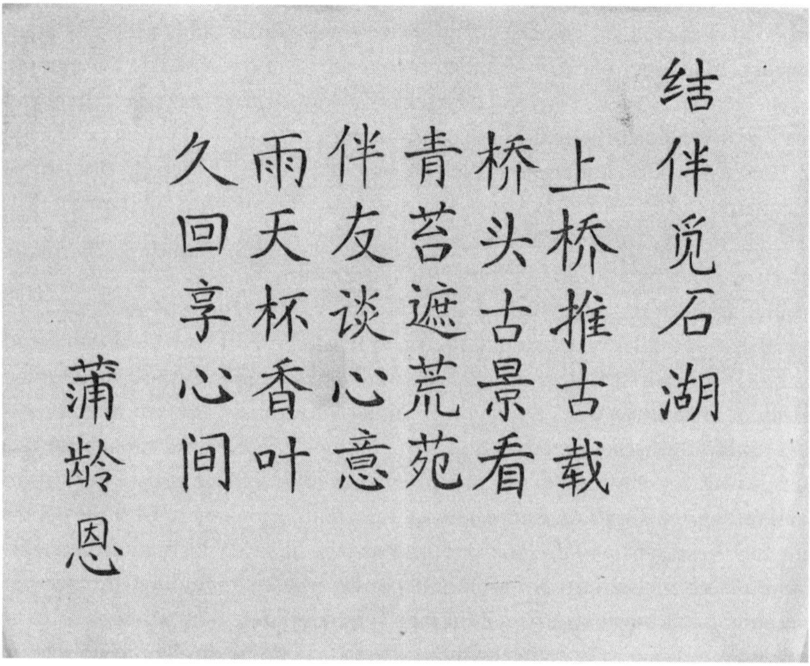

结伴觅石湖

上桥推古载
桥头古景看
青苔遮荒苑
伴友谈心意
雨天杯香叶
久回享心间

蒲龄恩

FIG. 6.1 [*Jie ban mi Shi Hu*]

But there is yet another option: we could learn Chinese. How could a poem or a poet have such power over us?[6] But this, I believe, is what Prynne invites us to do: learn to read the poem. For readers familiar with his poetry, this invitation is novel but not exceptional. From the early *Kitchen Poems* (1968) to *Each to Each* (2017), work is a prerequisite for interpretation. Prynne's poetry asks readers to learn specialized vocabularies, locate obscure references, research etymologies. ("Prynne's poems are incredibly difficult," the *Guardian* once announced. "At one stage, as if fearing a lapse into intelligibility, he actually started writing in Chinese.")[7] As Simon Jarvis argues, "Readers are requested to work at making sense through difficulties which are not ludic but the faultlines of a society and culture fractured in, but also constituted by, their multiple divisions of labour and divisions of intellectual labour."[8] In specific cases, these difficulties are resolvable: we could, for example, learn Chinese. But as a general poetic practice, they are not. Even if we were to accept the challenge of "Jie ban mi Shi Hu," we would gain access only to this one poem, and then only at the basic level of linguistic comprehension. We would still, so to speak, have the poem to read—and we would not be significantly closer to understanding Prynne's poetry as a whole.[9]

When viewed in this light, "Jie ban mi Shi Hu" exemplifies a problem for readers of Prynne's work, and for literary and social theory: How and why should we read texts that make extravagant, even impossible demands? The question asks us to justify the value of particular texts and the values of the world that receive them. To put this point a different way, when we ask for reasons to accept a poem's invitation to do work, we should also ask what kind of world would have to exist to make the invitation seem reasonable, and whether we would want to live in that world. What kind of institutions and incentives would have to be established or displaced to enable such a commitment to a single poem? Similar questions are relevant to debates about utopianism. How might we transform the world in the absence of clear and immediate incentives: money, pleasure, basic need? How might utopian ideas motivate us to act? How might they teach us about motivation?

2

To have great poets, there must be great audiences, too.

—WALT WHITMAN[10]

To address these questions about Prynne's poetry, and about difficulty and motivation in general, I begin with a discussion of Pound's own writing on and in Chinese.

In the early 1910s, Pound began to promote a conception of expertise—the knowledge (as know-how) needed to identify and produce great art. In spring

1913, the tenets of imagism were paramount: precision, concision, musicality. In three consecutive issues of *Poetry*, he outlines the tenets, provides a demonstration, and consolidates a community to confirm their value. The March issue features his manifesto, "A Few Don'ts by an Imagiste"; the April issue, his sequence "Contemporania," which ends with "In a Station of the Metro"; and the May issue, editorials by Harriet Monroe and Alice Henderson defending Pound's poetics, and Pound's reviews of books by Robert Frost and Maurice Hewlett, in which he promotes aspects of imagism.[11] "What the expert is tired of today the public will be tired of tomorrow," Pound declares in "A Few Don'ts." If a poem relies on "its music," he adds, "that music must be such as will delight the expert."[12]

In fall 1913, Pound defends the moral significance of expertise. In "The Serious Artist," published in three consecutive issues of the *New Freewoman*, he describes poetry as a science that reveals "a great percentage of the lasting and unassailable data regarding the nature of man, of immaterial man, of man considered as a thinking and sentient creature." Only experts, he argues, can interpret these data: "The touchstone of an art is its precision. This precision is of various and complicated sorts and only the specialist can determine whether certain works of art possess certain sorts of precision . . . It is no more possible to give in a few pages full instructions for knowing a masterpiece than it would be to give full instructions for all medical diagnosis."[13] Two claims are implicit here. First, that such special knowledge can be learned over many years—as a physician learns his or her craft. And second, that such knowledge is already possessed—by Pound and, to some extent, by his community of friends, artists, and editors.

Pound's poetry and poetics, in this way, represent more than the future of poetry: they represent the possibility of a just world. As A. David Moody argues, Pound "was proposing, in all seriousness, to found the ideal state upon the Image. Poetry, he argued, was the necessary basis of the just society, because to attain the good of the greatest number we must first establish accurately and precisely of what nature individuals are and what it is they desire."[14]

The challenge, for Pound, was how to train readers to become experts. In his pedagogical work from the 1920s and 1930s, he seems ready to give the "full instructions" sidestepped in "The Serious Artist." Yet rather than explain how to identify a masterpiece, he offers a list of masterpieces. "Let the student brace himself and prepare for the worst," he declares in *ABC of Reading* (1934), "I am coming to my list of the minimum that a man would have to read if he hoped to know what a given new book was worth."[15] The list is at once conservative and idiosyncratic: *The Odyssey*, *The Divine Comedy*, *The Canterbury Tales*, but not Petrarch's sonnets; Gavin Douglas's *Aeneid*, Arthur Golding's *Metamorphoses*, John Donne's "The Ecstasy," but not *Paradise Lost*. To learn to identify what Pound calls the "unknown best," readers must first acknowledge and become familiar with *his* best.[16]

This approach to training experts has at least one significant shortcoming. Why should readers submit to Pound's pedagogical program before making their own judgments about the value of a particular poem—or about value in general? Pound expects readers to respond to the power of his examples—and to the power of his prose.

Pound's work on and in Chinese offered a way to address this problem. In 1913, he received the notebooks of the orientalist Ernest Fenollosa and began to work on the material that would become *Cathay* (1915) and "The Chinese Written Character as a Medium for Poetry" (1919), among other texts.[17] In the notebooks, Pound discovered a way to hone and supplement the tenets of imagism.[18] He also discovered the central technique of *The Cantos*: the so-called ideogrammic method. But just as important, he discovered a poetry and poetics that did not require expertise of any kind.

In a two-part essay for *To-day* in 1918, Pound praises the "completeness" of classical Chinese poetry.[19] Readers, he argues, do not need any special training or knowledge to evaluate the poems' value. Discussing his translation of "The Jewel Stairs' Grievance," he notes that "upon careful examination we find that everything is there, not merely by 'suggestion' but by a sort of mathematical process of reduction."[20] (In *Cathay*, he includes a note performing the "reduction.")[21] Discussing his translation of "South-Folk in Cold Country," he notes that the only information the "writer expects his hearers to know [is] that Dai and Etsu are in the south, that En is a bleak north country. . . ." "Given these simple geographical facts the poem is very forthright in its manner."[22] Literary history is irrelevant: Homer and Ovid have no bearing on the author of "The Jewel Stairs' Grievance," of course, but if we take Pound as a guide, neither do the poets of the Tang and Sui Dynasties.[23]

A cynic might claim that expertise matters for Pound only insofar as he happens to possess it. He is his own ideal reader—and his pedagogy aims to promote his particular talents and worldview. This may be true in general. But in this specific case, his ascription of completeness is based on Fenollosa's account of classical Chinese poetry. According to Fenollosa, Chinese poetry makes expertise unnecessary because it appeals to innate and universal properties of mind.

The most famous aspect of Fenollosa's account concerns the iconicity of the Chinese ideogram. In the lecture that would become "The Chinese Written Character as a Medium for Poetry," Fenollosa writes, "Chinese notation is something very much more than . . . arbitrary symbols. It is based upon a vivid short-hand picture of the operations of nature. In the algebraic figure, and in the spoken word, there is no natural connection between thing and sign; all depends upon sheer convention. But the Chinese method proceeds upon natural suggestion."[24] The connection between "thing" and "sign" is natural: Fenollosa and Pound take this to mean that it need not be learned. As Pound declares in *ABC of Reading*, "The Chinese 'word' or ideogram . . . is based on something everyone KNOWS."[25]

But the iconicity of the ideogram is only one part of Fenollosa's account. He devotes most of his lecture (and the resulting essay) to promoting aspects of classical Chinese poetry relevant to English verse. Metaphor is central. The ideogram, he argues, juxtaposes concrete images to communicate abstract ideas. "The known interprets the obscure": metaphors give "color and vitality, forcing [words] closer to the concreteness of natural processes." The signs for "boat" and "water" combine to signify "ripple"; "rice-field" and "struggle" signify "male." Such juxtaposition conveys the interrelatedness of all things: "A true noun, an isolated thing, does not exist in nature," he writes. "The eye sees noun and verb as one: things in motion, motion in things." Verbs are concrete: "'is' not only means actively 'to have,' but . . . 'to snatch from the moon with the hand.'" Negative particles are absent; verbs serve in their place. (The "sign meaning 'to be lost in the forest'" expresses "a state of non-existence.") Chinese syntax follows "the transferences of force from agent to object, which constitute natural phenomena." "The sentence form," he declares, "was forced upon primitive men by nature itself. It was not we who made it; it was a reflection of the temporal order in causation."[26] Fenollosa's concern here is not Sinology but a poetics of natural law.[27]

This is Fenollosa's aim: to illuminate mental processes and provide raw materials for renewing English poetry. "I trust that this digression concerning parts of speech may have justified itself," he writes. "It proves, first, the enormous interest of the Chinese language in throwing light upon our forgotten mental processes . . . Secondly, it is indispensable for understanding the poetical raw material which the Chinese language affords."[28] At its core, "The Chinese Written Character as a Medium for Poetry" is a manifesto. (Pound appends "An Ars Poetica" to the title of the first stand-alone edition of the essay in 1936.) To give the manifesto urgency, Fenollosa marries his enthusiasm with a not-too-subtle chauvinism. "The Chinese problem alone is so vast that no nation can afford to ignore it. We in America, especially, must face it across the Pacific, and master it or it will master us."[29] The warning reinforces Pound's sense of art's political efficacy. If the health of a society is proportional to the accuracy of its language, China is both threat and guide: it provides the key to saving Western culture while signaling Western culture's obsolescence.

Ultimately, Fenollosa's account of classical Chinese poetry offered Pound a way to universalize his poetics. Instead of having to motivate readers to develop their critical capacities, he could write poems that would transcend their critical capacities. In the "Wisdom of Poetry" (1912), he seems to anticipate Fenollosa's program: "The function of an art is to free the intellect from the tyranny of . . . set moods, set ideas, conventions; from . . . experience induced by the stupidity of the experiencer and not by inevitable laws of nature."[30] Chinese, in short, promised to solve the problem of stupidity. The reception of Pound's poems would be defined by the "inevitable laws of nature," not the intellectual, artistic, and moral deficiencies of his readers.

The poems in *Cathay* attempt to make good on this promise. Consider "The Beautiful Toilet":

Blue, blue is the grass about the river
And the willows have overfilled the close garden.
And within, the mistress, in the midmost of her youth,
White, white of face, hesitates, passing the door.
Slender, she puts forth a slender hand,

And she was a courtesan in the old days,
And she has married a sot,
Who now goes drunkenly out
And leaves her too much alone.

BY MEI SHENG.
B.C. 140.[31]

In the poem, Pound juxtaposes its stanzas as an ideogram juxtaposes its constitutive parts. The first stanza represents a woman passing through the door of her home, wary of entering her garden. The second stanza describes her youth, marriage, and isolation. The juxtaposition of these stanzas captures her imprisonment, but also her agency and self-awareness, the careful pressure she exerts against circumstance.

Juxtaposition also governs the content of individual stanzas. The overfilled, enclosed garden contrasts with the flowing river; the woman's hesitancy contrasts with the motion of her hand; her present marriage contrasts with her past life. Even the repeated colors and conjunctions increase the tension between rest and motion, the woman's passive and active engagement with the world. The poem collects these concrete images to represent a dynamic environment, while providing a subtle music to make it cohere. The application of Fenollosa's techniques is flexible, fitted to the resources of English.

Or consider the opening of "Sennin Poem by Kakuhaku," a poem first published in the *New Age* in 1916 and revised for the expanded edition of *Cathay* published in *Lustra* (1916):

The red and green kingfishers
            flash between the orchids and clover,
One bird casts its gleam on another.[32]

The first line places the kingfishers before us; the second captures their flight between orchids and clover. In the third, the birds light each other's way. The diction is concrete. The images are distinct yet interrelated. Four discrete surfaces reflect light to illuminate the scene. The orchids and clover provide a reference point to track the birds' flight. Force flows from agent to object.

"Between" indicates both movement and relation. The images are not culturally specific: kingfishers, orchids, and clover populate every continent (save Antarctica) and are thus available to every mind's eye.[33] (Geographers call such distribution "cosmopolitan.") Context is unnecessary: readers need no special expertise to evaluate the poem.[34] This is universality as timelessness: an ancient poem that is perpetually present.

Much has been written about the inaccuracy of Pound's translations, and even more about their verisimilitude.[35] In light of these arguments, it is tempting to discuss *Cathay*'s influence or beauty or inventiveness, or to evoke T. S. Eliot's idea of aesthetic sanction, which proposes that "any way or view of life which gives rise to great art is for us more plausible than one which gives rise to inferior art or to none."[36] Pound's poems, in this way, can be made to justify his poetics and even Fenollosa's account of classical Chinese poetry. But these arguments miss the central claim of the work they defend: the poems are not open to justification.[37] The poems in *Cathay* deny the importance of expertise on ontological grounds. Their value hinges on their relation to nature, not the knowledge of individual readers.

3

In short, the great gamble continues. The method is being pressed to its logical conclusion. Either this is the waste of a prodigious talent, or else it is the poetry of the future.

—DONALD DAVIE ON CANTO 85[38]

In the aftermath of World War I and, especially, World War II, this denial of expertise became increasingly important for Pound's poetry.[39] Indeed, *Cathay* helps make sense of the seemingly impossible demands of the late cantos. Pound's epic is not a departure from *Cathay*'s populism but a commitment to its poetics of natural law. Consider Canto 85 from *Section: Rock-Drill de los Cantares LXXXV–XCV* (1955), the section of the poem with the greatest number and frequency of Chinese characters.[40] As A. Alvarez declares, "the work is no longer *like* ideograms, it actually *is* ideograms."[41]

"The mere look of Canto 85 on the page . . . announces it as 'unreadable,'" writes Donald Davie in *Ezra Pound: Poet as Sculptor* (1964): "bold black Chinese characters . . . interspersed with sparse print which includes Roman and Arabic numerals, Greek, Latin, French, and phonetic transcriptions of Chinese, as well as English."[42] In a contemporary review, Hugh Kenner notes that, "*Rock-Drill*, Pound's first post-*Pisan* sequence, opens with a Canto that defies the elocutionist; it is written for the printed page, as it were for stone tablets."[43]

How should readers approach Canto 85? Davie and Kenner agree that we should pair the canto with its main source, Séraphin Couvreur's Latin and French translation of the Confucian *Book of History*.[44] (Pound cites the book

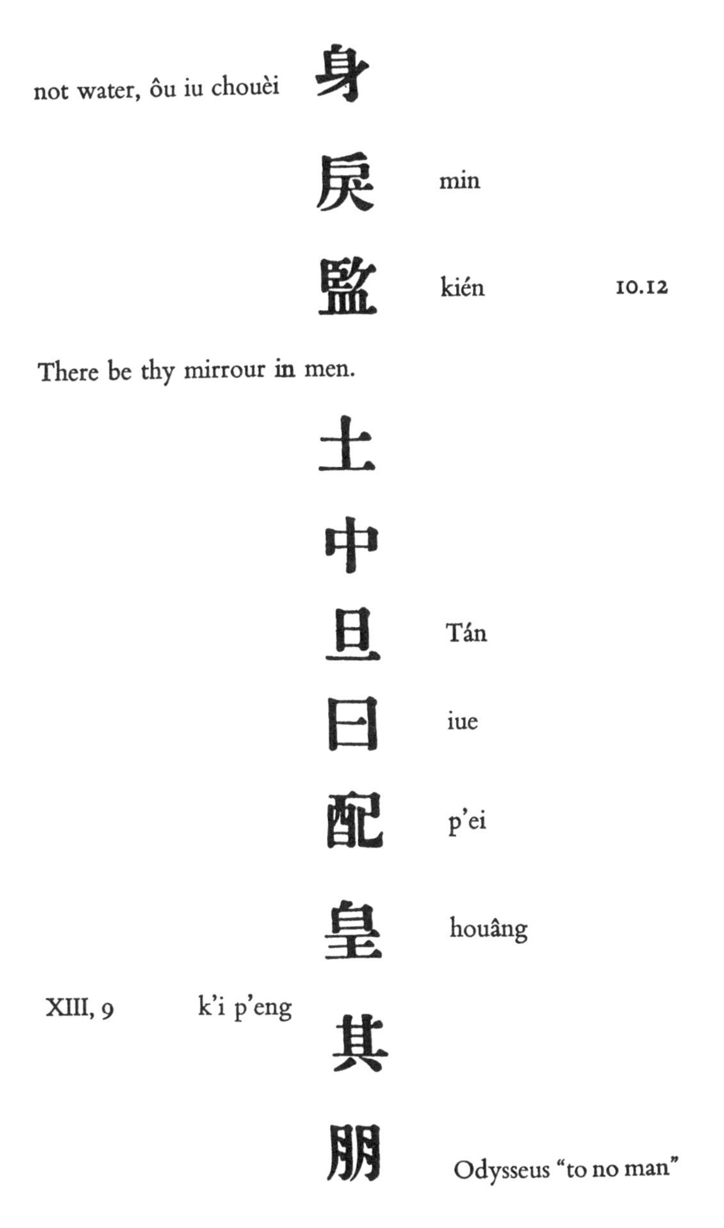

FIG. 6.2 From Canto 85

in a note at the end of the canto and in references throughout.)[45] The pairing reveals a series of correspondences that reinforce Pound's statements on statecraft.

Davie, for example, links the Chinese characters introduced by "not water, ôu iu chouèi" to Canto 90: "We have to follow the reference to the page of

Couvreur in order to unearth the ancient adage, 'Take not for glass the water's crystal, but other men'—a very important prefiguring of what will be the governing metaphor of Canto 90."[46] For Davie, such cross-checking is the only way to approach the poem. "Canto 85," he writes, "will tax the patience of even a devout Poundian, since it can be read only with the Chinese source in one's lap."[47] "Any one is at liberty to decide that he cannot afford to take this trouble."[48]

Kenner is more optimistic about this scholarly approach. He traces a "process of moral circulation," connecting, for example, the characters under "Right here is the Bill of Rights" (from an earlier passage in the canto) to the adage, "If one person lacks freedom to do good, the ruler will have one auxiliary the less, and his work will be incomplete."[49] The reference validates Kenner's scholarship: he completes Pound's poem by following its citations. The juxtaposition of American liberalism and Confucianism represents one version of Pound's utopia. This is the beginning of the poem's paradisiacal theme, which dominates *Rock-Drill* and the next section of *The Cantos, Thrones de los Cantares* (1959)—both written during Pound's thirteen-year incarceration at St. Elizabeths psychiatric hospital in Washington, DC.

According to these two accounts of the poem, readers should gloss Pound's references. But as Davie makes plain, it is unclear why we would ever do so. Kenner may accept what Wendy Flory calls the poem's "direct challenge to the reader," but I suspect most readers would not—even when presented with Kenner's findings.[50]

But this is not the only way to read the canto. Discussing *The Cantos* as a whole, John Wain recommends ignoring Pound's references: "[G]o into a trance with the book before you. Don't skip—that is the prime rule; your eyes must travel over every line that is on the page, including the ideograms. If, in this fashion, you sit there until the whole book has been read, you will find, when the last page is turned, that the experience was meaningful and even moving. It is merely that close attention destroys the effect."[51] Wain sounds insincere, but he is not. "[I]n the Cantos," he argues, "Pound has produced something unique: verse which doesn't need—is actually better without—close attention, and yet is anything but perfunctory or spurious."[52]

Brian M. Reed takes Wain's position to the extreme. Discussing the ideograms in *Rock-Drill,* he writes, "In rebellion against centuries of tradition, Pound proposes an alternative, freer mode of engagement with a text: a wandering, wondering perusal of a poem, in which the eye moves as readily backward, upward, or diagonally as well as down or to the right."[53] The canto, when approached in this way, is different for each individual reader. Yet each reader, Reed suggests, eventually loses his or her individuality when reading the poem: "Lost in a sea of noise, with one's moorings undone, one drifts." *Rock-Drill,* he concludes, is "poetry for the age of information overload."[54]

These radically different approaches find a synthesis in Peter Nicholls's work on the late cantos. Readers, he suggests, should oscillate between interpretation and what he calls "suspended meaning." After using Pound's sources to explicate Canto 85 and Canto 86, Nicholls notes, "Taken together, the ideograms are a body of signs which point to some ultimate fullness of meaning which the writing only gestures towards. As soon as we begin to explicate the passage, this semi-mystical sense of suspended meaning is lost; once the ideograms are anchored to specific concepts their doubleness disappears."[55] Nicholls claims that our oscillation is ultimately a way to cooperate with the poem. By participating in the poem's "play of disclosure and concealment," he argues, readers submit to its "paideutic spell" and receive its lessons on statecraft.[56]

Despite the differences among these approaches to Canto 85 (and *The Cantos* more generally), they share at least one feature: they foreground our responsibility as readers. According to Davie, Kenner, Flory, Wain, Reed, and Nicholls (and, indeed, most Pound scholars), the poem asks us to do certain things—identify sources, go into a trance, abandon linear reading practices, participate in the "play of disclosure and concealment." We are Pound's collaborators—we complete his poem.

But if we take Pound's earlier claims about Chinese poetry seriously, this cannot be the case. The poem is already complete. It does not need or want anything from readers. We can thus argue about the most rewarding way to read the poem, but not about how the poem asks to be read. The poem's presumed universality preempts questions about its actual reception.

How, then, should we understand the poem's citations? Does Pound want us to go and seek out Couvreur's Confucius? No. I believe that when Pound addresses readers directly in *The Cantos*—in citations, in asides—he is not asking us to supplement the poem. He is protecting the poem's integrity. *Cathay* helps make sense of this paradoxical claim. Recall the note to "The Jewel Stairs' Grievance." It confirmed the poem's completeness. It anticipated and inhibited our desire to look for meaning elsewhere. The citations in Canto 85 do the same thing.[57] They stop us from contaminating the poem—from undermining its completeness.

Pound's poetry thus unites two utopian traditions. The first presumes that human nature is invariable and benign—and yet under constant threat from convention. (Emerson is an important precursor here—his critiques of convention anticipate Pound's.) This tradition attempts to restore our humanity. The second tradition presumes that consciousness does not govern human action. (Here, behavioral engineering is an important precursor—from behaviorism to urban planning.) This tradition attempts to change our behavior without first having to change our minds.[58] These two traditions come together in Pound's poetry. *Cathay* may be his most accessible book and *Rock-Drill* his least, but both attempt to transform us, automatically, into the people we already innately are.

4

Our dogmatists are lazy-bones.

—MAO TSE-TUNG[59]

Embedded in Fenollosa's account of the ideogram's relation to nature is a brief account of its relation to history:

> In this Chinese shows its advantage. Its etymology is constantly visible. . . . After thousands of years the lines of metaphoric advance are still shown and, in many cases actually retained in the meaning. Thus a word, instead of growing gradually poorer and poorer as with us, becomes richer and still more rich from age to age, almost consciously luminous. Its uses in national philosophy and history, in biography and in poetry, throw about it a nimbus of meanings.[60]

Pound ignores the implications of this passage. By learning about Chinese philosophy and history, biography and poetry, we augment an ideogram's significance. By using an ideogram, we contribute to its meaning. Completeness is a fallacy.

This brief account anticipates contemporary scholarship on classical Chinese poetry. Stephen Owen, for example, writes, "in the Chinese poem fullness lies outside the text, as the end of the reading process. At its least complacent, a T'ang or Sung poem moves toward a fullness that is never attained—an ambiguous reality, a world of unmanageable complexity, or a true failure of intelligibility."[61] To begin to realize the "fullness" of a Tang or Sung poem, readers must investigate the contexts of its production and reception. Expertise matters.[62]

Prynne discusses these competing conceptions of classical Chinese poetry in a review of *New Songs from the Jade Terrace* (1982), an anthology of early Chinese love poems translated and edited by Anne Birrell. (The anthology was originally compiled by Hsü Ling around 545 CE.) Adapting Roman Jakobson's account of metaphor and metonymy, Prynne writes:[63]

> The Poundian theory of image had insisted on direct treatment of the thing, without an ascribed or intended meaning but metaphoric with an immediacy excluding even the act of comparison itself. Absolute metaphor was thus energetic and succinct, autonomous within the context of its presentation, and connected to it not by links of reference or idiom but by feeling and inner rhythm. . . . Chinese poetic practice, and the Chinese language itself, became for Pound at a critically formative stage in his career a demonstration against metonymy.[64]

This is Pound's ideal: precise word-object relations, denotation without connotation, aesthetic autonomy, metaphor. *New Songs from the Jade Terrace* undermines this ideal, revealing the metonymic character of Pound's sources:

> Literary figuration in Palace Style Poetry, and in the earlier kinds of writing assembled in the *Jade Terrace* anthology, emphasises what [Bernhard] Karlgren has in a more general context aptly called "metaphor with a history." The stylistic history, or occasionally the cosmology or other typological ordering, comprises the precursory system which makes the use of coded metaphor a metonymic rather than metaphoric procedure; and it is the subtlety of intelligible allusion, varied and superimposed, which here shews the power of metonymy both to support metaphor and to exceed it.[65]

In an extensive apparatus, Birrell illuminates this "stylistic history" and "typological ordering."[66] The poems in *Cathay* thus acquire the "nimbus of meanings" that Fenollosa describes and Pound attempts to suppress.

As an object lesson on the resources of metonymy, Prynne rereads "The Beautiful Toilet" in light of *New Songs from the Jade Terrace*. Pound's translation, quoted in full above, opens:

> Blue, blue is the grass about the river
> And the willows have overfilled the close garden.
> And within, the mistress, in the midmost of her youth,

When read in *Cathay*, the willows symbolize the mistress's connection to the natural world. "[T]he presence of the willows," Prynne argues, "is suggestive of delicate but over-luxuriant enclosure, the qualities of nature metaphorically transferred to the isolation of the mistress by a brilliant internal chiasmus of sound-values (*w<u>ill</u>ōws, ōverf<u>ill</u>ed*)."[67] When read in the context of the anthology, however, the willows symbolize the mistress's separation from the natural world. The "willow (*liu*)," Birrell notes, is "a pun for to detain, to keep someone from going away on a journey," which, of course, the mistress is unable to do.[68]

The poem's position in the anthology further emphasizes this separation. The poem (titled "Green, green riverside grass" in Birrell's translation) first appears in a series of nine anonymous first- and second-century CE lyrics. Seven imitations follow throughout the anthology, dating from the third to the sixth centuries. As Prynne observes, the poems, when taken together, chart "a polemical transfer of poetic values from the unsophisticated feeling for nature to a hypersophisticated and self-conscious acknowledgement of artifice."[69] The mistress's separation, in this way, comes to reflect the stylistic changes the anthology documents.

The last poems in the anthology vindicate Prynne's rereading of "The Beautiful Toilet." Hsiao Kang's sixth-century "Peach Pink," for example, makes the significance of the willows explicit:

> Peach pink, plum white like dawn cosmetics.
> I disgrace my wrecked self next to the fresh willow.

> I wouldn't mind living a while, then dying before you—
> But I'd be in despair without my west Reincarnation scent![70]

The blunt "I disgrace my wrecked self next to the fresh willow" glosses the delicate "willows have overfilled the close garden. / And within, the mistress." Both women are "wrecked" sophisticates. (The speaker of "Peach Pink" prefers death to living without her "west Reincarnation scent.") From this perspective, the mistress in "The Beautiful Toilet" is responsible for her abandonment and the artificiality of the poetry that depicts it.

What kind of reading is this? Context does more than enrich meaning—it transforms it. We read through the eyes of generations of readers. As Prynne notes:

> Birrell translates . . . not simply the traditionally quasi-simple poems from which the Chinese lyric traces some of its origins, but rather these same poems as seen in retrospect by the Liang court poets and as put into the anthology by Hsü Ling. It is what they read plus their reading of it which she reconstructs and transmits.[71]

As a result, images and themes from later poems have an impact on the meaning of earlier poems. Here, anachronism is not a mistake to be avoided but an opportunity to attend to a poem's relevance over time.

Our contemporary contexts also matter. For Anglophone readers of "The Beautiful Toilet," the dead metaphor "weeping willow" is an inevitable, if unintended, part of the poem's meaning. "Willow" recalls "weeping," and by means of pathetic fallacy characterizes the mistress's sorrow. The process is metonymic and anachronistic—and likely anathema to Pound.[72] Yet it has an impact on our reading—as a node of significance or an object of suppression or both.

Our contexts and the contexts supplied by *New Songs from the Jade Terrace* transform Pound's poem but do not supplant it. We do not have to choose between translations: we can read Pound's and Birrell's versions together. This is why Prynne celebrates "the power of metonymy both to support metaphor and to exceed it."[73]

This approach to reading is empowering, but also exhausting. As we read we must remain sensitive to intention and effect, denotation and connotation. Every poem is endlessly occasional, and we are part of its most recent occasion. (Indeed, we could ask whether it is possible to talk about *a* poem at all.) This is difficult work. Expertise is a daunting goal. Existing scholarship can certainly help. Birrell, for example, does much of the work for us—most significantly, by translating the poems. But we are often on our own, in a library with a new poem, struggling to understand its significance—and our contribution to its significance. Preference for Pound's translation thus might not simply be a matter of taste but of convenience.

Prynne's own scholarship attempts to honor this approach to reading. Consider his first monograph: *They That Haue Powre to Hurt: A Specimen of a Commentary on Shake-speares Sonnets, 94* (2001). The book reconstructs the sonnet's original linguistic environment. Prynne starts with a word or phrase and moves from its contemporary usage to its possible meanings in the sonnet as a whole. In a three-page gloss on "They," for example, he coordinates quotations from Thomas Wyatt, Abraham Fraunce, Philip Sidney, and others to delineate the pronoun's range of reference.[74] His aim is not to capture the poem's meaning for any individual reader or auditor (Shakespeare included). Instead, his aim is to capture its meaning (or its "fullness") for the world that first received the poem.

Prynne's focus on the sonnet's initial reception might seem to undermine the most compelling aspect of his review of *New Songs from a Jade Terrace*: the retroactive influence of future usage. *They That Haue Powre to Hurt* ignores connotations unavailable to the sonnet's first readers. (When Prynne glosses the poem's final line, for example, he does not mention that "lilies" could refer to the "bound feet of Chinese women"—a definition dating to 1841.)[75] But this reticence is central to the book's argument: Prynne is showing us what it means to *begin* to read a poem. Less rigorous approaches are both inadequate and impetuous. His monograph is a rebuke to scholars for their lack of diligence.[76]

5

Readers hoping to use this metonymic approach to explicate Prynne's own poetry will be frustrated. Unlike "The Beautiful Toilet" or "Peach Pink" or Sonnet 94 or even Canto 85, his poems lack an easily identifiable context and do not participate in a well-defined tradition. His poems solicit scholarship, but scholarship rarely leads to intelligibility.

Consider Prynne's sequence *Not-You* (1993), published one year after "Jie ban mi Shi Hu" and dedicated to the poets Che Qianzi and Zhou Yaping, and the "ORIGINALS," a collective of Chinese poets formed in the late 1980s.[77] The volume opens with epigraphs from David Lewis's "Languages and Language" (1975), and Thomas Nagel's *Equality and Partiality* (1991). In the first epigraph, Lewis argues that languages rely on conventions of truthfulness and trust, and that trust requires practical acts of communication: "Truthfulness-by-silence is truthfulness, and expectation thereof is expectation of truthfulness; but expectation of truthfulness-by-silence is not yet trust."[78] In the second epigraph, Nagel worries about the difficulty of separating the benefits of modern life from incentive structure of capitalism: "Love of semiconductors is not enough."[79] Both epigraphs, in this way, foreground the problem of motivation—albeit on radically different scales. Lewis highlights the connection between linguistic convention and language use, and Nagel highlights the connection between pecuniary incentives and innovation—and thereby mocks the presumption of parity in the idiomatic phrase "for love or money."

After these philosophical (and poetic) claims, the first poem in *Not-You* greets readers with a dense musicality and a series of obscure image-fragments:

> The twins blink, hands set to thread out
> a dipper cargo with lithium grease enhanced
> to break under heat stress. Who knows
>
> what cares arise in double streaks, letting
> the door slip to alternative danny boy in-
> decision. She'll cut one hand off to whack
>
> the other same-day retread, leaving its mark
> two transfiguration at femur length. Ahead
> the twins consult, shade over upon shade.[80]

Consonance and assonance brace a series of six-beat lines. "S" and "K" sounds dominate. Line breaks produce a number of puns: "Who knows" is phatic and part of a question completed in the second stanza. Line length maintains the poem's visual solidity. There is an intentional structure here. Yet readers must speculate to achieve even a weak sense of coherence. "[T]wins blink" might suggest a twin-engine plane or Gemini's twinkling stars. "[H]ands set to thread out" might suggest movement through the stars, a pilot's fingers wrapped around a throttle, or the plane's screws lined with lithium grease. The poem's focus is telescopic: stars become planes, which become plane parts. "Dipper cargo" suggests the constellation and the plane's load.

The second and third stanzas introduce a sense of urgency. A question about value ("Who knows // what cares") leads to an image of a plane's rising exhaust. These "double streaks," in turn, lead to outer space: the phrase was used by astronomers at the turn of the last century to describe canal-like formations on Mars, which were taken as signs of extraterrestrial life. (Percival Lowell, orientalist, astronomer, and brother of the poet Amy Lowell, was the main proponent of the theory.)[81] The "double streaks" also return us to earth: the phrase suggests planting patterns and a kind of tomato virus.[82] The pun connects to the reference to "Danny Boy" (1913) in the next line—a ballad that combines an exotic landscape with themes of departure and decay. (The lyrics, written by the English lawyer Frederic Weatherly, romanticize the Irish diaspora.) Implicit here is how a history of language use determines how we see the world. We see Martians in "double streaks" and Amy Lowell in exhaust fumes.

The poem revels in such wordplay. "She" recalls the speaker of "Danny Boy" and the anonymous "she" of Samuel Beckett's *Not I* (1972). The word "indecision" breaks in two to suggest a process of decision making. "[F]emur length" returns us to the Gemini twins, who appear to be about a femur-length apart in the night sky (the distance between the stars Wasat and Mebsuta). "[T]ransfiguration" is apt—words, under pressure from history and the poem itself, form a luminous network of associations. Yet Prynne's wordplay is not always sanguine. The plane imagery suggests military action; the overlapping shades suggest an approaching storm. The process of punning itself represents the poverty of our everyday lives—our constant need to abstract from circumstance to imagine new worlds, new possibilities.

The poem, in this way, is both overdetermined and underdetermined. Overdetermined because it generates an infinite number of readings. (One could, for example, read "twins blink" as an allusion to the Cocteau Twins' song, "Summer Blink" [1993]. The song, which mocks the narcissism of self-help rhetoric, is all about "me"—and thus constitutes its own "not you.") The poem is underdetermined because it does not offer a way to arbitrate between readings. Language is charged with significance, yet that significance cannot be captured in paraphrase. Readers struggle to make meaning, knowing they will only ever grasp a sliver of the poem's references. This is incredibly difficult work—but not as difficult as finding a reason to do the work in the first place. Peter Middleton asks exactly the right question: "No doubt about the task, but whose, to what end, with what promise?"[83]

To begin to answer Middleton's question, it is helpful to return to my discussion of Thoreau's linguistic idealism from chapter 1. "The Universe," Thoreau writes, "constantly and obediently answers to our conceptions."[84] According to Stanley Cavell, this is a claim about language: "the writer of *Walden* is as preoccupied as the writer of *Paradise Lost* with the creation of a world by a word." The problem for Thoreau is that his words are not his own. "As our lives stand," Cavell writes, "the meaning we give them [words] is rebuked by the meaning they have in our language—the meaning, say, that writers live on, the meaning we also, in moments, know they have but which mostly remains a mystery to us." In Cavell's reading, *Walden* is an attempt to remake the world by winning back "possession" of his words from a corrupt and corrupting culture, and from history itself.[85] This is an aesthetic, moral, and political project. We use words with denotations and connotations we did not establish and can, at most, tweak. Likewise, we live in a world we did not construct and cannot fully control. Ideology shapes and sustains our desires. History limits our independence. Thoreau treats this analogy as an identity. By mastering language—by developing what Nietzsche calls a *style*—he attempts to maximize his agency in the world.[86]

A version of this idealism is basic to Prynne's poetry as well. How we live depends on how we understand our lives, and how we understand our lives depends on how we use language. The world is shaped by linguistic convention. But this is not a callow idealism. New words do not fashion new worlds. By evading authority in language, we do not evade it in life. Instead, we begin to change the world by contributing to the linguistic conventions that compose it. This, for Prynne, is literary efficacy: the ability to augment consciousness by slowly augmenting language.

Prynne departs from Thoreau's example in a number of important ways. Thoreau's project is private, tailored to the contours of his life at Walden and in *Walden*. As I argued in chapter 1, readers do not participate in or directly benefit from his world-making. Prynne takes the opposite tack. His engagement with convention is public. He purges his poems of personality, drawing on public discourse rather than private experience. (He refuses to read his poems in England, where his voice conveys what he calls "life history.")[87] His aim is not to maximize his personal autonomy but to maximize our collective autonomy. His rejection of personality is an attempt to foreground the language itself—to create a common object, to prevent private interests from interfering with the common good. "It has mostly been my own aspiration," he tells Riley in the letter I quoted in my introduction, "to establish relations not personally with the reader, but with the world and its layers of shifted but recognisable usage; and thereby with the reader's own position within this world."[88]

Literature is the medium for this kind of impersonal engagement. It is a public record of a community's changing values. It is also how those values are changed and preserved. One way this happens is through an ever-expanding metonymic network. Conventions solidify and dissolve. Concepts become associated with sound patterns, phrases with once-lost antecedents. Puns become clichés, then clichés become bathos. Prynne wants us to participate in this process. We are meant to discover our values and their history in his poetry, and use his poetry as an occasion to share our discoveries. Prynne's ultimate goal, I believe, is a language that represents our collective needs as it fashions a world to satisfy them. But our work toward this end is also vital: by reading through Prynne's refraction of multiple discourses and events, we begin to take possession of our words and understand our agency (and responsibility) in the world.

The answer to Middleton's question, then, "No doubt about the task, but whose, to what end, with what promise?" is "ours" and "utopia." But to see this, readers must already be willing to read Prynne's work against an almost limitless series of texts and contexts. If we isolate a single poem and press it to justify the work it demands, we will miss its import. This hermeneutic circle can be off-putting. Yet even if we accept the challenge of Prynne's poetry, we still face a number of obstacles. At a recent conference in Guangzhou, China, Prynne remarked, "It's all too clear that, in whatever stage of social evolution, a discourse practice defaults in a wink to facile acceptance of the commonplace, to bending compliantly under commercial or political distortions, to accommodate by self-corruption."[89] The critique is more Adornian than Orwellian. We cannot trust language to represent our needs. But more importantly, we cannot trust our needs. Thoreau's response to this impasse is to distance himself from public life. By moving to Walden and writing *Walden*, he attempts to gain perspective on what Louis Althusser would call his "interpellation" by ideology.[90] (Hence Thoreau's focus on the "true necessaries and means of life.")[91] Prynne, in contrast, does not transform his everyday life. He continues to read and write and teach at Cambridge. His poetry attempts to resist "commercial or political distortions" and "self-corruption" by being, at once, recalcitrant and self-aware, oppositional and sincere. Transparency and opacity both threaten his project: the former submits to the "commonplace," while the latter remains inert outside it.

In light of these obstacles, there seems little chance of realizing Prynne's utopian vision of language possession—or even working toward its realization. We can know everything there is to know about his poetry (including its potential efficacy) and still not be able to accommodate its utopianism. The problem is not that it is insufficiently beautiful or cogent. (To demonstrate its full power, I would have to quote from his most compelling books—*The White Stones* [1969], *Brass* [1971], *Wound Response* [1974], *The Oval Window* [1983], *Triodes* [2000].)[92] The problem, instead, is that beauty and cogency, by themselves, rarely if ever facilitate such an intense commitment to a work of art—or any other object.

My analysis of *Not-You* is a case in point. Rather than read the poem in the contexts of Prynne's oeuvre, I isolated it. Rather than collaborate with fellow reader-researchers, I used Google to determine the poem's range of reference. My aim was to describe Prynne's difficulty, not participate in an aesthetic, moral, and political project.[93] As a result, I turned a practical proposal into a theoretical problem. My impropriety raises the question, if I won't commit to Prynne's poetry, who will?

This is not only a local problem. In its general form, it is common to all traditional utopian projects. Nagel defines utopianism as an ideal that "reasonable individuals cannot be motivated to live by."[94] Leninism, Stalinism, Maoism—these are the ideals Nagel has in mind.[95] But Prynne's poetry also exemplifies the impasse, albeit in miniature, imagining an ideal world we can endorse but not realize. The insight gained from reading *Not-You* is not simply that utopianism is unfeasible or requires a revolution in the structure of society or that powerful interests interfere with the common good. All this we know. It is that by reading a poem we can experience (and confront) the promise of collective life and its failure.[96]

6

> *A sinologue has no time to learn how to write poetry; a poet has no time to learn how to read Chinese.*
>
> —AMY LOWELL[97]

Under what conditions might readers be able to realize the potential of Prynne's poetry? Theodor W. Adorno, in his lecture "Why Is the New Art So Hard to Understand?" (1931), presents this counterfactual:

> [I]f the disposition of work and leisure time were different than [it is] today; if people, independent of cultural privilege, could spend their leisure time occupied substantively and extensively with artistic matters; if a demonically precise mechanism of advertising and anesthetization did not, in every instant of their leisure, prevent them from occupying themselves with actual art—then in principle, the consciousness of consumers could be changed in such a way that they could understand new art.[98]

Under such conditions, readers might be able to satisfy the demands of *Not-You*. Likewise, readers might be able to learn Chinese to read Prynne's pamphlet.

It is tempting to identify this counterfactual with the contemporary research university. This would be misguided for myriad reasons, of course. Yet as an ideal, the university seems designed to accommodate Prynne's work. (If the label "academic" could somehow be redeemed, it would apply to Prynne.) Indeed, at first glance, one university seems especially accommodating. Prynne's best readers are colleagues and former students at Cambridge: Keston Sutherland, Simon Jarvis, John Wilkinson, Drew Milne, Ian Patterson, and Ryan Dobran, to name a few. (Sutherland's thirty-five-page close reading of the two-page "L'Extase de M. Poher" is perhaps the most responsible critique of Prynne's poetry available.)[99] The little magazines *Parataxis*, *Quid*, and *Glossator*, edited by Milne, Sutherland, and Dobran, respectively, devote substantial space to Prynne's poetry.[100] The *nine* issues of *Parataxis*, for example, include *ten* essays on his work.

In the seventh issue of *Quid*, another former Prynne student, Li Zhimin, presents four English versions of "Jie ban mi Shi Hu"—translated as "Going Together to Seek for Stone Lake."[101] Here is the first:

> Stepping upon the bridge to push open ancient ages
> Standing on the bridge and watch the ancient views
> Green mosses cover deserted gardens
> With a friend, to talk in heartfelt words
> In a rainy day, to cup fragrant leaves
> Long echoing sweetly in the heart[102]

Li's versions illuminate more than the poem's conventionality—they illuminate Prynne's coterie reception at Cambridge. "Jie ban mi Shi Hu" has not, as far as I know, motivated anyone to learn Chinese, but it has motivated a coterie to work together to support Prynne's linguistic idealism. Li's version may be not inspiring as poetry, but it is a sincere contribution to a larger, collaborative project.

This coterie, however, reveals a contradiction at the project's center: Prynne's most devoted readers answer to the very thing his poems aim to transcend—personality. This is why Cambridge is a felicitous setting: it provides the means and intimacy necessary to begin to read his work. In a note accompanying his translations, Li writes, "Prynne once told me that he loves Chinese culture deeply and even finds himself somewhat addicted to it. This well explains the harmony of western and Chinese culture in his Chinese poem."[103] Such statements should be anathema to Prynne. Personal allegiance should play no part in the reception of his poetry.[104]

Why does this contradiction matter? Prynne's poetry does not ignore its relation to power—Cambridge included. Yet its relation to coterie presents a different set of concerns. Unlike other institutions, coteries maintain their power by guarding it. Their exclusivity is not simply a by-product of social inequality but a necessary, defining characteristic. Thus, as Prynne's coterie attempts to realize the potential of his poetry, it obstructs it. The commitment of some readers necessarily inhibits the commitment of others. (It is not a coincidence that every reader listed above is male.) When the British media derides Prynne's coterie as the "Cambridge School"—or when its members dismiss the term—these are, in part, the stakes: not simply the accessibility of his poetry but the accessibility of his coterie as well.[105]

Pound and Prynne embrace radically different conceptions of classical Chinese poetry. These conceptions lead to radically different utopian projects. Pound attempts to evade the "stupidity" of his readers. His goal is to separate the efficacy of his poetry from its reception. Prynne, in contrast, confronts the challenge of how to motivate readers. His goal is to catalyze an ever-increasing network committed to reshaping the conventions that determine our perception of the world. These utopian projects do not, of course, succeed. (Or, at least, they have not yet succeeded.) But Pound's and Prynne's respective reading and writing practices create versions of these utopias—for themselves alone. Pound only countenances his own experience of his poetry. Prynne, in turn, is his own ideal reader: by writing his poetry, he is able to maintain a rigorous engagement with convention. Both poets, in this way, inhabit utopias of one.

But my aim in this chapter is not simply to fit Pound and Prynne into a box (or paradigm) labeled "utopia of one." (Both poets come to inhabit their utopias of one reluctantly.) My aim, instead, is to understand how they tolerate their inability to adequately motivate readers. This aim connects to a larger question, which has motivated my book: What sustains such seemingly impossible literary projects in the face of constant failure? Potential answers include obsessiveness, careerism, and foolishness. (Ben Lerner suggests that failure is essential to poetry: "'Poetry' is a word for a kind of value no particular poem can realize: the value of persons, the value of a human activity beyond the labor/leisure divide, a value before or beyond price.")[106] My answer is different: some utopian writing has utopian effects. These effects are radically singular and specific but also genuine, dramatic, life-changing, and life-sustaining. One solution to the problem of motivation is self-motivation.

CONCLUSION

Utopias of Two

1

In late 1862 or early 1863, at the height of the American Civil War, Emily Dickinson wrote the following poem:

> The Soul unto itself
> Is an imperial friend –
> Or the most agonizing Spy –
> An Enemy – could send –
>
> Secure against it's own –
> No treason it can fear –
> Itself – it's Sovreign – Of itself
> The Soul should stand in Awe –[1]

In February 1863, Dickinson sent the poem to her friend and mentor Thomas Wentworth Higginson. Later that year, she sent it (with minor changes) to her sister-in-law, Susan Huntington Gilbert Dickinson. In the summer, she included it as the eleventh poem in her twenty-fifth fascicle book (also with minor changes).[2] A transcription of this fascicle version appears in R. W. Franklin's reading edition of Dickinson's poems as poem 579.

"The Soul unto itself" seems easy to understand. Edward Hirsch provides a gloss in his book, *How to Read a Poem and Fall in Love with Poetry* (1999). The first stanza, he argues, presents two options: "Dickinson powerfully defines what it means to face oneself at ground level, presenting it in the form of a single alternative: either the soul is a royal friend or a traitorous enemy."[3] The second stanza resolves the dilemma: Dickinson "presents the image of a house or fortress secure against insurrection."[4] For Hirsch, the poem is a defense of "Freedom within confinement"—one of Dickinson's "key subjects."[5]

The gloss is persuasive. Hirsch is a careful critic. He acknowledges the poem's context: the poem, he claims "takes civil war as its metaphor for inner spiritual division."[6] (The claim inverts the standard historicist approach.) He also attends to the poem's idiosyncratic capitalization and diction: "I assume the word 'friend' is not capitalized because Dickinson sought a secular term for an inner harmony—the soul's harmonious relationship to itself."[7] Finally, he recognizes the complexity of the poem's final line: "Awe is an emotion mingled with reverence, dread, and wonder inspired by something majestic or sublime. It is a radical move for Dickinson to take a word usually associated with the sublime . . . and to apply it to an interior realm."[8]

The gloss puts Dickinson in dialogue with a long tradition of stoicism. Hannah Arendt's account of Epictetus in "What Is Freedom?" (1958–61)—an essay I discuss in my introduction—anticipates Hirsch's account of Dickinson almost perfectly:

> According to ancient understanding, man could liberate himself from necessity only through power over other men, and he could be free only if he owned a place, a home in the world. Epictetus transposed these worldly relationships into relationships within man's own self, whereby he discovered that no power is so absolute as that which man yields over himself, and that the inward space where man struggles and subdues himself is more entirely his own, namely, more securely shielded from outside interference, than any worldly home could ever be.[9]

This was Epictetus's innovation: to transform a war without into a war within, and win. According to Hirsch, Dickinson follows suit.[10]

This gloss has at least one important implication: it subverts standard accounts of Dickinson's difficulty. In *Choosing Not Choosing* (1992), Sharon Cameron summarizes these accounts: "To look at the history of Dickinson criticism is to see that what is memorialized are her ellipses, her canceled connections, the 'revoked . . . referentiality' of the poetry."[11] Hirsch's gloss challenges this history. The poem's subject matter might be difficult, but the poem itself is not.

2

Does "The Soul unto Itself" represent Dickinson's utopia of one? Hirsch associates the poem's defense of "freedom within confinement" to "her self-imposed exile, her reclusion indoors."[12] Is the poem, then, an attempt to represent or even cultivate her own independence?

The poem certainly represents *a* utopia of one. Dickinson presents a soul at war with itself and then describes an ideal state of independence—total sovereignty, total security. Her use of "Awe" complicates this description, but does not invalidate it. Indeed, "awe" might be the perfect word to characterize the experience of inhabiting a utopia of one.

This utopia of one is different from the utopias I have been tracking in this book. Most significant, its efficacy does not depend on its difficulty or exclusivity or inimitability. Dickinson's description of independence can serve as a model for readers attempting to perfect their own lives. Want to be free? Self-regulate. Embrace stoicism.

Determining Dickinson's relation to "The Soul unto Itself," however, is much more difficult than determining the poem's ostensible import. Is she pursuing her own "freedom within confinement"—or mocking the concept? (Imperial friend? Agonizing spy? The poem's diction is ridiculously melodramatic.) Is Dickinson the poem's speaker? Is the poem's speaker sincere?

The other writers I discuss in *Utopias of One* have easily identifiable projects. Their poems and memoirs are instruments of independence. Even when their work is impersonal, their personal investment is clear. (This is one reason I categorized their work as nonfiction.) One of the major challenges of reading their work is determining *our* relation to their projects.

Dickinson's personal investment, in contrast, is ambiguous. This is the challenge of reading her work: not determining *our* relation to her project, but determining *her* relation to her project—and determining whether she has a project at all. "The Soul unto Itself" might be a response to her own "inner spiritual division"—or it might be a joke. Or it might be something else entirely.[13]

3

There are, I think, three ways to attempt to identify Dickinson's relation to "The Soul unto Itself"—all unsatisfying. First, one could read the poem in the context of her other poems. Hirsch, for example, cites Judith Farr's observation that "Dickinson speaks of the *soul* or *souls* 141 times in her poems" and tracks how she extricates the word from contemporary usage.[14] The poem, he argues, is part of a career-long attempt to "sever the soul from the power of the collective and scandalously reclaim it for the autonomous self."[15] Is the poem, then, an instrument of independence after all?

Yet contextualizing the poem against a different subset of poems points to a different conclusion. The twenty poems in Dickinson's twenty-fifth fascicle book all concern the ineluctable power of the collective. The first poem, which describes the intimacy of reading, opens—

A precious – mouldering pleasure – 'tis
To meet an Antique Book –
In just the Dress his Century wore –
A privilege – I think –

His venerable Hand to take –
And warming in our own –

A passage back – or two – to make –
To Times when he – was young – [16]

The second poem describes a prisoner struggling to gain access to his or her neighbor's cell—not the world outside the prison walls. Other poems depict encounters with God, fraught departures, and out-of-body experiences. The two poems that frame "The Soul unto Itself" describe acts of sympathetic identification. The fascicle, in this way, represents the impossibility of personal autonomy. The well-known line from Stéphane Mallarmé's "Le nénuphar blanc" ("The White Water Lily"; 1885) could serve as the fascicle's motto: "Apart, we are together."[17]

A second way to attempt to identify Dickinson's relation to "The Soul unto Itself" would be to read the poem in the context of contemporary accounts of "inner spiritual division"—or some other aspect of contemporary culture. Consider this passage from Horace Bushnell's *Sermons for the New Life* (1858)—a book owned by Dickinson's family:

> It is as if the soul were a thinking ruin; which it verily is. The angel and the demon life appear to be contending in it. The imagination revels in beauty exceeding all the beauty of things, wails in images dire and monstrous, wallows in murderous and base suggestions that shame our inward dignity; so that a great part of the study and a principal art of life, is to keep our decency, by a wise selection from what we think and a careful suppression of the remainder. A diseased and crazy mixture, such as represents a ruin, is the form of our inward experience.[18]

The connection is striking: Dickinson seems to adopt Bushnell's theme—and his Manichaeism. Her "Soul" echoes his "thinking ruin." Yet the connection does not reveal her personal investment in the poem. Would she endorse his view that our integrity depends on a "wise selection from what we think and a careful suppression of the remainder"? I do not know.

Indeed, one could just as easily connect "The Soul unto Itself" to a competing account of "inner spiritual division." Consider this passage from Emerson's "The Over-Soul" (1841)—Dickinson's family also owned a copy of *Essays* (1841):

> What we commonly call man, the eating, drinking, planting, counting man, does not, as we know him, represent himself, but misrepresents himself. Him we do not respect, but the soul, whose organ he is, would he let it appear through his action, would make our knees bend.[19]

For Emerson, our integrity depends on our receptivity—not a "wise selection from what we think and a careful suppression of the remainder." "The Over-Soul" is the likely source of Dickinson's use of "awe." Emerson uses the word three times—always to describe the feeling that results from the union of the "individual soul" and "universal soul."[20]

Is Dickinson a Bushnellian or an Emersonian? Neither? Both? The poem, one could claim, explores different accounts of "inner spiritual division." Yet even this modest claim would be speculative.

A third way to attempt to identify Dickinson's relation to "The Soul unto Itself" would be to read the poem in the context of its initial circulation. When she sent the poem to Higginson, he had just taken command of a regiment of black soldiers, the First South Carolina Volunteers. Her letter begins:

> Dear friend
>
> I did not deem the Planetary forces annulled – but suffered an Exchange of Territory, or World –
>
> I should have liked to see you, before you became improbable. War feels to me an oblique place – Should there be other Summers, would you perhaps come?
>
> I found you were gone, by accident, as I find Systems are, or Seasons of the year, and obtain no cause – but supposed it a treason of Progress – that dissolves as it goes. Carlo – still remained – and I told him –
>
> Best Gains – must have the Losses' Test –
> To constitute them – Gains –
>
> My shaggy Ally assented –
>
> Perhaps Death – gave me awe for friends – striking sharp and early, for I held them since – in a brittle love – or more alarm, than peace.[21]

Later in the letter, Dickinson mentions her upbringing, prayer, and the "Supernatural." War and death remain constant themes. She concludes with a plea for Higginson's safety: "Could you, with honor, avoid Death, I entreat you – Sir – It would bereave."[22] She then signs the letter, "Your Gnome," and adds a postscript: "I trust the 'Procession of Flowers' was not a premonition."[23]

Now imagine you are Higginson. You know Carlo refers to Dickinson's dog. You know "Procession of Flowers" refers to your essay, "The Procession of the Flowers" (1862), recently published in the *Atlantic*. You do not know the meaning of "Your Gnome." ("I cannot explain this extraordinary signature," Higginson wrote in 1891.)[24] What can you say about Dickinson's relation to the poem? Not much. Indeed, you might even find fault with Hirsch's gloss—assuming, of course, you had access to it. Is civil war a metaphor for the soul—or is the soul a metaphor for civil war? Is the poem about "freedom within confinement"—or death? You might point to a passage from "The Procession of the Flowers":

> Harriet Prescott says that some souls are like the Water-Lilies, fixed, yet floating. But others are like this graceful purple blossom, floating unfixed, kept in place only by its fellows around it, until perhaps a breeze comes, and, breaking the accidental cohesion, sweeps them all away.[25]

Is the poem a plea for fixity? Is Dickinson's use of "secure" a synonym for "fastened" rather than "protected"—as Hirsch seems to assume? Did Dickinson write the poem to keep you (Higginson) alive?

One could extend and refine all these approaches. There is more to learn about the poem's connection to Dickinson's other poems, her connection to contemporary culture, and the poem's initial circulation. One could read the poem in dialogue with her poem "The Robin is the One," which was also enclosed in the letter.[26] One could read the poem in dialogue with the poems embedded in the letter. (Notice Dickinson's use of "awe" in the sentence beginning "Perhaps death." Once lineated, the sentence is an even more beautiful poem than "The Soul unto Itself.")[27] In addition, one could read the poem in dialogue with contemporary debates about slavery. The First South Carolina Volunteers was a regiment of escaped slaves. Does that fact complicate Hirsch's argument about "freedom within confinement"? (What about the fact that Abraham Lincoln issued the Emancipation Proclamation on January 1, 1863?) One could also read the poem in dialogue with mid-nineteenth-century accounts of same-sex desire. Some scholars believe that the poem's other recipient, Susan Dickinson, was Dickinson's lover.[28]

This, ultimately, is my argument: Contextualization will never reveal Dickinson's personal investment in the poem. The problem is not merely a lack of sources. The problem is also the ambiguity of the sources we have. For other writers, context delimits interpretation. The more one learns about the contexts of Pound's "The Beautiful Toilet," for example, the less ambiguous the poem becomes. Pound's utopianism becomes clear. For "The Soul unto Itself," the opposite is true: the more one learns about the poem's contexts, the more ambiguous the poem becomes. As Virginia Jackson writes, "the difficulty of reading Dickinson's manuscripts is that even in their fragmentary extant forms, they provide so much context that individual lyrics become practically illegible."[29]

4

Questions about Dickinson's relation to the poem are, ultimately, questions about her intentions and beliefs. Why did she write "The Soul unto Itself"? What did she want it to accomplish? How was it supposed to work?

Why do Dickinson's intentions and beliefs matter? For two reasons. First, they matter to me: *Utopias of One* is about why writers write—and about how they sustain and realize their utopian desires.[30] Second, Dickinson's intentions and beliefs matter because they have always mattered to Dickinson critics. In 1890, four years after her death, Higginson introduced her first book by observing that "these verses will seem to the reader like poetry torn up by the roots."[31] Ever since, critics have attempted to re-root the poems. (R. P. Blackmur's notorious quip from 1956 updates Higginson's observation: "One exaggerates, but it sometimes seems as if in her work a cat came at us speaking English.")[32] Even Susan Howe's influential claim, from 1991, that the poems "checkmate inscription to become what a reader offers them" concerns Dickinson's intentions and beliefs.[33] According to Howe, Dickinson is an "unconverted antinomian," refusing to conform to any standard of conduct.[34] In a discussion of Dickinson's variants—the nonexclusive substitute words that appear in the margins of her poems—Howe asks, "What if the author went to great care to fit these words onto pages she could have copied over?"[35]

Was Dickinson writing lyrics? What is the significance of her punctuation and spelling and capitalization and lineation and calligraphy?[36] Are her fascicle books actually books? These questions all concern her intentions and beliefs. The same is true for questions about the connection between her poems and what Hirsch describes as her "self-imposed exile, her reclusion indoors."

"The Soul unto Itself" is not a special case. Or to be more precise: it is a special case, but only insofar as it is a comparatively easy poem to understand. Dickinson's other poems often present an array of hermeneutic challenges—before one even attempts to identify her intentions and beliefs. "The Soul unto Itself" is an exception: its ostensible import is clear. There are no dramatic differences among manuscript versions. These versions do not include variants. The poem's difficulty, in other words, is basic.

In *Choosing Not Choosing*, Cameron offers a powerful account of this basic difficulty. The critical question is not whether the poems "make no sense or the sense that they make is completely unproblematic." The critical question, instead, is how to make sense of her "extraordinarily complex, perhaps even conflicted, set of intentions, beliefs, desires."[37] As Cameron notes, "we know that Dickinson intended something. After all, she copied the poems into the fascicles."[38] Yet we do not know what, specifically, she intended. Cameron focuses on the fascicle books, but her insights apply to Dickinson's oeuvre. "[T]he reader," Cameron observes, "experiences the necessity for choosing, without access to the criteria by which she could make a choice."[39]

Cameron, in the end, follows Howe and re-roots the poems by speculating about Dickinson's refusal to put down roots: "[Dickinson] refused to make up her mind about how her poems should be read. This refusal—another aspect of what I have called choosing not to choose—is crucial to the problematic of reading her poetry."[40] From this perspective, Dickinson is a utopian writer. Her refusal to choose represents her resistance to "all forms of totalizing closure"—to quote the passage from Jacques Rancière's *Politics of Aesthetics* (2000) that I quoted in the introduction to this book.[41]

This reading is, of course, speculative—and necessarily so. To successfully choose not to choose, Dickinson must choose not to choose not to choose. Her utopianism prohibits identification of any kind—for identification is a form of "totalizing closure." This prohibition prevents readers from identifying her utopianism in the first place.

This is why I did not (and could not) devote a chapter to Dickinson in *Utopias of One*: her utopianism is unknowable. She might be a successful utopian writer; she might not be a utopian writer at all.[42] A comparison to Thoreau is illuminating. Both Thoreau and Dickinson isolate themselves: Thoreau retreats to the woods at Walden Pond, Dickinson to her garret. Both participate in the intellectual climate of mid-nineteenth-century New England. Both are innovative, difficult, beautiful writers. Both write about personal sovereignty. Both seem obvious writers to discuss in a book titled *Utopias of One*. Yet Thoreau's personal investment in his work is clear. Dickinson's is not. Readers can identify Thoreau's project at Walden and in *Walden*—even if they cannot share it or fully evaluate its efficacy. *Walden*'s utopia of one is Thoreau's utopia of one—and his alone. In contrast, readers cannot identify Dickinson's relation to her own work.

5

"The Soul unto Itself" represents a limit case of difficulty. Readers cannot even be sure that the poem is difficult. Howe writes, "Form and content collapse the assumption of Project and Masterpiece."[43] But that is not quite right: the impossibility of identifying Dickinson's intentions and beliefs collapses the assumption of project and masterpiece—and many other assumptions as well.[44]

The basic difficulty of "The Soul unto Itself" and Dickinson's other poems clarifies an implicit claim of this book. There are obvious benefits to reading difficult texts: wonder; pleasure; self-estrangement; philosophical, philological, historical, and sociological insight. And there are less obvious benefits. Most significantly: difficult texts teach us how to live without reciprocity—to cultivate care for persons and things independent of our personal interests. Difficult texts, in other words, teach us to be altruistic.

Is altruism compatible with the other benefits mentioned above? Probably not. But the other benefits might help us recognize the importance of altruism in the first place. Wonder; pleasure; self-estrangement; and philosophical, philological, historical, and sociological insight might be an effective delivery system for an ethics that circumvents our need for acknowledgment.

This description of the social utility of difficult literature may seem out of place at the conclusion of a book about the antisocial utility of difficult literature. In the preceding chapters, I have been careful to avoid narratives of redemption. *Utopias of One* details the efficacy of utopian literature—and attempts to understand why writers devote their lives to such seemingly impossible projects. These projects are always morally ambiguous. To celebrate their social utility is to risk obscuring their complexity and precariousness. But perhaps this conclusion is an appropriate place to take that risk.

The basic difficulty of Dickinson's poems clarifies another implicit claim of this book. When we read difficult texts, we create an occasion for collective inquiry. We might not be able to share Dickinson's project (if she even has one!) or the projects of the other writers I discuss in *Utopias of One*. But we can share a project among ourselves.[45] Our estrangement is an invitation to work together and be together—and to learn how to be together more effectively. In this way, a utopia of one might lead to a utopia of two or three or four.

6

There are at least two paradoxes (or, less generously, contradictions) at the core of this book. The first is clear from the book's title: Can there be a utopia of just one person? Indeed, can there be a utopia at all? The second paradox is clear from the book's table of contents: Can writers from such disparate contexts illuminate a single concept? Can a series of specific claims about aesthetics and politics lead to a general claim about aesthetics and politics?

In the preceding pages, I have tried to elucidate these paradoxes by tracking how utopian desire survives the failure of utopia. The projects I have discussed are unimaginable outside their particular contexts. Even Stevens, who seems wholly uninterested in context, develops a project that reflects his relative freedom and privilege. Yet the projects, together, represent a limit case of literary efficacy—what literature can and does make happen. Writers perfect their lives by alienating the readers they purportedly address.

Does my general claim illuminate the specific claims on which it is based? Does *Utopias of One* tell us anything new about liberalism and communism, for example? My first answer should be uncontroversial: the book reveals how liberalism and communism created specific opportunities for dissent at specific moments in history. My second answer might be more tendentious: the book reveals that liberalism and communism were not (and are not) discrete ideologies or political systems. Writers in the United States and England were not immune to the effects of anticapitalist conceptions of art and life, and writers in the Soviet Union were not immune to the effects of capitalism—from reification to alienation. The October Revolution may have led to a "New Man," but it did not shield that man from the world. *Utopias of One* begins to capture the connections between radically different ideas and historical events as it disentangles literary efficacy from the public good, and utopianism from failure.

ACKNOWLEDGMENTS

Lauren Berlant, Robert Bird, Oren Izenberg, and Robert von Hallberg supervised the dissertation that led to *Utopias of One*. I am incredibly grateful for their guidance and trust. They have been (and continue to be) models of intelligence, receptivity, and integrity.

I also benefited from advice from other faculty members at the University of Chicago. Bradin Cormack, Boris Maslov, Srikanth Reddy, Richard Strier, Kenneth W. Warren, and John Wilkinson commented on individual chapter drafts and provided helpful feedback. David W. Galenson introduced me to new ways of thinking about literature and art, and the value and aims of scholarship. I owe him a special debt.

A community of friends supported *Utopias of One* from the beginning. For more than ten years of camaraderie, I thank V. Joshua Adams, Robert P. Baird, Michael Hansen, Michael Kindellan, John Lennox, Eirik Steinhoff, Johanna Winant, and Nathan Wolff.

I am also grateful for the brilliance and generosity of my colleagues at Princeton. Anne Cheng, Bradin Cormack (again), Jeff Dolven, Diana Fuss, William Gleason, John Logan, Meredith Martin, Sarah Rivett, Susan Stewart, and Susan Wolfson read chapter drafts and provided excellent, useful feedback. Susan Stewart, especially, gave me detailed and incisive advice, which made (and continues to make) a significant impact on my thinking about poetry and philosophy. I thank my other colleagues at Princeton as well, especially Zahid Chaudhary, Sarah Chihaya, Maria DiBattista, Sophie Gee, Simon Gikandi, Claudia Johnson, Russ Leo, Kinohi Nishikawa, Deborah Nord, Katherine Hill Reischl, Effie Rentzou, Esther Schor, Nigel Smith, and Michael Wood. (My conversations with Russ and Effie over the last five years have been vital to my thinking about literature.) In addition, I thank my current and former students, especially Carl Adair, Danny Braun, Ian Davis, Elspeth Green, Cate Mahoney, Jesse McCarthy, Orlando Reade, and Roy Scranton.

Many colleagues in the profession read chapter drafts and offered challenging advice. I thank Charles Altieri, Ryan Dobran, Rachel Galvin, Eric Hayot, Walt Hunter, Lee Konstantinou, Douglas Mao, Britt Rusert, and Avery Slater for sharing their expertise with me.

Many other individuals made important contributions, large and small, to the book. Thank you to Jennifer Ashton, Kelly Austin, Venus Bivar, Daphne Brooks, Steph Burt, Joel Calahan, Hillary Chute, Moacir de Sá Pereira, Abby Dean, Michael Dickman, Peter Gizzi, Mollie Godfrey, Jackie Goldsby, Pat Guglielmi, Christian Hawkey, Megan Heffernan, Alison James, William Junker, Lena Kamenskaia, Heather Keenleyside, Maggie Kilgour, John Lacombe, Amy

Langstaff, Robert Lecker, Olga Livshin, W. Martin, Kerry McSweeney, Kevin Mensch, Mark Miller, Karen Mink, Deborah Nelson, Phoebe Nobles, Peter Ohlin, Liesl Olson, Richard Parker, Mark Payne, Lloyd Pratt, Harsha Ram, Michael Robbins, Jeremy Rosen, Jennifer Scappettone, Lytle Shaw, Nancy Shillingford, Dustin Simpson, Eric Slauter, Richard So, Kate Soto, Hilary Strang, Gabriel Swift, Nick Torrey, Brian Trehearne, Adam Weg, and Leila Wilson.

I also thank my family: Beth Applebaum, Noha Applebaum, Teddy and Alyssa Applebaum, Frederick and Margot Barnard, Ben Kotin, Dan Kotin, David Kotin and Colleen Darragh, Ilana Kotin and Peter Lowe, Joel Kotin and Lyda Hill, Paul and Pauly Kotin, Nick and Carrie Patch, Randy Patch, and Yvonne Patch and Joe McGlynn.

During my research for this book, I received support from the Social Sciences and Humanities Research Council of Canada, the University of Chicago, the University Center for Human Values at Princeton, the Dodd Research Center at the University of Connecticut, the European University Institute, and the Center for the Humanities at Tufts. I thank Jonathan Wilson at Tufts in particular for creating an environment that allowed me to complete a full draft of the book.

I also thank the editors of *Modernism/modernity* and *PMLA* for their feedback on earlier versions of chapters 3 and 5, respectively, and the scholars who responded to my work at conferences, seminars, and lectures. I thank Anne Birrell, Li Zhimin, and J. H. Prynne for permission to quote from their work. They retain all rights to their poetry and prose.

Finally, I thank the editors and staff at Princeton University Press, especially my editor, Anne Savarese, for her guidance and support; Cathy Slovensky for her copyediting; Thalia Leaf for her help with permissions; David Luljak for the index; and Mark Bellis for overseeing the production process.

I dedicate *Utopias of One* to Rachel Applebaum, who has made the most significant impact on this book. She is a true partner in every aspect of my life. I am grateful for the world we have made together and continue to remake with and for our daughter, Eleonora Taubelle.

NOTE ON TRANSLITERATION & TRANSLATION

Throughout *Utopias of One*, I use the Library of Congress system to transliterate Russian names and titles. (I make an exception for the names of Russian writers who also write for English-speaking audiences—Joseph Brodsky, for example.) When I cite published translations of Russian writers in my notes, I adopt the spelling used in the translations. In the bibliography, however, I use the Library of Congress system, but note alternative spellings. (For example, all texts by Nadezhda Mandel'shtam are collected under a single entry, "Mandel'shtam, Nadezhda," but I indicate when texts use the spelling, "Mandelstam.") Translations are my own unless otherwise indicated in the bibliography.

Introduction: Utopias of One

1. Similar claims have been made about other political and philosophical concepts. "It will be seen," George Orwell writes in "What Is Fascism?" (*Collected Essays* [1944]), "that, as used, the word 'Fascism' is almost entirely meaningless" (113). In *Existentialism Is a Humanism* (1946), Jean-Paul Sartre writes, "For now that it has become fashionable, people like to call this musician or that painter an 'existentialist.' . . . Indeed, the word is being so loosely applied to so many things that it has come to mean nothing at all" (20).

2. Rancière, *Politics of Aesthetics*, 40.

3. Some utopias succeed and by succeeding reveal their spuriousness. As Theodor W. Adorno notes, "I would like to remind us right away that numerous so-called utopian dreams—for example, television, the possibility of traveling to other planets, moving faster than sound—have been fulfilled. However, insofar as these dreams have been realized, they all operate as though the best thing about them had been forgotten—one is not happy about them. . . . [O]ne sees oneself almost always deceived: the fulfillment of the wishes takes something away from the substance of the wishes." See Bloch and Adorno, "Something's Missing," 1.

4. Winter, "Minor Utopias," 72.

5. Bloch and Adorno, "Something's Missing," 12. Fredric Jameson makes a similar point in the introduction to *Archaeologies of the Future* (2005): "Utopia," he writes, "can serve the negative purpose of making us more aware of our mental and ideological imprisonment . . . therefore the best Utopias are those that fail the most comprehensively" (xiii). Later in the introduction, he argues, citing Sartre, that for "those mindful of the very real political function of the idea and the program of Utopia in our time, the slogan of anti-anti-Utopianism might well offer the best working strategy" (xvi).

6. In "Utopia deferred . . ." (originally published as "L'utopie a été renvoyée . . ."), Baudrillard writes, "There could be no model for utopia nor utopian function, because utopia denies the inscription of all finality, whether unconscious or in the class struggle. . . . In the topic of the sign, Utopia is the gap, the fault, the void that passes between the signifier and the signified and subverts every sign" (61, 62). In *Utopia, Limited*, Nersessian argues that "Romantic literature functions as utopian thought insofar as it takes its own formalism to mime a minimally harmful relationship between human beings and a world whose resources are decidedly finite" (16).

7. von Hallberg, *Charles Olson*, 41.

8. Buck-Morss, *Dreamworld*, x.

9. Clover and Sutherland, "Always Totalize."

10. These overlapping categories—the critical, analytical, aspirational, inspirational, sentimental, representational—are not exhaustive, but they do index most work on literary efficacy. Consider two recent and influential defenses of poetry. In "The Poetic Case" (2007), Christopher Nealon identifies poetry's "political unconscious" as "a tone that makes both affirmation and exploitation audible at once" (886). ("[L]earning how to listen for it is the central task of aesthetic theory today," he adds.) In *Being Numerous* (2011), Oren Izenberg identifies poetry as "a site for the articulation of a new humanism." His thesis: "Against a poetics of poems that enters deeply into the texture of the experience of persons (whether as representation of that experience or occasion for it), the poets I will describe

here seek ways to make their poetic thinking yield accounts of personhood that are at once *minimal*—placing as few restrictions as possible upon the legitimate forms a person can take—and *universal*—tolerating no exemptions or exclusions. Finally, they will also demand that our concepts of personhood identify something *real*: not political fictions we could come to inhabit together, or pragmatic ways of speaking we might come to share, but a ground on which the idea of a 'we' might stand. This poetry, I argue, is an important site for the articulation of a new humanism: it seeks a reconstructive response to the great crises of social agreement and recognition in the twentieth century" (4). For critics as different as Nealon and Izenberg, poetry is critical and aspirational: it helps us understand the world and promotes (or "articulates") a program to change the world.

11. Thoreau, *Walden*, 51.

12. For a brief account of the turmoil within in the abolitionist movement in the 1840s, see Lowance, general introduction to *Against Slavery*, xxv–xxvi.

13. For an account of the slow dissolution of Brook Farm, see Delano, *Brook Farm: The Dark Side of Utopia*.

14. Thoreau, *Walden*, 134.

15. Cavell, *Senses of Walden*, 49.

16. A case in point: the controversy that followed the publication of Kathryn Schulz's *New Yorker* essay, "Pond Scum: Henry David Thoreau's Moral Myopia" (2015). Schulz writes, "Thoreau was, in the fullest sense of the word, self-obsessed: narcissistic, fanatical about self-control, adamant that he required nothing beyond himself to understand and thrive in the world. From that inward fixation flowed a social and political vision that is deeply unsettling" (http://www.newyorker.com/magazine/2015/10/19/pond-scum). A flurry of responses defending Thoreau followed—from, among others, Jedediah Purdy in the *Atlantic*, Donovan Hohn in the *New Republic*, Richard B. Primack and Abraham J. Miller-Rushing in the *Boston Globe*, and Simon Waxman in the *Boston Review*.

17. Judith Butler makes the general point eloquently in *Undoing Gender* (2004): "One is dependent on this 'outside' to lay claim to what is one's own. The self must, in this way, be dispossessed in sociality in order to take possession of itself" (7). Earlier in the book, she notes, "If I have any agency, it is opened up by the fact that I am constituted by a social world I never chose. That my agency is riven with paradox does not mean that it is impossible. It only means that paradox is the condition of its possibility" (3).

18. Guillame Budé, letter to Thomas Lupset, included in the ancillary materials to the 1517 edition of *Utopia*, 114–15.

19. Kumar, *Utopia and Anti-Utopia*, 82. Roland Barthes, in his lectures at the Collège de France in 1977 and 1978, makes a related claim: "there can be no solipsistic utopia." See Barthes, *The Neutral*, 40. For a brief discussion of solipsism, see chapter 5, note 46.

20. White, "A Slight Sound," 295.

21. Thoreau, *Walden*, 323.

22. Emerson, *Essays and Lectures*, 259.

23. Thoreau gave public lectures about his project at Walden as early as January 1847. See Dean and Hoag, "Thoreau's Lectures before *Walden*," 169–75.

24. In *Isolated Cases* (2004), Nancy Yousef discusses the connection between the terms "independence" and "autonomy": "The terms *autonomy* and *independence* share as primary definitions the idea of being 'self-governing.' Earliest usages of both terms in this sense—referring either to the will of a political entity or of a person—date to roughly the same period (between 1611 and 1640, the age of Hobbes and Descartes). *Independence*, with its extended definitions of freedom from authority, influence, and other forms of reliance on others, has broader application than *autonomy*, but the terms are largely synonymous. To be independent, as the *Oxford English Dictionary* defines it, is to be 'self-governing, autonomous, free'; to be autonomous is to be 'self-governing, independent'" (12).

25. Berlin, "Two Concepts of Liberty," 122. Berlin's "body of men" should be read expansively to include a range of factors that interfere with our independence—social norms, state power, capital, and so on. Yet this list reveals the complexity of independence: social norms, for example, interfere with our independence while determining our understanding of, and desire for, independence.

26. Ibid., 146.

27. Arendt, "What Is Freedom?," 163.

28. Ibid., 167.

29. Hartman, *Scenes of Subjection*, 122.

30. Balibar, "Subjection and Subjectivation," 8.

31. This inquiry into the meaning and effects of independence only scratches the surface. The inquiry does not, for example, consider the relation between independence and luck—or the relation between independence and mood. In *The Poet's Freedom* (2011), Susan Stewart discusses how weather limits our independence: "Recent studies show that our moods are responsive as well to positive and negative ions in the atmosphere. The warm, dry conditions that facilitate air pollution and result in positive ions produce negative moods, whereas the negative ionic concentrations characterizing the period after rain, or the atmosphere that surrounds circulating water like waterfalls and seashores, or even running shower water, inversely result in good moods" (64). In *Isolated Cases*, Yousef considers why "critiques of the self-determining subject" are today "virtually commonplace" (6).

32. Macpherson, *Political Theory*; Bersani, *Culture of Redemption*, 3.

33. Berlin, "Two Concepts of Liberty," 140.

34. Ibid.

35. This inquiry does not attempt to explain why so many of us prize independence despite its impracticality and perniciousness. Yousef notes that "The power of the idea of an originally independent or self-made individual never derived from its being mistaken for a fact (insofar as it claimed that status, it was contested from the outset) but from the theoretical and imaginative implications of conceiving the individual as such, from the barely articulated needs and desires such an idea could meet, and the barely acknowledged anxieties and fears it could attempt to quell" (*Isolated Cases*, 19). Lauren Berlant's account of "cruel optimism" provides a model for understanding how our attachments can simultaneously protect and threaten us. "'Cruel optimism,'" she writes, "names a relation of attachment to compromised conditions of possibility. What is cruel about these attachments . . . is that the subjects who have x in their lives might not well endure the loss of their object or scene of desire, even though its presence threatens their well-being" ("Cruel Optimism," 21). The desire for independence might be an instance of this x—a source of both sustenance and harm, and thus not easily abandoned. From this perspective, independence is not a zero-sum game—it is a social trap. Social traps, to quote John Platt, are situations in which individuals or groups get "started in some direction or some set of relationships that later prove unpleasant or lethal and that they see no easy way to back out of or to avoid" ("Social Traps," 641).

36. I thank one of the book's anonymous reviewers for the term "nonnational."

37. Gates, "Bad Influence," 94.

38. Halfin, *Terror in My Soul*, 19.

39. The history of utopian literature is coextensive with the history of literature itself—beginning, at least, with Hesiod's account of the golden age. Indeed, many critics believe that utopianism is coextensive with humanity. Bloch, for example, identifies the desire for utopia as the "pervading and above all only honest quality of all human beings" ("Something's Missing," 5). Frank E. Manuel and Fritzie P. Manuel begin their history of utopian thought by noting, "Anthropologists tell us that blessed isles and paradises are part of the dreamworld of savages everywhere" (*Utopian Thought*, 1).

40. Adorno, *Aesthetic Theory*, 33.

41. Thoreau, *Walden*, 297–98.

42. In *Ways of Worldmaking* (1978), Nelson Goodman argues that fictional worlds are also part of our world—"albeit metaphorically." "'Don Quixote,' taken literally, applies to no one," he admits, "but taken figuratively, applies to many of us—for example, to me in my tilts with the windmills of current linguistics" (103–4). Goodman's qualifications ("albeit metaphorically," "but taken figuratively") point to the difference I want to emphasize.

43. In "The Logical Status of Fictional Discourse" (1974–75), John Searle argues that the sole criterion for determining the difference between nonfiction and fiction is the intentions of the author: "the identifying criterion for whether or not a text is a work of fiction must of necessity lie in the illocutionary intentions of the author. There is no textual property, syntactical or semantic, that will identify a text as a work of fiction. What makes it a work of fiction is, so to speak, the illocutionary stance that the author takes toward it, and that stance is a matter of the complex illocutionary intentions that the author has when he writes or otherwise composes it" (65). Searle's claim reverberates in Dirk Eitzen's less precise but more straightforward claim in "When Is a Documentary" (2005): "'Might it be lying?' is what distinguishes documentaries, and nonfiction in general, from fiction" (89). ("A lie," Arnold Isenberg writes, "is a statement made by one who does not believe it with the intention that someone else shall be led to believe it" [466].) The value of Eitzen's claim will become clear in the paragraphs that follow.

44. Stevens, *Collected Poetry and Prose*, 55.

45. As Jonathan Culler points out in *Theory of the Lyric* (2015), most critics assume that all poems have "speakers," which they equate with fictional characters. (For example, even skeptics of critical orthodoxy such as Virginia Jackson and Yopie Prins refer to "poetic fictions," and to the "first-person speaker of the lyric," as "a fictional person" [general introduction, *The Lyric Theory Reader*, 5].) Culler argues, in contrast, that lyric poetry is not "a form of fiction": "To claim that lyric is not, at bottom, a form of fiction seems a significant advance and in particular helps to identify the disadvantages of the most prominent current theory of the lyric, which treats the poem as the speech act of a fictional persona: the fictional imitation of a real-world speech act" (7).

46. Prynne, *Poems*, 321.

47. The passage is from a letter from Prynne to the poet Peter Riley. Riley quotes the passage as the epigraph to his pamphlet, *The Reader* (1992), and appends the date, September 15, 1985. See Riley, *The Reader*.

48. Stevens, *Collected Poetry and Prose*, 53, 55.

49. *Walden* contains fictional elements—the "artist in the city of Kouroo," for example. But the book is still a work of nonfiction. In *Bird Relics* (2016), Branka Arsić describes the combination of the "miraculous and natural" in Thoreau's writing: "Thoreau is not a fiction writer. The generic characteristics of all of his writings—*A Week* is a memoir, *Walden* is autobiography, the *Journal* is a record of perceptions and thoughts, while the natural history essays are structured according to the logic of scientific writing of the day—require that we treat their content not as fiction but as truth, and their utterances not figuratively but declaratively, as testimonies. Yet, his declarations are sometimes so eccentric, they so radically blur the distinction between what is possible and what is not, between miraculous and natural, that one must raise the question of whether to take them seriously" (1).

50. *Typee* is a rare case. In most cases, one can, at least eventually, distinguish between fake memoirs (*Go Ask Alice* [1971] and James Frey's *A Million Little Pieces* [2003]) and fictional memoirs (*Moby Dick* [1851] and Vladimir Nabokov's *Lolita* [1955]). *Typee* is almost certainly a fictional memoir—in other words, a novel—but scholars are still not certain about exactly what happened to Melville on Nuku Hiva. The difference matters. Melville's critique of cultural imperialism would resonate differently if it were, in fact,

based on firsthand experience. One way to determine *Typee*'s status as a work of fiction or nonfiction would be to adopt Eitzen's advice and ask, can *Typee* lie? Answer yes, and you're reading a work of nonfiction; answer no, and you're reading a novel. See Eitzen, "When Is a Documentary?," 89.

51. Vogler, "The Moral of the Story," 15.

52. In a review of Jeremy Glick's *The Black Radical Tragic* (2016) in the *Los Angeles Review of Books*, Slavoj Žižek writes, "That's why one needs narrative fiction, from Glissant to O'Neill, from Eisenstein to Fanon. Art plays with possible alternatives and thus provides the dense cobweb against the background of which the reality of what happened acquires its true profile" (https://lareviewofbooks.org/article/prophetic-vision-haitis-past/). For Žižek, here, art (that is, narrative fiction) illuminates reality's "true profile."

53. An exception—one of many, perhaps: In "Bernhard's Way" (2013), Michael Clune demonstrates how a novel might create a utopia of one, reading Thomas Bernhard's *Woodcutters* (1984) by way of Samuel Beckett's trilogy. Clune summarizes his argument: "Bernhard thus endows the first person narrative with an entirely new meaning and value. That meaning and value utterly exhausts itself in the experience of its creator. What is verifiable from our readers' perspective is the following: 1) Bernhard thinks, in good postmodern fashion, that the problem of art is a social problem. 2) He thinks through this postmodern problem to conclude that the ideal form of art will not be dependant [*sic*] on social relations. 3) *Logically, such a form can give satisfaction only to its creator, never to its audience.* 4) In freeing life from recognition, such a form will 'transform' its creator, and give him the only 'real satisfaction' possible in art or life. 5) The end of *Woodcutters* suggests that Bernhard sees in his novel just such a form. 6) *Woodcutters*' exploitation of the first person narrative techniques of Beckett's *Molloy* provides some limited evidence that the joy expressed at the end of the novel *is the joy of real satisfaction at total transformation*" (my italics). See Nonsite.org at http://nonsite.org/feature/bernhards-way.

54. I thank Steph Burt for this phrase.

55. Izenberg catalogs the ways critics have attempted to justify the difficulty of experimental poetry: "So variously fragmented, occulted, difficult, and silent; so assertively trivial, boring, or aleatory are the types of poetry on the 'experimental' side of the critical divide, that critics who champion the work have gone to great didactic and theoretical lengths to imagine, explain, justify, and market alternative species of pleasure and interest to compensate for the loss of traditional aesthetics. Such justifications include 'the fascination with what's difficult,' the penetration of the veil of the esoteric, the masochistic pleasures of derangement, the politicized shock of estrangement, the tranquilizing or meditative dwelling in the ambient" (*Being Numerous*, 11). Daniel Tiffany challenges what he calls "the common presumption, associated with models of textual difficulty, that obscurity is principally a feature of works considered to be arcane, virtuosic, or deliberately experimental . . . [O]ne must consider the possibility," he argues, "that literary conceptions of obscurity may be rooted in the social *misunderstanding* of demotic speech, thereby shifting the phenomenology of obscurity away from its conventional association with elite culture and toward the lyric vernacular—especially poems composed in slang, jargon, or dialect" (*Infidel Poetics*, 8).

56. Siraganian, *Modernism's Other Work*, 4.

57. A note about art and instrumentality. Art is instrumental. Writers write to achieve certain effects in the world. Indeed, anti-instrumentality is itself an instrumental aim. Michael Robbins quotes Izenberg: "Critics writing about poetry usually assume, without thinking about it, that the poem has priority. Izenberg has challenged this assumption: 'the *a priori* conviction that all poetic projects imagine the crucial relation to poetry to be a relation to an object—an object of labor, of perception, of interpretation—is an unwarranted assumption; even a sort of fetishism.' He insists that '*what the poet intends by means of*

poetry is not always the poem.' Commitments might come first" (Robbins, forthcoming, Izenberg quotation from *On Being Numerous*, 11–12). I would go further than Robbins and argue that commitments *always* come first. The commitment to write a poem is always a commitment to the value of poetry in the world. Perhaps the greatest theorist of art and autonomy, Adorno, did not repudiate instrumentality as such—he repudiated instrumental reason, which might be defined as a focus exclusively on means, and as a refusal to reason about ends. For Adorno, art can be (and is) an instrument of truth and resistance—a way to undermine narrow and false conceptions of rationality and value. For an additional account of art's instrumentality, see note 30 in the conclusion.

58. A note about frustration. *Utopias of One* discusses texts that it cannot fully understand, let alone explicate. Some readers of the book have detected a frustration with these texts. These readers might be correct—I do not exempt myself from my claims about the connection between ostracism and efficacy. But my frustration is not disappointment, irritation, or exasperation—despite the etymology of "frustration." I am full of wonder for the texts I discuss—for their artistry and commitment and, especially, their power. Their ability to frustrate readers (myself included) is, paradoxically, an index of their greatness—and their relevance to politics, history, and philosophy. I would not change them (or resolve their moral ambiguity) if I could. Frustration, in these cases, is almost an experience of beauty.

Chapter 1: Learning from Walden

1. Francis, *Transcendental Utopias*, 223.

2. Marshall, "Freedom through Critique," 395; Richardson, "Social Ethics of Walden," 238; Cavell, *Senses of Walden*, 85; Boone, "Delving and Diving," 135; Cafaro, "Thoreau's Living Ethics," ix. Jane Bennett claims that "Thoreau's is an eminently practical model of individuality. It includes not only the 'what' and the 'why' of individuality but also its 'how'" (*Thoreau's Nature*, xxi).

3. The lecture would eventually serve as the basis for the first chapter of *Walden*. Thoreau gave seventeen lectures based on material from *Walden* before the book's publication. He gave "Economy" at least nine times. For a discussion of these lectures and of the occasion that led to the review, see Dean and Hoag, "Thoreau's Lectures," 169–75. Milette Shamir discusses the *New-York Daily Tribune* review in *Inexpressible Privacy* (2006), 175–83.

4. *New-York Daily Tribune*, April 2, 1849.

5. Thorough, letter to the editor, *New-York Daily Tribune*, April 7, 1849. I suspect that Greeley authored the entire exchange—perhaps as an attempt to address his own uncertainty about *Walden*'s pedagogy. The letter is signed "Timothy Thorough, Le Roy Place, April 2, 1849." I have not been able to locate any record of "Timothy Thorough." Le Roy Place was a wealthy development built in New York in the 1820s on both sides of Bleeker Street, between Mercer Street and Greene Street. The address would have been read as a synecdoche for ostentatious, upper-middle-class wealth. See Pelletreau, *Early New York Houses*, 77–78; Lockwood, *Manhattan Moves Uptown*, 52–54. Timothy Thorough's letter is the first in a long history of skeptical readings of *Walden*. Later readings include James Russell Lowell's "Thoreau" (1865), Richard Bridgman's *Dark Thoreau* (1982), and Kathryn Schulz's "Pond Scum: Henry David Thoreau's Moral Myopia" (2015).

6. Greeley, editorial comments, *New-York Daily Tribune*, April 7, 1849.

7. Leo Marx, "The Machine in the Garden," 244. As evidence of the conventionality of *Walden*'s underlying message, consider Irina Paperno's account of the values of the intelligentsia tradition in nineteenth-century Russia: "alienation from the establishment; rejection of accepted living forms; valorization of poverty, suffering, and self-denial; reliance on the written word for self-expression and self-preservation; staunch belief in literature as a

source of moral authority; and an overwhelming sense of the historical significance of one's personal life" (*Stories of the Soviet Experience*, 60). Or consider Seneca's advice: "Philosophy calls for simple living, not for doing penance, and the simple way of life need not be a crude one" (*Letters from a Stoic*, 37).

8. "What Would Thoreau Do?," T-shirt at the Thoreau Society Shop at Walden Pond, http://www.shopatwaldenpond.org/product_p/tts30071par.htm.

9. Thoreau, *Walden*, 70, 118. Further citations are from the 2004 Princeton edition and are given parenthetically by page number in the main text. Italics in quoted text are in the original unless otherwise noted.

10. Richardson, "The Social Ethics of *Walden*," 237.

11. Johnson, "A House, a Bay Horse, and a Turtle Dove," 37, 43.

12. In "The Divinity School Address" (1838), Emerson writes, "Truly speaking, it is not instruction, but provocation, that I can receive from another soul" (79). Alternatively, one might read *Walden*'s inconsistencies, ambiguities, and clichés as a reflection of Thoreau's inconstant moods and opinions. In his essay "Everybody Hates Henry," Donovan Hohn writes, "[Thoreau] was flawed, full of contradictions, and in *Walden* endeavored to document the changing seasons of his changing thoughts and moods as painstakingly as he did the depths and temperatures of Walden. So he liked trains, and also didn't. My feelings about air travel and iPhones are similarly conflicted" (*New Republic* magazine online, October 21, 2015, https://newrepublic.com/article/123162/everybody-hates-henry-david-thoreau).

13. Freire, *Pedagogy of the Oppressed*, 53.

14. Ibid.

15. Emerson, *Essays and Lectures*, 390.

16. Cameron, "The Way of Life by Abandonment," 7.

17. Emerson, *Essays and Lectures*, 385–86.

18. Johnson, "A Hound, a Bay Horse, and a Turtle Dove," 40.

19. Michaels, "Walden's False Bottoms," 138.

20. Compare Thoreau's account of doubleness to W.E.B. Du Bois's less benign (and justly more influential) account in *The Souls of Black Folk* (1903), 3–4. I return to the similarities between Thoreau and Du Bois at the end of chapter 3.

21. Thoreau also plays with the religious connotations of "to wake." His use of the concept recalls Romans 11:13: "And that, knowing the time, that now it is high time to awake out of sleep: for now is our salvation nearer than when we believed" (King James Version). His use of the concept also recalls the Great Awakening. In "A Faithful Narrative of the Surprising Work of God" (1737), Jonathan Edwards describes awakening as a process of reform: "Others have awakenings that come upon them more gradually; they begin at first to be something more thoughtful and considerate, so as to come to a conclusion in their minds that 'tis their best and wisest way to delay no longer, but to improve the present opportunity; and have accordingly set themselves seriously to meditate on those things that have the most awakening tendency, on purpose to obtain convictions; and so their awakenings have increased, till a sense of their misery, by God's Spirit setting in therewith, has had fast hold of them" (68).

22. Cavell, *Senses of Walden*, 98.

23. Michaels, "Walden's False Bottoms," 145. Michaels borrows the phrase "literary anarchy" from Charles Feidelson Jr.'s *Symbolism and American Literature* (1966).

24. Walls, "*Walden* as Feminist Manifesto," 142–43.

25. Cavell, *Senses of Walden*, 110.

26. In a report for Princeton University Press, a reader of *Utopias of One* argued that "we can still agree on things that Thoreau would *not* want us to do. He would not want

us to wrap ourselves in arid contemplation and ignore the things happening in the world around us." But the generality of this claim reinforces my argument: "When Thoreau's advice is consistent and unambiguous, it often is clichéd or empty." In *Walden*, Thoreau might advise us to be ethical and observant, but he does not delineate an ethics or teach us how to respond to our observations. Be ethical; do not be oblivious: these injunctions are so general as to be meaningless.

27. Deleuze and Guattari, "Percept, Affect, and Concept," 167.

28. Ibid., 196–97.

29. Ibid., 197.

30. Pound and Cummings, *Pound/Cummings*, 143. The letter from Pound is dated December 17, 1939.

31. For accounts of *Walden*'s composition, see Clapper, "The Development of *Walden*," and Shanley, *The Making of "Walden."*

32. See Delano, *Brook Farm: The Dark Side of Utopia*, 193.

33. Cavell, *Senses of Walden*, 8.

34. In this passage, "Fisherman" is a pun on "fishers of men." The scene is a parable about proselytizing—about how the desire to share one's experience can interfere with one's experience. I thank John Lennox for this reading.

35. White, "A Slight Sound at Evening," 295.

36. Thoreau's arrest is a scene of immense goodwill. Concord tax collector Sam Staples offered to pay the tax on Thoreau's behalf, an offer Thoreau refused. Thoreau was then arrested, but later that same day, someone paid the tax. Instead of releasing Thoreau from jail and forcing him to return to Walden Pond in the dark, Staples let him spend the night in jail. The arrest is also a scene of imitation: Bronson Alcott was arrested two years earlier for refusing to pay his taxes. For a fuller account of Thoreau's arrest and its aftermath, see Cramer, *Walden: A Fully Annotated Edition*, 166. Compare Thoreau's account of the arrest in *Walden* with his account in "Resistance to Civil Government" (1849). In "Resistance to Civil Government," he writes: "When I was let out the next morning, I proceeded to finish my errand, and, having put on my mended shoe, joined a huckleberry party, who were impatient to put themselves under my conduct; and in half an hour,—for the horse was soon tackled,—was in the midst of a huckleberry field, on one of our highest hills, two miles off; and then the State was nowhere to be seen" (272). Notice the "huckleberry *party*" and Thoreau's use of "our."

37. Sattelmeyer, "The Remaking of Walden," 498.

38. Warner, "Thoreau's Bottom," 64–65.

39. Emerson, *Essays and Lectures*, 34.

40. Cavell, *Senses of Walden*, 62.

41. My account coordinates two seemingly incompatible readings of *Walden*. In *Bird Relics*, Branka Arsić argues that Thoreau, in *A Week* and *Walden*, works "not toward individualism but toward its opposite, toward a radical weakening of the self, advocating a precarious self that doesn't conform to any Jacksonian American value" (22). In *Inexpressible Privacy*, Shamir argues that Thoreau's experiment in *Walden* "reflects and promotes a general model of manhood based on solitariness and boundedness" (185). *Walden*, from Shamir's perspective, is an attempt to realize a "liberal fantasy of independence qua withdrawal into the private sphere" (179).

42. Kant, *Critique of the Power of Judgment*, 297.

43. Discussing the "paradox of not voting," Timothy J. Feddersen notes, "In a large election, the probability that an individual vote might change the election outcome is vanishingly small" ("Rational Choice Theory," 99).

44. Woolf, "Thoreau," 137.

45. Sattelmeyer, "The Remaking of Walden," 494.

46. Warner, "Thoreau's Bottom," 60.

47. Shamir offers a compelling gloss of the passage: "The only full dramatization in *Walden* of an encounter between two middle-class men of equal social position appears in 'Brute Neighbors,' in which Thoreau recounts a meeting between his friend, the 'Poet,' and himself, the 'Hermit.' This encounter is striking because it never really happens: it is both an evasion of an encounter and a hint of an encounter yet to happen. . . . This scene, more a conjoining of two monologues than a dialogue, encapsulates Thoreau's ideal intimacy: always intrusive on one's privacy; approximated to be immediately shunned; when it finally takes place, it takes place in silence, outside the boundaries of the text" (*Inexpressible Privacy*, 222).

48. Does reading "Crossing Brooklyn Ferry" not count as an aesthetic experience? Or does the poem undermine Deleuze and Guattari's argument? Whitman underscores our different subject positions—writer, reader—and then collapses them. The poem concludes with a mesmerizing account of the Over-soul: "You have waited, you always wait, you dumb beautiful ministers, / We receive you with free sense at last, and are insatiate henceforward, / Not you any more shall be able to foil us, or withhold yourselves from us, / We use you, and do not cast you aside—we plant you permanently within us, / We fathom you not—we love you—there is perfection in you also, / You furnish your parts toward eternity, / Great or small, you furnish your parts toward the soul" (*Complete Poetry and Collected Prose*, 312, 313).

49. Cavell, *Senses of Walden*, 63.

50. For an account of the diffusion of meaning, see David Lewis, "Languages and Language," 168.

51. Bakhtin, *The Dialogic Imagination*, 294.

52. Cavell, *Senses of Walden*, 92.

53. I thank Diana Fuss for suggesting this argument.

54. Barthes, *The Rustle of Language*, 54.

55. Shamir provides a different touchstone for understanding Thoreau's imagined reader: Seyla Benhabib's essay "The Generalized and the Concrete Other: The Kohlberg-Gilligan Controversy and Feminist Theory" (1985). Shamir writes, "What liberalism's early annals reveal, in Seyla Benhabib's summary, is 'the fear of being engulfed by the [male] other' or the 'brother,' 'the anxiety that the other is always on the look to interfere in your own space and appropriate what is yours.' This anxiety makes imperative liberalism's construction of the 'disembedded and disembodied' generalized other, the view of the other solely based on the nonconcrete and universal. Such a view allows individuals to relate to other individuals without interfering with their privacy or risking interference with their own. The invention of the generalized other relies, therefore, on the suppression and concealment of private differences, on an 'epistemological blindness' to the particulars of private affairs of the self, now deliberately hidden behind a 'veil of ignorance'" (*Inexpressible Privacy*, 214–15). The "suppression and concealment of private differences" recalls Barthes's "man without history, without biography, without psychology" (*The Rustle of Language*, 54).

56. Ilgunas, "Thoreau's Disciple."

57. Even Thoreau's harshest critics assume his exemplarity. (In their view, he exemplifies undesirable characteristics.) Schulz, for example, writes, "[Thoreau's] claim that he doesn't want others to imitate him can't be taken seriously. For one thing, 'Walden' is a guide to doing just that, down to the number of chairs a man should own. For another, having dismissed all other life styles as morally and spiritually desperate, he doesn't leave his readers much choice" ("Pond Scum," *New Yorker* online, http://www.newyorker.com

/magazine/2015/10/19/pond-scum). Does Schulz truly believe that Thoreau thinks that everyone should own just three chairs—and not four or two or five?

58. Ibid.

59. See, for example, Harding and Meyer, "Thoreau's Reputation," 202–24.

60. Buell, *The Environmental Imagination*, 313–14.

61. Ilgunas, "Thoreau's Disciple."

62. For an account of the "enabling cliché," see Berlant, "Remembering Love, Forgetting Everything Else: *Now, Voyager*," 202–4.

Chapter 2: W.E.B. Du Bois's Hermeticism

1. Roy Wilkins, quoted in Euchner, *Nobody Turn Me Around*, 183. David Levering Lewis and James C. Hall, among others, also discuss the speech. See David Levering Lewis, *W.E.B. Du Bois: Biography of a Race*, 2; and Hall, *Mercy, Mercy Me*, 189.

2. Du Bois, *The Souls of Black Folk*, 3. The passage about becoming a "co-worker in the kingdom of culture" is a site for debates about Du Bois's philosophical and political commitments. Cornel West reads the passage as evidence of Du Bois's pragmatism—and, more specifically, his Emersonianism (*The American Evasion of Philosophy*, 142–43). Robert Gooding-Williams challenges West's reading, linking the passage to Josiah Royce's reading of Hegel ("Evading Narrative Myth," 526). Shamoon Zamir claims that the passage "adapts" the *Phenomenology of Spirit* (1807) (*Dark Voices*, 113–99). Both Gooding-Williams and Ross Posnock challenge Zamir's claim—albeit from different perspectives. Gooding-Williams argues that Zamir "overstates" Du Bois's indebtedness to Hegel, while Posnock reasserts Du Bois's commitment to pragmatism (Gooding-Williams, "Evading Narrative Myth," 855–56; and Posnock, "Going Astray, Going Forward," 187–89).

3. King, "I Have a Dream," 105.

4. See Harcourt, Brace, and Company to Du Bois, June 13, 1950, W.E.B. Du Bois Papers; and Du Bois, *Russia and America: An Interpretation*, W.E.B. Du Bois Papers. For a discussion of the aims of *Russia and America: An Interpretation*, see Rasberry, *Race and the Totalitarian Century*, 187–237. In 1953, Du Bois published a eulogy for Stalin in the *National Guardian*. The eulogy begins: "Joseph Stalin was a great man; few other men of the 20th century approach his stature. He was simple, calm and courageous. He seldom lost his poise; pondered his problems slowly, made his decisions clearly and firmly; never yielded to ostentation nor coyly refrained from holding his rightful place with dignity." See Du Bois, "On Stalin."

5. For an account of Shirley Graham Du Bois's life and her influence on Du Bois, see Horne, *Race Woman*.

6. Du Bois moved to Ghana to edit the *Encyclopedia Africana*—a project that was to be funded by the Ghana Academy of Learning, a government organization. For a discussion of the project, see David Levering Lewis, *W.E.B. Du Bois: The Fight for Equality and the American Century*, 566–70.

7. "The writings of DuBois," writes J. Saunders Redding, "have the lucidity of a series of anatomical drawings showing the progressive stages in the development of an organism" ("Portrait: W. E. Burghardt du Bois," 94). An important question in Du Bois scholarship is why there are so many competing assessments of Du Bois's intellectual commitments and development—despite his own constant self-assessments. West, Posnock, and others claim that Du Bois is a pragmatist. Zamir claims that Du Bois is a Hegelian. Horne and Bill V. Mullen claim that Du Bois is a radical Marxist. Adolph L. Reed Jr. claims that Du Bois is a Fabian socialist. Reed argues that the "confusion about locating Du Bois programmatically has two sources." The first source of confusion has to do with "temporal or contextual

focus": "Du Bois lived and acted through several discrete social and political situations that seemed to him to require different strategic responses for the race. Sometimes, especially when sundered from the situations to which they were responses, the strategies that he proposed appear to contradict one another. Analysts, then, have chosen and defended one or another set of strategies or one or another period as authentically Du Boisian." The second source of confusion, Reed claims, has to do with "conceptual focus": "If examination is restricted to Du Bois's various racial strategies, which were usually the central concerns of his writing, analysis will record a mélange of discrete political positions, but will gloss the normative and conceptual logic that organized his worldview." Reed, of course, believes (and convincingly argues) that "the normative and conceptual logic that organized his worldview" was "essentially Fabian." I think there is one additional source of confusion. Du Bois's most canonical writing invites identification: its openness encourages readers to discover their own philosophical and political commitments. It is not a coincidence that West and Posnock identify as pragmatists, Zamir as a Hegelian, and Horne and Mullen as Marxists. Reed is an exception: he criticizes Du Bois's supposed Fabianism. See Reed, *W.E.B. Du Bois and American Political Thought*, 71, 88.

8. For bibliographies of Du Bois's writing, see Aptheker, *Annotated Bibliography of the Published Writings of W.E.B. Du Bois*; Partington, *W.E.B. Du Bois: A Bibliography of His Published Writings*; and Andrews, "Checklist of Du Bois's Autobiographical Writings." In 1961, Du Bois recorded an autobiography for Folkways Records. See Du Bois, *W.E.B. DuBois: A Recorded Autobiography*. The recording recounts the same events as the earlier autobiographies but not verbatim. Lewis notes that Du Bois began a new memoir after his move to Ghana. See Lewis, *W.E.B. Du Bois*, 567. An eleven-page outline for that memoir, titled "Pan-Africa: The Story of a Dream" is extant; see Du Bois, "Pan-Africa: The Story of a Dream," Du Bois Papers.

9. Du Bois, *Dusk of Dawn*, xxxiii.

10. I use "pragmatism" here in a nontechnical sense—to describe Du Bois's responsiveness to evidence, and his resistance to "dogma" and "artificiality" (to adopt William James's terms in *Pragmatism*, 509). Reed's account of the "collectivist outlook" that characterized a new generation of intellectuals in late nineteenth-century America would serve as well. According to Reed, these intellectuals shared three characteristics: "(1) a disposition toward puzzle solving as an orientation to purposeful activity; (2) an inclination to think in terms of systems and wholes and parts; and (3) a commitment—at least in principle—to self-correcting, reflexive language which delegitimizes claims to validity based on references to ascriptive authority and grounds validation on a relatively impersonal standard of truth" (*W.E.B. Du Bois and American Political Thought*, 17).

11. Du Bois, "My Evolving Program for Negro Freedom," 57.

12. Ibid.

13. Ibid.

14. For an account of *Phylon* at its founding and its changing aims, see Warren, *What Was African American Literature?*, 44–56.

15. Du Bois, *The Souls of Black Folk*, 108. Du Bois makes a similar point about the importance of mutual understanding earlier in *Souls*: "the future of the South," he writes, "depends on the ability of the representatives of these opposing views to see and appreciate and sympathize with each other's position,—for the Negro to realize more deeply than he does at present the need of uplifting the masses of his people, for the white people to realize more vividly than they have yet done the deadening and disastrous effect of a color-prejudice that classes Phillis Wheatley and Sam Hose in the same despised class" (89).

16. Du Bois, *Darkwater*, 50.

17. Du Bois, *Dusk of Dawn*, 144.

18. Ibid., 151.

19. Du Bois, *In Battle for Peace*, 107.

20. Ibid., 113.

21. As American liberalism threatens the world, it threatens Du Bois as well. In *Autobiography*, he describes his treatment after his acquittal in 1951: "All this made my enemies and the Federal government take a determined stand to insure my destruction. The secret police swarmed my neighborhood asking about my visitors; whether I entertained and whom. . . . My manuscripts and those of Shirley Graham were refused publication by reputable commercial publishers. My mail was tampered with or withheld. . . . From being a person whom every Negro in the nation knew by name at least and hastened always to entertain or praise, churches and Negro conferences refused to mention my past or present existence. The white world which had never liked me but was forced in the past to respect me, now ignored me or deliberately distorted my work" (271, 255). Notice how Du Bois extricates himself from the "We" in "We threaten the world" and identifies with the "men, women, and children who dare refuse to do what we want done."

22. Ibid., 20. The phrase "sifting of democracy" reflects what Reed describes as "the intrinsic tension between centralized planning—as the expression of macrological, technical interests—and democratic decision making" (*W.E.B. Du Bois and American Political Thought*, 86).

23. Du Bois, *Autobiography*, 275.

24. Ibid., 258.

25. Werner Sollors notes that Du Bois "started writing the *Autobiography* when he turned ninety in 1958" (introduction to *The Autobiography of W.E.B. Du Bois*, xxix).

26. Shirley Graham Du Bois to the Afro-Asian Writers Bureau, ca. 1968, Du Bois Papers.

27. Alfred A. Knopf Inc. to Du Bois, April 13, 1960, Du Bois Papers.

28. Du Bois, "A Negro Student at Harvard at the End of the 19th Century," 439–58.

29. See Du Bois, *Vospominaniia*. The chapter divisions and titles in the Russian version are identical to the chapter divisions and titles in the English-language version published in 1968. The Russian version opens with a five-page introduction from the publisher, detailing Du Bois's conversion to communism. The introduction also includes a note from Gus Hall, general secretary of the National Committee of the Communist Party USA (CPUSA), discussing the significance of Du Bois's membership in the CPUSA. In 1965, *Autobiography* was published in German by Dietz Verlag in East Berlin.

30. Osofsky, "The Master of the Grand Vision," 42.

31. Duberman, "Du Bois as Prophet," 39. Osofsky and Duberman gloss over the critical differences between the Black Power movement and the CPUSA.

32. King, "Honoring Dr. Du Bois," 37.

33. Ibid., 36.

34. Du Bois had plans to publish *Autobiography* in China and Ghana as well. The Du Bois Papers include receipts for the translation of nine chapters (including the postlude) into Chinese. See Translation receipts, December 17, 1964, and December 26, 1964, Du Bois Papers. For a note about Du Bois's plans to publish *Autobiography* in Ghana, see Shirley Graham Du Bois to the Afro-Asian Writers Bureau, ca. 1968, Du Bois Papers. I assume that the Chinese edition was never published because of the Sino-Soviet split.

35. See Du Bois, "A soliloquy on viewing my life from the last decade of its first century," Du Bois Papers. The dedication of this draft of *Autobiography* was revised in Du Bois's hand presumably after the death of his only daughter, Yolande, in 1961.

36. Du Bois, *Autobiography*, 275.

37. The address of Du Bois's work in the 1950s is often obsessively inclusive. For the fiftieth-anniversary edition of *The Souls of Black Folk*, for example, published in 1953 by

Blue Heron Press, Du Bois revised eight passages critical of Jews. ("[U]nscrupulous Jews," for example, became "unscrupulous immigrants.") The revisions reflect Du Bois's growing concerns about anti-Semitism—as well as his desire not to offend his Jewish friends, including the book's publisher, Howard Fast. (Fast, who was blacklisted in 1950, had started Blue Heron Press in 1952 to keep his novel *Spartacus* [1951] in print.) See Du Bois, *The Souls of Black Folk*, 81; Du Bois, *The Souls of Black Folk* (1953), 169. See, also, Aptheker, "The Souls of Black Folk," 15–17; Bornstein, "W.E.B. Du Bois and the Jews," 64–74.

38. Mostern, *Autobiography and Black Identity Politics*, 76.

39. Hall, *Mercy, Mercy Me*, 201.

40. Du Bois, *Autobiography*, 31.

41. Ibid., 35.

42. Ibid.

43. Huggins, *Writings*, 1308–9.

44. Du Bois, *Autobiography*, 39.

45. Du Bois, *Darkwater*, 3. The sentence first appeared in the *Crisis* in 1918. See Du Bois, "The Shadow of Years," 167.

46. Du Bois, *Dusk of Dawn*, 18.

47. Du Bois, *Autobiography*, 87.

48. Mullen notes that passages about Du Bois's trips to the Soviet Union and China in 1926 and 1936 replicate material first published in the *Crisis* (*Un-American*, 6).

49. Byerman, "The Children Ceased to Hear My Name," 85–86.

50. Rampersad, *The Art and Imagination of W.E.B. Du Bois*, 263.

51. Irving Howe, "Remarkable Man, Ambiguous Legacy," 143.

52. Mostern, *Autobiography and Black Identity Politics*, 237.

53. Melamed, "W.E.B. Du Bois's UnAmerican End," 540.

54. Letter from Alfred A. Knopf Inc. to Du Bois, April 13, 1960, Du Bois Papers.

55. Some of Du Bois's political opponents doubted his sanity. Lewis notes, "Du Bois's opposition to the Marshall Plan, NATO, the Point Four program for the developing world, and the Korean War as instruments of capitalist imperialism were heresies that most of the spokespersons for the race deemed to be evidence of unreality bordering on the certifiable, an opinion Walter White [Wilkins's predecessor at the NAACP] allowed to be attributed to him over the Voice of America" (*W.E.B. Du Bois: The Fight for Equality and the American Century, 1919–1963*, 555, 569–70). In 1962, Du Bois underwent a series of surgeries that seriously compromised his physical health.

56. Ibid., 564.

57. Ibid., 565.

58. Irving Howe, "Remarkable Man, Ambiguous Legacy," 149.

59. Ibid., 148.

60. Ibid., 149.

61. Melamed, "W.E.B. Du Bois's UnAmerican End," 535.

62. Garrison, preface to *Narrative of the Life of Frederick Douglass*, 4.

63. Melamed, "W.E.B. Du Bois's UnAmerican End," 543.

64. Baldwin, *Beyond the Color Line*, 199, 200.

65. Ibid., 200.

66. Melamed, for example, writes, "In providing a black witness against US neocolonialism to counter liberal nationalist stories of a black witness for America, Du Bois's declaration of belief in communism comes across as something other than a dogmatic show of support for the Soviet Union" ("W.E.B. Du Bois's UnAmerican End," 543).

67. Another way to avoid these pitfalls might be to refer to Theodor W. Adorno's theory of late style. "[P]sychological interpretation" cannot explain late style, Adorno argues; the

"thought of death" outstrips the "subjectivity" of the artist. Adorno describes Goethe's late work: "Touched by death, the hand of the master sets free the masses of material that he used to form . . . Hence the overabundance of material in *Faust II* and in the *Wanderjahre*, hence the conventions that are no longer penetrated and mastered by subjectivity, but simply left to stand" (*Essays on Music*, 566). In an essay on Adorno's theory, Edward Said suggests that late style involves a "deliberately unproductive productiveness" (*On Late Style*, 7). "Overabundance of material," "conventions . . . left to stand," "deliberately unproductive productiveness"—these phrases seem to describe *Autobiography* almost perfectly. But Adorno's theory of late style also obscures *Autobiography*'s specificity—its links to anticolonialism, Jim Crow, the Cold War. *Autobiography* is excessive—but it is also the story of a particular life.

68. Shaw, "The Uses of Autobiography," 142. Shaw's remark could serve as an epigraph for *Utopias of One*.

69. Gates, "The Black Letters on the Sign: W.E.B. Du Bois and the Canon," xii.

70. Du Bois, "The Atlanta Conferences," 85. Du Bois would repeat this definition throughout his career. See, for example, Du Bois, *Dusk of Dawn*, 3; and Du Bois, "My Evolving Program for Negro Freedom," 48.

71. James, "The Dilemma of Determinism," 123.

72. Du Bois, "My Evolving Program for Negro Freedom," 53.

73. Marx and Engels, *The Communist Manifesto*, 85.

74. West argues that "it is possible to be a prophetic pragmatist and belong to different political movements, e.g., feminist, Chicano, black, socialist, left-liberal ones" (*The American Evasion of Philosophy*, 232).

75. Engels, *Engels*, 105.

76. Marx and Engels, *The Communist Manifesto*, 77.

77. Du Bois, *The Correspondence of W.E.B. Du Bois*, 394, 396.

78. Aptheker to Du Bois, January 20, 1956, Du Bois Papers.

79. Rampersad, *The Art and Imagination of W.E.B. Du Bois*, 263.

80. Stalin, *Dialectical and Historical Materialism*, 22.

81. Ibid., 14.

82. Engels, *Engels: 1892–1895*, 266. Aptheker cites a different passage from Engel's letter; see Aptheker, *History and Reality*, 34.

83. For an account of Du Bois's contribution to the development of sociology, see Morris, *The Scholar Denied*.

84. Du Bois, *Autobiography*, 4.

85. Engels, *Engels*, 105.

86. See Aptheker, *History and Reality*, 161–62.

87. Engels, *Engels*, 106.

88. Gusdorf, "Conditions and Limits of Autobiography," 41.

89. Gilroy, *The Black Atlantic*, 69.

90. Clark, *The Soviet Novel*, 16.

91. Nelson, "W.E.B. DuBois: Prophet in Limbo," 76–79.

92. In a discussion of Baltimore's "geographical disparities in wealth and power," Harvey writes, "So the wealth moves, either further out to ex-urbs that explicitly exclude the poor, the underprivileged, and the marginalized, or it encloses itself behind high walls, in suburban 'privatopias' and urban 'gated communities'" (*Spaces of Hope*, 148). Milette Shamir calls Thoreau "the philosopher of the great migration of the middle class to the suburb, a spatiosocial transformation that has the liberal myth of private manhood as its underlying rationale" (*Inexpressible Privacy*, 18).

93. Consider Du Bois's "I Won't Vote" (1956), which defends his refusal to vote in the 1956 presidential elections. In the essay, Du Bois does not attempt to absolve his complicity

in American militarism. Instead, he attempts, yet again, to be exemplary: "Is the refusal to vote in this phony election a counsel of despair?" he asks. "No, it is dogged hope. It is hope that if twenty-five million voters refrain from voting in 1956 because of their own accord and not because of a sly wink from Khrushchev, this might make the American people ask how much longer this dumb farce can proceed without even a whimper of protest" (324–25). Compare this to Thoreau's anxieties about complicity in "Resistance to Civil Government" (1849): "It is not a man's duty, as a matter of course, to devote himself to the eradication of any, even the most enormous wrong; he may still properly have other concerns to engage him; but it is his duty, at least, to wash his hands of it, and, if he gives it no thought longer, not to give it practically his support" (263). Lawrence Rosenwald notes that this passage is at least partially ironic: "As if in half-conscious self-criticism, Thoreau links himself by this phrase to Pontius Pilate, who, refusing to resist the multitude's call to crucify Jesus, 'washed his hands before the multitude, saying, I am innocent of the blood of this just person: see ye to it'" ("The Theory, Practice, and Influence of Thoreau's Civil Disobedience," 175–76).

94. In *X: The Problem of the Negro as a Problem for Thought* (2013), Nahum Dimitri Chandler describes one aspect of Du Bois's commitment to his exemplarity: "Du Bois took the status of the African American subject as an exemplary path by which to trace the theme (or develop the topic) of the problem of racial distinction, and hence, the problem of difference in general" (75). According to Chandler, this is the "guiding question" of Du Bois's work: "Is it possible for the most particular or 'subjective' history to tell the most general of truths, perhaps precisely because such histories do distort, or magnify, and so on in particular sorts of ways?" (77). Posnock suggests that Du Bois resented his exemplarity: "Sacrificing himself to group identity, viscerally enduring Jim Crow's mania for frozen classification, Du Bois' lifelong challenge becomes to find a margin of freedom, a way to mitigate, if not evade, the twin sacrifice demanded by the repressions of coerced identity—as race man and as 'a colored man in a white world'" ("Going Astray, Going Forward," 179). Posnock's claim is misleading for at least two reasons. First, Du Bois presents an ambivalent account of his "coerced identity": in *Dusk of Dawn*, for example, he writes, "Had it not been for the race problem early thrust upon me and enveloping me, I should have probably been an unquestioning worshipper at the shrine of the social order and economic development into which I was born" (14). Second, Posnock's claim obscures Du Bois's true objection to his "coerced identity": not that he must represent all African Americans, but that he cannot represent everyone—black and white Americans, humans in general. Du Bois is not a radical individualist. For an additional discussion of Du Bois and exemplarity, see Balfour, *Democracy's Reconstruction*, 71–95.

Chapter 3: Osip and Nadezhda Mandel'shtam's Utopian Anti-Utopianism

1. By the mid-1930s, the Gulag was the largest construction organization in the Soviet Union. For accounts of the canal's construction, see Ruder, *Making History for Stalin*, especially 12–38; and Baron, "Conflict and Complicity." For a discussion of the economics of prison labor in the Soviet Union, see Morukov, "The White Sea–Baltic Canal."

2. The estimate only includes deaths that occurred during the construction process itself—not from malnutrition or illness. Aleksandr Solzhenitsyn estimates that 100,000 prisoner laborers died during the first year of construction. Official Soviet numbers put the mortality rate for the entire Gulag system in 1933 at 15.3 percent, almost one in six, and the total number of deaths between 1931 and 1933 at 87,777. See Baron, "Conflict and Complicity," 643; and Solzhenitsyn, *The Gulag Archipelago*, vol. 2: Parts 3–4, 98–99.

3. Struve, *Osip Mandel'shtam*, 73. See Gor'kii et al., *Belomorsko-Baltiiskii Kanal imeni Stalina*. For accounts of the book's composition and reception, see Ruder, *Making History for Stalin*, 39–153; Dobrenko, *The Making of the State Writer*, 372–76; and Clark, "'The History of the Factories' as a Factory of History."

4. Solzhenitsyn describes the book as the "first in Russian literature to glorify slave labor." See Solzhenitsyn, *The Gulag Archipelago*, vol. 1: Parts 1–2, xii. In 1935, the book was translated into English and published in London and New York. The translation departs from the original; for example, it reduces the original fifteen chapters to ten and omits Aleksandr Tikhonov from the list of contributors. See Gor'kii et al., *Belomor*.

5. Gor'kii et al., *Belomorsko-Baltiiskii Kanal imeni Stalina*, 11.

6. The slogan is adapted from Karl Marx, *Capital* (1867): "Through this movement he acts upon external nature and changes it, and in this way he simultaneously changes his own nature" (283). Rodchenko was one of several photographers who contributed to the volume. In the book, all the photographs are uncredited. In the archives for the book, many photos are credited, but not this one. See Gosudarstvennyi arkhiv Rossisskoi Federatsii (GARF) f.R-7952, op. 7, d. 74, l. 139. I thank Katherine Hill Reischl and Aglaya Glebova for information about the photograph and for the citation.

7. Hellbeck, "Working, Struggling, Becoming," 341–42.

8. Ibid., 343. The use of autobiography as a moral and political instrument was coextensive with, and dependent on, the rise of literacy in the Soviet Union. Between 1897 and 1937, the literacy rate rose from 28.4 percent to 75 percent. See Fitzpatrick, *Stalin's Peasants*, 225–26.

9. Nadezhda Mandelstam, *Hope against Hope*, 159.

10. Struve speculates about the connection between Gor'kii's book and Mandel'shtam's decision to compose and perform the epigram. See Struve, *Osip Mandel'shtam*, 73–74. Mandel'shtam's reasons for performing the Stalin epigram are complex. During his interrogation by the state secret police—the OGPU, the forerunner of the NKVD and the KGB—Mandel'shtam reveals that he lost his "sense of ease in society" owing to Stalin's policy of dekulakization: "In 1930 a great depression afflicted my political outlook and my sense of ease in society. The social undercurrent of this depression was the liquidation of the kulaks as a class. My perception of that process was expressed in the poem 'A Cold Spring' ['Холодная весна'] . . . written in the summer 1932." See Shentalinsky, *The KGB's Literary Archive*, 177–78.

11. Osip Mandelstam, *Critical Prose and Letters*, 316.

12. To protect Mandel'shtam, Nikolai Bukharin had contacted Stalin and argued that the poet's death would upset other writers (especially Pasternak) and would thus negatively impact the first Soviet writers' congress, planned for later in 1934. For accounts of Bukharin's involvement, see Shentalinsky, *The KGB's Literary Archive*, 175–76, 183; and Lekmanov, *Mandelstam*, 135–40. For an account of Pasternak's own conversations with Stalin about Mandel'shtam, see Ivinskaya, *A Captive of Time*, 60–67. In her memoirs, Nadezhda Mandel'shtam notes that her husband had originally been sentenced to hard labor on the White Sea–Baltic Canal: "The sentence originally suggested—that M. should be sent to a forced-labor camp on the White Sea Canal—had been commuted, by this same supreme authority, to exile in the town of Cherdyn" (*Hope against Hope*, 32).

13. Heaney, "Osip and Nadezhda Mandelstam," 72.

14. Osip Mandelstam, *Critical Prose and Letters*, 90.

15. See Alter, "Osip Mandelstam"; Berlin, "A Great Russian Writer"; Chatwin, introduction to *Journey to Armenia*; Coetzee, "Osip Mandelstam"; Davenport, "The Man without Contemporaries"; Dimock, "Literature for the Planet"; Littell, *The Stalin Epigram*; Miłosz, *A Year of the Hunter*, 228; Prieto, "Reading Mandelstam"; Rich, "What Would We Create?," 19; Rushdie, "Whither Moral Courage?"; Steiner, "Death of a Poet"; Stewart, *The*

Poet's Freedom, 186–89. Robert Littell's contribution to the epigram's reception is the mass market thriller *The Stalin Epigram: A Novel*. In a back cover blurb for the book, Martin Cruz Smith writes, "When Josef Stalin declared war on poetry, Osip Mandelstam, Russia's greatest poet, declared war on dictators."

16. Shelley, *Shelley's Poetry and Prose*, 513.

17. Cavanagh, *Lyric Poetry and Modern Politics*, 115.

18. Osip Mandel'shtam, *Polnoe sobranie sochinenii i pisem*, 1:184. In the 1967 edition of Mandel'shtam's collected poems, the epigram is divided into eight couplets. (This is why Heaney refers to it as "eight stony couplets.") See Osip Mandel'shtam, *Sobranie sochinenii*, 202. More recent editions follow the version in Mandel'shtam's police file, written in his own hand, which is divided into two eight-line stanzas. The poem was not included in the first collected edition of Mandel'shtam's poems in 1955. In a 1964 edition, it is divided into three quatrains and a concluding couplet. In the 1967 edition, G. P. Struve notes an alternative version of the third and fourth lines: "Только слышно кремлевского горца / Душегубца и мужикоборца" [Only the Kremlin highlander is heard / Murderer and peasant-killer]. See the editorial apparatus in Osip Mandel'shtam, *Sobranie sochinenii*, 511.

19. To put this point another way, the epigram would have been effective in paraphrase. In "Conversation about Dante" (1933), Mandel'shtam writes, "where there is amenability to paraphrase, there the sheets have never been rumpled, there poetry, so to speak, has never spent the night." See Osip Mandelstam, *Critical Prose and Letters*, 397.

20. Nadezhda Mandel'shtam quoting Pasternak in "Zametki o peresechenii biografii Osipa Mandel'shtama i Borisa Pasternaka," 316. Mandel'shtam describes other reactions to his performance in the transcript of his interrogation. The poet Vladimir Narbut, for example, supposedly responded, "This did not happen." See Shentalinsky, *The KGB's Literary Archive*, 180.

21. Nadezhda Mandelstam, *Hope against Hope*, 161.

22. There is a long history in Russia of poets speaking truth to power—and having it matter. For an overview of the relationship between Russian poets and Russian politics (and an account of Vladimir Maiakovskii's own martyrdom), see Boym, *Death in Quotation Marks*, especially 119–89.

23. Jennifer Baines provides an excellent description of the music of the epigram's thirteenth line: "the staccato 'к', the vindictive splitting of 'пах' [groin] and 'лоб' [head], the brilliant use of the anaphoric 'кому' [to one] in such a way that the whole stress in each foot lands, like a violent blow, on its last syllable—on those vulnerable parts of the body where the blow of each iron 'указ' [decree] indeed falls." See Baines, *Mandelstam*, 85.

24. For an account of the importance of the poem's oral transmission, see Cavanagh, *Lyric Poetry and Modern Politics*, 113–19.

25. Osip Mandelstam, *Critical Prose and Letters*, 421, 414.

26. In his interrogation, Mandel'shtam connects the epigram with a tradition of "old Russian literature of using a simplified presentation of the historical situation and reducing it to a confrontation between 'the country and its ruler.'" "Indubitably," Mandel'shtam adds, "this lowered the level of historical understanding of the group . . . to which I myself belong. Yet it was precisely this way that the poster-like expressiveness of the lampoon was attained, which makes it a widely applicable weapon of counterrevolutionary struggle which could be used by any social group." I discuss the relevance of this conception of the epigram in section 3 of this chapter. See Shentalinsky, *The KGB's Literary Archive*, 181.

27. For a history of Acmeism, see Doherty, *The Acmeist Movement*. In "Concerning Beautiful Clarity" (1910), an essay that inspired the Acmeist movement, Mikhail Kuzmin writes, "I implore you, be logical—may I be forgiven this cry from the heart!—logical in design, construction, syntax . . . be economic in means and parsimonious in words, precise and genuine—and you will discover a wonderful secret: beautiful clarity" (*Selected*

Writings, 226, 230). Mandel'sham, in his essay "The Morning of Acmeism" (1919), takes Kuzmin's advice to its logical conclusion, proclaiming, "A = A: what a splendid theme for poetry!" Brown, "Mandelshtam's Acmeist Manifesto," 50.

28. Osip Mandelstam, *Critical Prose and Letters*, 407. "Mineral rock," Mandel'shtam notes, "is an impressionistic diary of weather accumulated by millions of natural disasters" (ibid., 439).

29. Ibid., 407.

30. Ibid., 409.

31. For an account of the relationship between purity and the history of abstract art, see, for example, Cheetham, *The Rhetoric of Purity*.

32. Bukharin, *Poetry, Poetics*, 246–47. The congress adopted socialist realism as the official "guiding line" of Soviet art but did not give the term a clear definition. "Many of us try to be too clever about socialist realism," notes A. I. Stetskii, the head of the Central Committee Department for Culture and Propaganda (Kul'prop). "Socialist realism is not some set of tools that are handed out to the writer for him to make a work of art with. Some writers demand that they be given a theory of socialist realism complete in all its details. . . . [T]here is only one answer which we can give here, at this congress of writers: socialist realism can best be shown in those works of art which Soviet writers produce" (Stetsky, "Under the Flag of the Soviets," 265). Boris Groys offers the following definition of socialist realism: to be a socialist realist "means to avoid being shot for the political crime of allowing one's personal dream to differ from Stalin's. The mimesis of socialist realism is the mimesis of Stalin's will, the artist's emulation of Stalin, the surrender of their artistic egos in exchange for the collective efficacy of the project in which they participate. 'The typical' of socialist realism is Stalin's dream made visible, a reflection of his imagination" (*The Total Art of Stalinism*, 53).

33. Clark, "Utopian Anthropology as a Context for Stalinist Literature," 180.

34. Ibid., 189, 186.

35. In his portraits of contemporary poets, Il'ya Erenburg describes Mandel'shtam as "frail and small," and compares him to a chicken. See Erenburg, *Portrety sovremennykh poetov*, 82.

36. For a discussion of Mandel'shtam's creation of a cult of personality, see Freidin, *A Coat of Many Colors*, especially 15–16.

37. Shentalinsky, *The KGB's Literary Archive*, 180.

38. Vitalii Shentalinskii suggests that Mandel'shtam's interrogator may have gotten "carried away" and "decorat[ed] his charge's replies with his own extravagant labels." Ibid.

39. Serguei Alex. Oushakine writes, "To become involved in a discourse is possible only by entering the discursive field that is already there, that is, only by accepting existing discursive conventions" ("The Terrifying Mimicry of Samizdat," 206). Alexander Zholkovsky makes a different though complementary point: "Warring parties tend to develop mutual affinities. In the so-called 'Stockholm syndrome,' hostages adopt the value system of their captors" ("The Obverse of Stalinism," 62).

40. Mandel'shtam's performance represents the paradoxical affinity between submission and resistance. By submitting to the power of his own poetry, he successfully resisted Stalin's power. For a discussion of the "antimony" in Mandel'shtam's poetry between "submission and resistance," see Vaingurt, "Introduction: Mastery and Method in Poetry."

41. Berlin, "Two Concepts of Liberty," 140.

42. Ibid.

43. Rancière, *Politics of Aesthetics*, 19.

44. This counterfactual illuminates an important aspect of the epigram that I haven't adequately discussed: its implied audience was not only Mandel'shtam's friends and

neighbors but average Russians, including, for example, Russian chauvinists who might object to a Georgian in the Kremlin. (Stalin was Georgian.) The final line about the "broad chest of the Ossetian" signals Stalin's ethnic difference. Nadezhda Mandel'shtam notes that her husband wrote "the poem with a view to a much wider circle of readers than usual, though he knew, of course, that nobody would be able to read it at the time." See Nadezhda Mandelstam, *Hope against Hope*, 162. See, also, Mandel'shtam's comments about the poem during his interrogation, cited in note 26.

45. Other translations appeared across Europe at the same time: Swedish in 1970, German in 1971, and French and Italian in 1972. Tamizdat versions in Czech and Polish appeared in the mid-1970s. The title, *Hope against Hope*, is a play on Nadezhda Mandel'shtam's first name, which means "hope" in Russian.

46. See Mandel'shtam, *Vospominaniia.*

47. Nadezhda Mandelstam, *Hope against Hope*, 320.

48. Holmgren, *Women's Work in Stalin's Time*, 140.

49. Davenport, "The Man without Contemporaries," 298.

50. See Mandel'shtam, *Kniga Tret'ia.*

51. Davenport, "The Man without Contemporaries," 298.

52. Nadezhda Mandelstam, *Hope against Hope*, 3.

53. The slap has a complex backstory: Nadezhda Mandel'shtam accused the novelist Sergei Borodin (who wrote under the pseudonym Amir Sargidzhan) of assaulting her at a party. Tolstoi, a popular Soviet writer and former anti-Bolshevik émigré turned communist, presided over an investigation that exonerated Borodin. See the appendix to Nadezhda Mandelstam in *Hope against Hope*, 422, and Freidin, *A Coat of Many Colors*, 383.

54. Freidin, *A Coat of Many Colors*, 270.

55. Nadezhda Mandelstam, *Hope Abandoned*, 235.

56. Gershtein published her own memoirs in 1998. The book, which sparked a series of controversies in Russia, disputes many of Nadezhda Mandel'shtam's claims. See Gershtein, *Memuary*; and Gerstein, *Moscow Memoirs*. For an overview of the memoir and the ensuing controversies, see Rylkova, review of *Memuary*, by Emma Gershtein, and *Vospominaniia*, by Nadezhda Mandel'shtam.

57. In "Trauma and Ineloquence" (2001), Lauren Berlant describes the challenge of witness literature: "Mobilizing the putative universality of pain and suffering, . . . testimonials challenge you to be transformed by the knowledge of what you cannot feel directly: to re-hardwire your viscera, enabling your bodily impulses to archive the encounters of which you read. . . . To the degree that actual numbers are involved—so many dead, so many imprisoned, so many marked out for violence—the dialectic of testimony and witnessing has material consequences. One either commits to compelling new laws and practices, or not. One decides to count, or not. One makes further publics with one's knowledge, or not" (44).

58. Brodsky, "Beyond Consolation."

59. Brown, "Memories of Nadezhda," 486.

60. Ibid.

61. Brown's account of the operation is thrilling—in his words, "a scene from a Grade B thriller." See ibid., 487–88.

62. Ibid., 488.

63. Ibid.

64. Proffer, "The Attack on Mme Mandelstam."

65. Nadezhda Mandel'shtam had written, among other things, "Tynianov declared that poetry had had its day and we were now in an era of prose. M. put it another way: jailers, he said, have more need of novels than anyone" (*Hope Abandoned*, 342–43). Tynianov appears in a positive light in the transcript of Mandel'shtam's integration after his second arrest,

in May 1938. Mandel'shtam notes that Tynianov gave him "material help" during visits to Leningrad. See Shentalinsky, *The KGB's Literary Archive*, 190.

66. Proffer, "The Attack on Mme. Mandelstam."

67. Ibid.

68. Susan Sontag's response to the memoirs captures their influence among New York intellectuals: "the shock came first," she writes, "before Solzhenitsyn, from the book *Against All Hope* by Nadeshda Mandelstam [*sic*], this implacable testimony on what happened in the Soviet Union in the thirties and later" (*Conversations with Susan Sontag*, 99).

69. A reviewer of my manuscript for Princeton University Press suggested I put the point more bluntly: "Mandelstam became a Cold War prop for the *New York Review of Books*."

70. George Kennan quoted in Gaddis, *George F. Kennan: An American Life*, 420.

71. For information on CIA support of culture during the Cold War (and a brief discussion of the Ford Foundation and Chekhov Publishing House), see Saunders, *The Cultural Cold War*, especially 139–44; and Barnhisel, *Cold War Modernists*.

72. Paperno, "Personal Accounts of the Soviet Experience," 610.

73. Kaverin publicly defended Solzhenitsyn and other persecuted Soviet writers in the late 1960s.

74. Nadezhda Mandelstam, *Hope Abandoned*, 6, 5.

75. Ibid., 5.

76. Miłosz, *A Year of the Hunter*, 228.

77. Osip Mandel'shtam, *Critical Prose and Letters*, 561–62; translation slightly modified. See, also, Shentalinsky, *The KGB's Literary Archive*, 185.

78. "To judge by formal features alone," Freidin writes, "the poem belongs to one of the most difficult genres of panegyric poetry, the Pindaric ode. The exuberant imagery framed in the rhetoric of praise, triadic divisions within stanzas that follow the pattern of strophe, antistrophe, and epode, and finally the lines of unequal length combining hexameter, pentameter, and tetrameter conform to the basic scheme of the ancient genre of glorifying a supreme leader" (*A Coat of Many Colors*, 260). Svetlana Boym notes how almost every sentence of the "manic" ode "is a quote either from the Russian poetic tradition or from Stalin's slogans." "The landscape of the poem is epic and Soviet," she continues, "remade in the image of a larger-than-life leader who can move mountains" (*Another Freedom*, 71, 72).

79. Osip Mandel'shtam, *Polnoe sobranie sochinenii i pisem*, 1:309.

80. Ibid., 310.

81. Ibid.

82. See Jangfeldt, "Osip Mandel'štam's Ode to Stalin," 41.

83. Stavskii, quoted in Lekmanov, *Mandelstam*, 159.

84. Pavlenko, quoted in Shentalinsky, *The KGB's Literary Archive*, 187.

85. Coeztee, "Osip Mandelstam," 73.

86. Freidin, *A Coat of Many Colors*, 255.

87. Nadezhda Mandelstam, *Hope against Hope*, 205.

88. Freidin, *A Coat of Many Colors*, 255. See, also, Zholkovsky's comments about Stockholm syndrome in note 39 above.

89. Gasparov, *O. Mandel'shtam*, 88. Gasparov dates this desire to at least 1935 and Mandel'shtam's short sequence "Стансах" ["Stanzas"].

90. Coetzee, "Osip Mandelstam," 80–81.

91. See McGarry, "'Ode to the Great Leader'," 75. McGarry's claims are anticipated and undermined by Gasparov, Coetzee, and others, who note that the authorities charged with identifying such Aesopian descriptions found none. (Coetzee writes, "such [descriptions] mean nothing unless they can be detected, and no one is more skilful at such detection than the paranoid and therefore *overdetecting* censor" ["Osip Mandelstam," 74].)

92. Osip Mandel'shtam, *Polnoe sobranie sochinenii i pisem*, 1:309.

93. Nadezhda Mandelstam, *Hope against Hope*, 47.

Chapter 4: Anna Akhmatova's Complicity

1. Berlin, "Conversations with Akhmatova and Pasternak."

2. See Akhmatova, *Sobranie sochinenii*, 4:474.

3. Chukovskii's analysis is meant as praise. He concludes his paper, "For me there is no such question as 'Akhmatova or Mayakovsky?' That Old Russia that Akhmatova stands for—so sensitive and so restrained—is very dear to me; as is the riotous and drumbeating element incarnated in Mayakovsky. As I see it, the two elements are not mutually exclusive; rather they complement one another, and are both equally necessary" ("Akhmatova and Mayakovsky," 53).

4. See Reeder, *Anna Akhmatova: Poet and Prophet*, 174.

5. See Sarnov, *Stalin i Pisateli*, 2:614–15. Boris Pasternak also wrote to Stalin on Akhmatova's behalf. See Sarnov, *Stalin i Pisateli*, 1:241–42.

6. For more on the fates of Gumilov and Punin, see Reeder, *Anna Akhmatova: Poet and Prophet*, especially 305–6, 306–10, and 319–23. Akhmatova wrote Stalin again in 1939 to try to secure her son's release, but the letter never reached its intended recipient. See Golovnikova and Tarkhova, "'Iosif Vissarionovich! Spasite sovetskogo istorika . . .'"

7. Zhdanov, quoted in Clark and Dobrenko, *Soviet Culture and Power*, 365.

8. Akhmatova, *Sobranie sochinenii*, 4:272–73. The poem appeared in *Pravda* on March 8, 1942.

9. See Chukovskaia, *Zapiski ob Anne Akhmatovoi*. The diary would eventually cover twenty years of Akhmatova's life, from 1938 to 1942, and 1952 to 1966. Only the first volume, covering 1938 to 1941, has been translated into English. See Chukovskaya, *The Akhmatova Journals*.

10. Chukovskaia, quoted in Paperno, *Stories of the Soviet Experience*, 85.

11. Paperno, *Stories of the Soviet Experience*, 85.

12. For more details of the meeting, see, for example, Dalos, *The Guest from the Future*, especially 15–52.

13. Berlin, "Conversations with Akhmatova and Pasternak."

14. Ibid.

15. Zhdanov, *The Central Committee Resolution*, 43.

16. Ibid., 53, 56.

17. Stalin, quoted in Clark and Dobrenko, *Soviet Culture and Power*, 424.

18. Berlin, "Conversations with Akhmatova and Pasternak."

19. Akhmatova, *Stikhotvoreniia*. Another volume followed in 1961, and a book of prose in 1965.

20. "The last decade of Akhmatova's life," writes Galina Rylkova, "coincided roughly with the Khrushchev Thaw. During that period her position in the cultural hierarchy changed from that of a famous persona non grata to that of a Soviet and international celebrity. Her poems were no longer circulated only among a group of devoted friends and admirers but also reached a wider audience through Soviet periodicals and publishers that were engaged in preparing her collected works. Akhmatova received international awards and was allowed to travel to receive them. She was blessed with the friendship of young poets in Leningrad and Moscow who sought her guidance and worshiped her" (*The Archaeology of Anxiety*, 155–56).

21. Akhmatova, *Sobranie sochinenii*, 3:21. Further references to this volume are given parenthetically by page number in the text.

22. For a description of the *Requiem*'s form, including its prosody, references, antecedents, and narrative structure, see, for example, Amert, *The Later Poetry of Anna Akhmatova*, 2–59; and Crone, "Antimetabole in *Rekviem*."

23. Bird, "Voices of Silence," 337.

24. Cavanagh, *Lyric Poetry and Modern Politics*, 123.

25. Naiman refines his claim about *Requiem*'s affinity to Soviet poetry: "What differentiates [*Requiem*] from, and thus contrasts it to, even ideal Soviet poetry is the fact that it is personal, just as profoundly personal as her early poetry . . . This is what makes *Requiem* poetry—not Soviet poetry, but simply poetry" (Nayman, *Remembering Anna Akhmatova*, 127). Naiman's point is that the poem doesn't reduce Akhmatova to a type; it preserves her individuality even as it speaks for "the people."

26. Akhmatova, quoted in Paperno, *Stories of the Soviet Experience*, 102.

27. In 1964, Joseph Brodsky was arrested for "social parasitism"—that is, for refusing to find gainful employment. His exchange with the trial judge is well known: "Judge: What is your profession? Brodsky: Translator and poet. Judge: Who has recognized you as a poet? Who has enrolled you in the ranks of poets? Brodsky: No one. Who enrolled me in the ranks of the human race?" Brodsky was sentenced to five years of hard labor. His sentence was commuted in 1965 and he was forced to emigrate in 1972. See McFadden, "Joseph Brodsky."

28. Nayman, *Remembering Anna Akhmatova*, 135.

29. Ibid.

30. Brodsky, *Less than One*, 51.

31. See Robert Lowell, *Collected Poems*, 897–905. Amanda Haight, who interviewed Akhmatova in Oxford in 1965, describes the poet's "extreme distress" after reading Lowell's translation (*Akhmatova: A Poetic Pilgrimage*, 108). For an analysis and bibliography of the English translations of *Requiem*, see Rosslyn, "*Requiem*," 27–28.

32. Barringer, "Anti-Stalin Poem."

33. Reagan, "Remarks at a Luncheon." The poet Evgenii Evtushenko attended the speech and describes its reception in a short memoir. The luncheon was hosted by Vladimir Karpov, the head of the Writers' Union and a war hero. According to Evtushenko, Reagan received a standing ovation from everyone except the "unreconstructed Stalinists." Karpov was overjoyed: "You, Comrade Reagan and Mister Gorbachev, you . . . you . . . you . . . both of you in our, so to speak, difficult century, are our, so to speak, our collective Jesus Christ." Reagan supposedly cried in response. See Evtushenko, "Reigan i Akhmatova."

34. Nadezhda Mandelstam, *Hope Abandoned*, 436.

35. Auden, "In Memory of W. B. Yeats," 242.

36. Cavanagh, *Lyric Poetry and Modern Politics*, 128.

37. "The poem returned again," Akhmatova writes in a notebook entry from 1963. "It demands a second epigraph for the first chapter." See Akhmatova, *The Word that Causes Death's Defeat*, 297.

38. Cavanagh, *Lyric Poetry and Modern Politics*, 121.

39. Vsevolod Kniazev (1891–1913) committed suicide after being spurned by his lover, the ballerina Ol'ga Glebova-Sudeikina (who was Akhmatova's close friend). The "silver age" refers to the Russian writers who came of age during the first two decades of the twentieth century—Innokentii Annenskii, Fedor Sologub, Viacheslav Ivanov, Konstantin Bal'mont, Valerii Briusov, Maksimilian Voloshin, Aleksandr Blok, Mikhail Kuzmin, Gumilev, Akhmatova, Mandel'shtam, Velimir Khlebnikov, Ivan Bunin, Sergei Esenin, and Marina Tsvetaeva, among others.

40. See Akhmatova, *Sobranie sochinenii*, 5:40.

41. The scholar Lev Loseff argues that the "unequivocal 'identification' of prototypes . . . is impossible" ("Who Is the Hero of the Poem without One?," 96).

42. For a synopsis of the poem, especially its first section, see Wells, *Anna Akhmatova: Her Poetry*, 96–129.

43. The identity of the source text is the subject of debate. The date of the dedication—December 27, 1940—suggests that it is a poem by Mandel'shtam, who died on December 27, 1938. But a case can be made for a poem by other writers as well, including Kniazev, Gumilev, and Tsvetaeva. See, for example, Loseff, "Who Is the Hero of the Poem without One?," 91–95.

44. Akhmatova, *Word that Causes Death's Defeat*, 291. The angle brackets represent Nancy K. Anderson's emendations.

45. Ibid., 294.

46. Ibid., 221.

47. Wells, for example, structures his analysis of the poem around three general themes, "the political theme," "the metapoetic theme," and "the lyrical theme" (*Anna Akhmatova: Her Poetry*, 107–25).

48. Akhmatova, *Word that Causes Death's Defeat*, 296.

49. Berlin, "Conversations with Akhmatova and Pasternak."

50. For a description of an open text, see Hejinian, "The Rejection of Closure," 43.

51. For a defense of this claim, see Loseff, "Who Is the Hero of the Poem without One?"

52. Amert, *The Later Poetry of Anna Akhmatova*, 17, 106, 130.

53. Berlin, "Conversations with Akhmatova and Pasternak."

54. Rylkova, *The Archaeology of Anxiety*, 163.

55. Nadezhda Mandelstam, *Hope Abandoned*, 442.

56. Ibid., 437, 436.

57. Wells, *Anna Akhmatova: Her Poetry*, 104.

58. Cavell, *Contesting Tears*, 66.

59. Yurchak, *Everything Was Forever*, 80.

Chapter 5: Wallace Stevens's Point of View

1. Wittgenstein gave the lecture to the Heretic Society in Cambridge—an audience with "no particular interest or training in philosophy" (to quote James C. Klagge and Alfred Nordmann) (361). For information on the lecture (and the lecture itself), see Wittgenstein, "A Lecture on Ethics," 3–12. For a more detailed account of the occasion, see Klagge and Nordmann, *Ludwig Wittgenstein*, 361–62.

2. Wittgenstein, "A Lecture on Ethics," 6.

3. Ibid., 6–7.

4. For a brief history of the fact/value dichotomy "from David Hume to the present day," see Putnam, "The Collapse of the Fact/Value Dichotomy," especially 7–19. Putnam discusses Hume's conception of "matters of fact" and its relation to what has become known as the "is-ought problem." Putnam's first chapter begins with a passage from Hume's *An Enquiry concerning the Principles of Morals* (1751) that clearly anticipates Wittgenstein's lecture: "where is that matter of fact, which we here call *crime*," Hume asks; "point it out; determine the time of its existence; describe its essence or nature; explain the sense or faculty, to which it discovers itself. It resides in the mind of the person, who is ungrateful. He must, therefore, feel it, and be conscious of it. But nothing is there, except the passion of ill-will or absolute indifference. You cannot say, that these, of themselves, always, and in all circumstances, are crimes. No: They are only crimes, when directed towards persons, who have before expressed and displayed good-will towards us. Consequently, we may infer, that the crime of ingratitude is not any particular individual *fact*; but arises from a complication of circumstances, which, being presented to the spectator, excites the *sentiment*

of blame, by the particular structure and fabric of his mind" (*An Enquiry concerning the Principles of Morals*, 158–59).

5. Stevens, *Collected Poetry and Prose*, 579. Further references to this edition are given parenthetically by page number in the text.

6. Introducing the concept of metaphysical need, Schopenhauer writes, "Temples and churches, pagodas and mosques, in all lands, in all ages, testify, in their splendor and grandeur, to that human need for metaphysics which follows, strong and ineradicable, upon the heels of physical need" (*The World as Will and Presentation*, 184).

7. For an account of Stevens as a philosophical poet, see Eeckhout, "Stevens and Philosophy." As Eeckhout notes, Stevens is usually "considered the most philosophical among modernist poets in English" (103). For an argument about Stevens's contribution to philosophy, see the introduction to Altieri, *Wallace Stevens and the Demands of Modernity*.

8. Wittgenstein, "A Lecture on Ethics," 7.

9. Jameson, "Exoticism and Structuralism in Wallace Stevens," 220–21.

10. Alvarez, *Stewards of Excellence*, 133–34.

11. Cunningham, "The Styles and Procedures of Wallace Stevens," 381.

12. Jarrell, "Reflections on Wallace Stevens," 122.

13. Kenner, *A Homemade World*, 57. Helen Vendler identifies Stevens as "one of the last of our writers to experience fully the nineteenth-century crisis of the death of God." See Vendler, *Wallace Stevens*, 30.

14. Paglia, "Final Cut," 21.

15. As Vendler repeatedly emphasizes, "Stevens is our great poet of the inexhaustible and exhausting cycle of desire and despair." "Never was there a more devout believer," she writes, "in love, in the transcendent, in truth, in poetry. . . . And never was there a more corrosive disbeliever—disillusioned in love, deprived of religious belief, and rejecting in disgust at their credulousness the 'trash' of previous poems" (*Wallace Stevens*, 39–40, 40–41).

16. For an account of "cruel optimism," see Berlant, "Cruel Optimism," 21. I quote Berlant's definition in my introduction, note 35.

17. Miller, *Poets of Reality*, 222.

18. The ending of the final version of the poem differs from the ending of the version published in *Poetry* magazine in 1915. Stevens submitted the full (and final) version to *Poetry*, but Harriet Monroe, the magazine's editor, asked to publish cantos 1, 4, 5, 7, and 8. Stevens acquiesced and suggested the following order: 1, 8, 4, 5, 7. The redacted version thus ends with the community of men and a completely different perspective on metaphysical need.

19. For an account of the relation between mortality and value, see Williams, "The Makropulos Case," 82–100.

20. See Galenson, "Literary Life Cycles," 149.

21. The question places us squarely in the realm of what W. K. Wimsatt Jr. and Monroe C. Beardsley call, in the "Intentional Fallacy" (1946), "author psychology." ("There is criticism of poetry," they claim, "and there is author psychology" [10].) In their view, critics should bracket "the author's attitude toward his work, the way he felt, what made him write" (4)—the very concerns that motivate this chapter and the book as a whole. My view is that to follow this advice would be to ignore a central feature of Stevens's poetry: how it relies on "author psychology" to evaluate its own efficacy. Stevens's poetry is literally about the poet's attitude toward his work—accordingly, it asks us to privilege his sense of adequacy over our own. In a contemporary review of Stevens's *Selected Poems* (1953), Dunstan Thompson notes, "After reading these fascinating poems and thinking about them and the brilliant poet who wrote them, one is left wondering how it is that they themselves have not resolved Mr. Stevens's perplexities" ("The Poetry of Wallace Stevens," 396). I thank Danny Braun for recommending Thompson's review.

22. Fernandez's appearance in the poem is also a repudiation of another form of collective action: communism. In the months leading up to the publication of "The Idea of Order at Key West" in *Alcestis* in October 1934, Fernandez, a prominent French critic, published a series of responses to the February 6, 1934, riots in Paris, including an open letter to André Gide in *La Nouvelle Revue Française* (a magazine Stevens read regularly) and a personal commentary in *Commune*, which was quickly translated and published in *Partisan Review* as "I Came Near Being a Fascist." (Walter Benjamin quotes a passage from the open letter as the epigraph to his 1934 lecture, "The Author as Producer.") The responses narrate Fernandez's conversion from "une éthique de droite" (an ethic of the right) to an unaffiliated Marxism to a committed communism. "The Idea of Order at Key West" rewrites this conversion by including Fernandez in a community formed in response to an aesthetic experience rather than class consciousness. Late in his career, Stevens denied the reference. "When I was trying to think of a Spanish name for *The Idea of Order*," he wrote to Renato Poggioli in 1951, "I simply put together by chance two exceedingly common names . . . The real Fernandez used to write feuilletons in one of the Paris weeklies and it is true that I used to read these. But I did not consciously have him in mind." The denial corroborates Hugh Kenner's claim that "The Stevens world is empty of people." See Fernandez, "Lettre ouverte à André Gide," 708; Kenner, *A Homemade World*, 75; Stevens, *Letters of Wallace Stevens*, 823. For additional accounts of Fernandez's role in the poem, see Longenbach, *Wallace Stevens*, 161–63; and Surette, *The Modern Dilemma*, 199–232.

23. Wittgenstein, "A Lecture on Ethics," 7.

24. Michael Szalay makes a similar point in his reading of "The Idea of Order at Key West." The poem, he argues, presents an "inquiry into the origin of phenomena—such as collectivities, economies and . . . poems—that cannot be understood as having, or being the product of, an individual mind" (*New Deal Modernism*, 125).

25. Rorty, introduction to *Empiricism*, 1.

26. Gardner, "Wallace Stevens and Metaphysics."

27. Critchley, *Things Merely Are*, 26–30.

28. Altieri, *Wallace Stevens and the Demands of Modernity*.

29. Other philosophical traditions (and philosophers) are relevant to this discussion of Stevens's critique of sense-data empiricism—and his avoidance of naive forms of idealism. One could, for example, cite Kant's claim that "Thoughts without content are empty, intuitions without concepts are blind" (*Critique of Pure Reason*, 193–94); or C. S. Peirce's insight that "there is no thing which is in-itself in the sense of not being relative to the mind, though things which are relative to the mind doubtless are, apart from that relation" ("Some Consequences of Four Incapacities," 155). With respect to the second canto of "Credences of Summer," Husserl's practice of epoché (or phenomenological reduction or bracketing) is apposite. Indeed, one could argue that the canto attempts to motivate a strange, collective epoché. Finally, one could cite Stevens himself. In his essay "The Noble Rider and the Sound of Words" (1942), he writes, "The subject-matter of poetry is not that 'collection of solid, static objects extended in space' but the life that is lived in the scene that it composes; and so reality is not that external scene but the life that is lived in it. Reality is things as they are" (658).

30. Sellars, *Empiricism and the Philosophy of Mind*, 43, 87.

31. In *Empiricism and the Philosophy of Mind*, Sellars writes, "Now the idea that epistemic facts can be analyzed without remainder—even 'in principle'—into non-epistemic facts, whether phenomenal or behavioral, public or private, with no matter how lavish a sprinkling of subjunctives and hypotheticals is, I believe, a radical mistake" (19).

32. McDowell, "Sellars and the Space of Reasons," 2. In *Mind and World* (1994), McDowell presents a more precise version of the same claim: "Conceptual capacities, whose interrelations belong in the *sui generis* logical space of reasons, can be operative not only in judgments—results of a subject's actively making up her mind about something—but already

in the transactions in nature that are constituted by the world's impacts on the receptive capacities of a suitable subject: that is, one who possesses the relevant concepts" (xx).

33. Ibid.

34. Stevens, *Voice of the Poet.*

35. Wiggins, "Truth, Invention, and the Meaning of Life," 108.

36. As Eleanor Cook notes, "The auroras are unpredictable in their occurrence and in their trajectory, unlike the stars and the planets; they come in the autumn and in the north, but no one can predict exactly when or where" ("Wallace Stevens and the King James Bible," 244).

37. "Wherever he found the symbol," writes Vendler in *On Extended Wings* (1969), "whether in literature or in nature, it corresponds perfectly to the bravura of his imagination, even more so than the slower transformations of 'Sea-Surface Full of Clouds.' And certainly these changing auroras match his solemn fantasia better than the effort, so marked in 'Credences of Summer,' to hold the imagination still" (246). Later in the book, she adds, "These transformations of the sky occur as an enormous relief to Stevens, as he feels momentarily that he can give up the difficult labor of willed imagination transformation: the sky will do it all for him" (260).

38. Bloom, *Wallace Stevens*, 265.

39. Doggett and Emerson, "A Primer of Possibility," 53.

40. Riddel, *The Clairvoyant Eye*, 235.

41. Kenner, *The Poetry of Ezra Pound*, 200.

42. Cook, *A Reader's Guide to Wallace Stevens*, 240.

43. To clarify this point: person x could know everything there is to know about lovers y and z, and still not be able to comprehend their love for each other. Identity, not knowledge, is the impediment.

44. For additional readings of the poem, see, for example, Altieri, *Wallace Stevens and the Demands of Modernity*, 186–89; Berger, *Forms of Farewell*, 34–80; Costello, *Shifting Ground*, 73–85; Perloff, *The Poetics of Indeterminacy*, 18–23; and Vendler, *On Extended Wings*, 231–68.

45. Cook, "Wallace Stevens and the King James Bible," 244–49.

46. Ibid., 249.

47. There are insurmountable obstacles to becoming a true solipsist—to actually believing that one's self is all that can be known to exist: the publicness of language, the normativity of perception, the undeniable presence of the external world. As Stanley Cavell writes in *The Claim of Reason* (1979), "with respect to the external world, an initial sanity requires recognizing that I cannot live my skepticism" (451). Even solipsism as self-absorption is a matter of degree—one can be excessively self-absorbed but not completely self-absorbed. Accordingly, solipsism can be a risk and even a strategy—but solipsism cannot be an all-encompassing subject position.

48. Wittgenstein, *Philosophical Investigations*, 51e.

49. Winters, *In Defense of Reason*, 459.

50. Vendler, *On Extended Wings*, 268.

Chapter 6: Reading Ezra Pound and J. H. Prynne in Chinese

1. Prynne, ["Jie ban mi Shi Hu"]. Between 1985 and 1994, Poetical Histories published sixty pamphlets in a similar format, all featuring contemporary British poets or poets visiting Cambridge from abroad. Prynne's pamphlet, the twenty-second, is the only one that does not include an English-language poem. For more information, see Riley, "Bibliography (b)."

2. See, for example, Prynne, *Poems*, 379–80.

3. Riley, "Bibliography (b)."

4. Ibid.

5. See Eliot, introduction to *Selected Poems*, by Ezra Pound, xvii. Eliot is making a subtle point about translation: "As for *Cathay*, it must be pointed out that Pound is the inventor of Chinese poetry for our time. . . . I predict that in three hundred years Pound's *Cathay* will be a 'Windsor Translation' as Chapman and North are now 'Tudor Translations': it will be called (and justly) a 'magnificent specimen of XXth Century poetry' rather than a 'translation.' Each generation must translate for itself." "This is as much as to say," Eliot adds, "that Chinese poetry, as we know it today, is something invented by Ezra Pound. It is not to say that there is a Chinese poetry-in-itself, waiting for some ideal translator who shall be only translator; but that Pound has enriched modern English poetry" (xvi–xvii).

6. Readers often learn foreign languages to read their favorite authors. To cite two famous examples: James Joyce learned Norwegian to read Henrik Ibsen, and Willa and Edwin Muir learned German to read (and translate) Franz Kafka. But these cases have little in common with the case at hand. "Jie ban mi Shi Hu" is Prynne's only poem in Chinese, and, to my knowledge, his only published poem not written in English.

7. Mullan, "Prynne's Progress."

8. Jarvis, "Soteriology and Reciprocity," 30.

9. As Peter Middleton writes in "Dirigibles" (2001): "Prynne's poetry reaches out to so many registers that the fully consonant reader who would have to [be] situated in so many linguistic communities does not yet exist in our culture" (41).

10. Whitman, *Complete Poetry and Selected Prose*, 1058. Harriet Monroe, the editor and founder of *Poetry* magazine, lineated and repunctuated Whitman's sentence and used it as a motto for the magazine. "To have great poets / there must be great audiences too" appeared on the back cover of many issues. Pound hated the motto. In 1917, *Poetry*'s competitor, the *Little Review*, adopted the motto, "Making No Compromise with the Public Taste," which Pound much preferred.

11. Pound praises Frost for "the good sense to speak naturally and to paint the thing, the thing as he sees it"; and Hewlett for "his skillful use of harsh rime to check the verse suddenly and to keep it in swift motion." See Pound, review of *A Boy's Will*, 72–73; and Pound, review of *Helen Redeemed*, 75. For a brief account of Frost's resistance to the association, see, for example, Moody, *Ezra Pound*, 233; see, also, Frost, *Letters of Robert Frost*, 1:132.

12. Pound, "A Few Don'ts by an Imagiste," 202, 203.

13. Pound, *Early Writings*, 234, 241.

14. Moody, *Ezra Pound*, 226–27.

15. Pound, *ABC of Reading*, 41.

16. Pound, "Praefatio," 12.

17. Pound met Fenollosa's widow, the poet Mary McNeil Fenollosa, at a dinner party on September 29, 1913. Her husband had died five years earlier and she was looking for a literary executor for his work on Japanese Noh and Chinese poetry. She had read Pound's poems and essays in *Poetry*, and considered him an excellent candidate for the position. Pound already had an interest in Japanese and Chinese literature—he had written haiku and had begun to read Confucius under the guidance of Allen Upward. Within two months of the meeting, Pound received the first of several packets in the mail. "I know you are pining for hieroglyphs and ideographs," Mary McNeil Fenollosa wrote, "but I must keep to our plan and send the Nō stuff first." The "Nō stuff" became *Certain Noble Plays of Japan* (1916) and *"Noh," or, Accomplishment* (1916). The "hieroglyphs and ideographs," which soon followed, became *Cathay* and "The Chinese Written Character as a Medium for Poetry." See Mary McNeil Fenollosa to Pound, November 24, 1913, in Pound, *Ezra Pound and Japan*, 6. For a more detailed account of the meeting and its aftermath, see Qian, *Orientalism and*

Modernism, 9–64; and Saussy, "Fenollosa Compounded," especially 2–11. For an account of Pound's relationship with Upward, see Moody, "Pound's Allen Upward."

18. In "Imagisme and England: A Vindication and an Anthology" (1915), Pound declares, "we have sought the force of Chinese ideographs *without knowing it*" (185). For an overview of Pound's early poetics, including the influence of Fenollosa's work, see, for example, Hermans, *The Structure of Modernist Poetry*, 85–117.

19. Pound, *Early Writings*, 303.

20. Ibid., 299.

21. Pound, *Cathay*, 13. Paradoxically, the note simultaneously confirms and undercuts Pound's claims for completeness. For a discussion of the note's significance, see Hayot, *Chinese Dreams*, 23–26.

22. Pound, *Early Writings*, 299. *Cathay* also includes a note providing these "geographical facts." See Pound, *Cathay*, 31.

23. Pound never addresses the development of Chinese poetry, despite having access to Herbert Giles's *History of Chinese Literature* (1901). (In *Lustra* [1916], Pound retranslated some of Giles's translations of classical Chinese poetry.) This neglect, however, represents Pound's faithfulness to Giles's description of the poems' reception in China. Giles writes, "Native scholars with their endless critiques and appreciations of individual works, do not seem ever to have contemplated [a history of Chinese literature], realising, no doubt, the utter hopelessness, from a Chinese point of view, of achieving even comparative success in a general historical survey of the subject" (v). Pound, following Fenollosa, attributes "The Jewel Stairs' Grievance" to "Rihaku," the Japanese name for Li Bai (also known as Li Po).

24. Fenollosa and Pound, *The Chinese Written Character*, 80.

25. Pound, *ABC of Reading*, 22. Pound is discussing the ideogram for "red," which, he claims, combines "pictures" of "rose," "cherry," "iron rust," and "flamingo." Earlier in *ABC of Reading*, he recounts how the sculptor Henri Gaudier-Brzeska could understand Chinese ideograms without knowing Chinese: "Gaudier Brzeska, who was accustomed to looking at the real shape of things, could read a certain amount of Chinese writing without ANY STUDY. He said, 'Of course, you can *see* it's a horse' (or a wing or whatever)" (21). For a discussion of Pound's account of the ideogram for red, and a more general discussion of Pound and pedagogy, see Kindellan and Kotin, "*The Cantos* and Pedagogy." The essay is, in many ways, a companion to sections 2 and 3 of this chapter.

26. See Fenollosa and Pound, *The Chinese Written Character*, 54, 54–55, 46, 46, 46, 46, 49–50, 49, 44, 47. These quotations and all subsequent quotations from *The Chinese Written Character* are from the published version of the essay edited by Pound.

27. Fenollosa's debt to Emerson's *Nature* (1836) is impossible to miss. For a discussion of the connection between Emerson's theory of language and Fenollosa's, see Kern, *Orientalism, Modernism*.

28. Fenollosa and Pound, *The Chinese Written Character*, 53.

29. Ibid., 42.

30. Pound, *Early Writings*, 191.

31. Pound, *Cathay*, 7.

32. Pound, *Lustra*, 97.

33. Pound constructs the scene's topography to maximize its universality. As Susan Stewart points out, the trio of kingfishers, orchids, and clover represents a "category mistake of topography," which conflates three distinct landscapes: "Kingfishers famously lay their eggs in nests built on the sea in the heart of winter (hence their association with the Nativity); orchids grow in the air in forest (and occasionally meadow) environments; clover requires lots of water and sunlight and grows in open fields—so water, air, and earth" (e-mail message to author, August 9, 2016).

34. Hayot quotes a contemporary review of *Lustra* in the *Times Literary Supplement*: "The Chinese poems are full of content and of a content interesting to everyone." Hayot also quotes George Steiner's claim that "Pound can imitate and persuade with utmost economy not because he or his reader knows so much but because both concur in knowing so little." See Hayot, *Chinese Dreams*, 20, 21. See also Clutton-Brock, "The Poems of Mr. Ezra Pound," 545; and Steiner, *After Babel*, 359.

35. For a succinct (and early) summary of the debate, see Miner, *The Japanese Tradition*, 28–31.

36. Eliot, "Poetry and Propaganda," 601.

37. In *Solid Objects* (1998), Douglas Mao anticipates a version of this argument: for Pound, Mao argues, "the most significant communication is founded not on clear, systematic, and logical unfolding of the speaker's or writer's reasoning but rather upon some form of connection that finally exceeds rational articulation" (171).

38. Davie, "Bed-Rock," 317.

39. In this chapter, I do not discuss Pound's political and economic views in detail because they are so well documented elsewhere. The best book on the subject remains Tim Redman's *Ezra Pound and Italian Fascism* (1991). The one fact I should emphasize, although it might go without saying: Pound's political and economic views did not meet with success. Fascism failed and his economic theories were never fully tested. This lack of success is vital for understanding his poetry—and the relevance of one of the central questions of *Utopias of One*: What sustains utopianism in the face of constant failure?

40. Brian M. Reed, "Ezra Pound's Utopia of the Eye," 62.

41. A. Alvarez, review of *Section: Rock-Drill de los Cantares*, 442.

42. Davie, *Ezra Pound: Poet as Sculptor*, 204–5.

43. Kenner, "Under the Larches of Paradise," 280.

44. See *Chou King: Les Annales de la Chine*, trans. Séraphin Couvreur (Paris: Cathasia, 1950). This was the specific edition Pound used while composing *Rock-Drill.*

45. The numbers, justified left and right in the text, refer, chapter and verse, to the third and fourth sections of *Annales*.

46. Davie, *Ezra Pound: Poet as Sculptor*, 206. Davie translates Couvreur's French and Latin: "Ne prenez pas pour miroir le cristal des eaux, mais les autres hommes"; "Homo ne in aquis inspiciat se; oportet in hominibus inspicere." See *Chou King*, 252. The adage, which appears in a section entitled "The Announcement about Drunkenness," is translated by James Legge as, "Let not men look into water; let them look into the glass of other people." See *The Sacred Books of China*, 178.

47. Davie, "Bed-Rock," 316.

48. Davie, *Ezra Pound: Poet as Sculptor*, 206.

49. Pound, *The Cantos*, 561. Kenner, "Under the Larches," 291, 289. Kenner's translation condenses Courveur's French and Latin: "Si un homme ou une femme du peuple n'a pas la liberté de s'appliquer de toutes ses forces (à faire le bien), le maître du peuple aura un secours de moins, et le bien qu'il doit faire ne sera pas complet"; "Si privatus vir privatave mulier non assequatur ut se omnino impendant (in bene agendo), populi rector non habebit quicum perficiat suum opus." See *Chou King*, 131.

50. Flory, *Ezra Pound and "The Cantos,"* 233.

51. Wain, "The Shadow of an Epic," 453.

52. Ibid.

53. Brian M. Reed, "Ezra Pound's Utopia of the Eye," 66.

54. Ibid., 68.

55. Nicholls, *Ezra Pound*, 197.

56. Ibid., 200. Nicholls develops Eric Havelock's account of the "paideutic spell" supposedly cast by early Greek epics. In *Preface to Plato* (1963), Havelock writes, "You did not learn your ethics and politics, skills and directives, by having them presented to you as a corpus for silent study, reflection and absorption. You were not asked to grasp their principles through rational analysis. You were not invited to so much as think of them. Instead you submitted to the paideutic spell. You allowed yourself to become 'musical' in the functional sense of that Greek term" (159). Pound took the word "paideuma" from the anthropologist Leo Frobenius and used it to refer to the innate intelligence of a culture—the ideas, assumptions, and habits that transcend "book learning." See Pound, *Guide to Kulchur*, 58. Davie, in his second book on Pound, *Ezra Pound* (1975), supplements his earlier account of how to read *The Cantos*. His later account resembles Nicholls's: "They must be taken in big gulps or not at all," Davie writes. "Does this means [*sic*] reading without comprehension? Yes, if by comprehension we mean a set of propositions that can be laid end to end. We are in the position of not knowing 'whether we have had any ideas or not.' Just so. Which is not to deny that some teasing out of quite short excerpts, even some hunting of sources and allusions, is profitable at some stage. For the *Cantos* are a poem to be lived with, over years. Yet after many years, each new reading—if it is a reading of many pages at a time, as it should be—is a new bewilderment" (*Ezra Pound*, 84–85).

57. In an interview with Donald Hall in 1962, Pound praises Henry James's use of parentheses: "I'll tell you a thing that I think is an American form, and that is the Jamesian parenthesis. You realize that the person you are talking to hasn't got the different steps, and you go back over them." Pound adopts this technique to protect the integrity of Canto 85. "(No, that is *not* philological)," he writes after juxtaposing "chueh" and "cohere." The aside helps readers understand the canto, and, more importantly, protects the canto from supplementation. The aside is defensive. See Pound, "The Art of Poetry," 54.

58. "The relationship between urban planning and utopia is obvious and banal," writes Robert Klein. "By organizing in detail the material setting of public (and up to a point, private) urban life, one will reinforce or modify certain aspects of the social structure" (*Form and Meaning*, 89).

59. Mao Tse-Tung, *Four Philosophical Essays*, 37.

60. Fenollosa and Pound, *The Chinese Written Character*, 55.

61. Owen, *Traditional Chinese Poetry and Poetics*, 70.

62. Qian Zhongshu demonstrates the importance of just such an investigation in the contexts of a poem's production and reception. In his essay "The Corruption of Consciousness" (1979–80), he focuses on a single line by the Song Dynasty poet Wang Anshi: "The withered chrysanthemums scatter their petals, covering the ground with gold." The line, Qian notes, presents a puzzle: chrysanthemums, unlike most flowers, retain their petals as they fade. Is the line a mistake or an intentional distortion? To resolve the puzzle, Qian examines the use of chrysanthemums and other yellow flowers in the Chinese canon. He concludes that the line is the result of a false syllogism. Wang combines two sources: "Chrysanthemums have yellow blossoms" from the *Book of Rites*, and "Yellow blossoms look like scattered gold coins" from a poem by the fourth-century poet Zhang Han. By identifying these sources, Qian glosses the line while illuminating how art mediates our understanding of the natural world—how artifice shapes consciousness. See Qian Zhongshu, "The Corruption of Consciousness," 56–60.

63. In "Two Aspects of Language and Two Types of Aphasic Disturbances" (1956), Jakobson associates metaphor with similarity and metonymy with contiguity. A "rose" is a metaphor for "love" because of shared attributes—beauty, fragility, and so on. A "crown" is a metonymy for "king" because of a shared context. Yet Prynne's understanding of context is more expansive than Jakobson's. For example, Prynne would read "rose" as a metonymy for "love" because of their long history of association. Indeed, all stock metaphors are, for

Prynne, metonymies—"bridge" for "hope," "pork" for "government spending," and so on. Only *novel* substitutions based on similarity count as metaphors, and such substitutions always become metonymies through a history of use. Jakobson bases his claims on his research on aphasia. One group of aphasiacs could not make substitutions based on similarity: for example, they would claim that "lamp" is a synonym for "table." The other group could not recognize and manipulate contextual relations, including syntactic relations. See Jakobson, ibid., 95–119. For an overview of Jakobson's dichotomy and its influence in literary studies, see Lodge, *Modes of Modern Writing*, 73–124.

64. Prynne, "China Figures," 367.

65. Ibid., 368.

66. Prynne describes Birrell's apparatus as follows: "Dr Birrell . . . combine[s] a plain-text presentation of each poem with a detailed and extensive apparatus, not of commentary on each poem or representative samples of them . . . but of notes on idioms, images, names of persons and places and tunes, distinctive locutions, fables and particular associations, all arranged alphabetically at the end of the book. This she has combined with summary biographical profiles of the poets and their interconnections, and with an index of her adapted titles alongside their literally translated originals, which allows the identification of those later poems which imitate or 'harmonise with' previous originals (most of them included in the earlier chapters of this anthology)" (ibid., 364–65).

67. Ibid., 369–70. In "China Figures" (1983, 1986), Prynne notes his debt to Kenner for this reading. See Kenner, *The Pound Era*, 194.

68. Birrell, *New Songs from a Jade Terrace*, 333.

69. Prynne, "China Figures," 372.

70. Birrell, *New Songs from a Jade Terrace*, 256.

71. Ibid., 374.

72. The connection between willows and weeping has a long history in English—and in French and German, which adopt the same metaphor (*saule pleureur* and *Trauerweide*). In Psalm 137, for example, weeping is associated with willows: "By the rivers of Babylon, there we sat down, yea, we wept, when we remembered Zion. We hanged our harps upon the willow in the midst thereof" (King James Version). In the medieval ballad "The Bitter Withy [Willow]," Mary spanks the young Jesus with a willow branch for tricking three "lords' and ladies' sons": "Our Saviour built a bridge with the beams of the sun, / And over He gone, He gone He; / And after followed the three jolly jerdins, / And drownded they were all three" (Roud 452). The earliest example of "weeping willow" that I could find in English is in Mary Wroth's *Countesse of Montgomeries Urania* (1621). Wroth also uses the willow as a symbol for sorrow. (The *OED* cites a gardening dictionary from 1731 as its earliest example, and Nathaniel Baxter's *Sir Philip Sydneys Ourania* [1606] as its earliest example of a weeping tree of any kind, a weeping elm.) The association between willows and weeping is alive in popular song—in, for example, Ann Ronell's "Willow Weep for Me" (1932) and Johnny Cash's "Big River" (1958). I thank Susan Stewart for recommending "The Bitter Withy" and Robert von Hallberg for recommending "Willow Weep for Me." To read four versions of "The Bitter Withy," see Gerould, "The Ballad of *The Bitter Withy*," 142–43.

73. This approach to reading recalls a central claim of T. S. Eliot's "Tradition and the Individual Talent" (1919): "The existing monuments form an ideal order among themselves, which is modified by the introduction of the new (really new) work of art among them. The existing order is complete before the new work arrives; for order to persist after the supervention of novelty, the *whole* existing order must be, if ever so slightly, altered; and so the relations, proportions, values of each work of art toward the whole are readjusted; and this is conformity between the old and the new. Whoever has approved this idea of order, of the form of European, of English literature will not find it

preposterous that the past should be altered by the present as much as the present is directed by the past. And the poet who is aware of this will be aware of great difficulties and responsibilities" (5).

74. Prynne, *They That Haue Powre to Hurt*, 3.

75. See "Lily," definition 4d. in the *OED*, dating from 1841.

76. I owe this final point to a conversation with V. Joshua Adams about Prynne's second monograph, *Field Notes: "The Solitary Reaper" and Others* (2007). The rebuke is especially ironic in relation to Sonnet 94, which, according to Stephen Booth, is "the most frequently interpreted of the sonnets" (*Shakespeare's Sonnets*, 305). Peter Middleton notes that "Prynne's recent 86 page essay on a single Shakespeare sonnet might be intended as a demonstration of the persistence of the uninterpreted in even the most overrun of texts" ("Dirigibles," 33). I suspect that the rebuke has two specific targets: William Empson and Veronica Forrest-Thomson. Both Empson and Forrest-Thomson use Sonnet 94 to develop theories about how to manage literary ambiguity. See Empson, *Some Versions of Pastoral*, 89–118; and Forrest-Thomson, *Poetic Artifice*, 1–17.

77. For more information on the Originals, see Twitchell and Huang Fan, "Avant-Garde Poetry in China," 33–35; and Prynne, afterword in a special issue of the journal *Parataxis* devoted to the Originals, with translations by Twitchell. The issue is reprinted in the twentieth issue of the online journal *Jacket*.

78. David Lewis, "Languages and Language," 169, 187. See, also, Prynne, *Not-You*, 5.

79. Nagel, *Equality and Partiality*, 121. See, also, Prynne, *Not-You*, 5. In Nagel's original, the line appears as "Even love of semiconductors is not enough."

80. Prynne, *Not-You*, 7.

81. Percival Lowell wrote a series of books about Mars—*Mars* (1896), *Mars and Its Canals* (1906), and *Mars as the Abode of Life* (1908).

82. "Double Streak" virus is a combination of two viruses: Tobacco Mosaic Tobamovirus and Potato X Potexvirus. See Horst, *Westcott's Plant Disease Handbook*, 675. For a discussion of Prynne and botany, see Katko, "Relativistic Phytosophy."

83. Middleton, "Dirigibles," 42.

84. Thoreau, *Walden*, 97.

85. Cavell, *Senses of Walden*, 112, 92.

86. See Nietzsche, *The Gay Science*, 163–64.

87. In a speech at the Second Pearl River International Poetry Conference in Guangzhou, China, in 2008, Prynne remarks, "Separating from its origins in a life history (personal beliefs, memory, emotion, and physiology of personhood) is an essential step in the generation of poetic thought; but once again by negative description it is necessary to understand how this step does not mean that prior activity in consciousness transfers into something less active, more like a result of activity. The case is quite the reverse: the focus of poetic composition, as a text takes shape in the struggle of the poet to separate from it, projects into the textual arena an intense energy of conception and differentiation, pressed up against the limits which are discovered and invented by composition itself" ("Poetic Thought," 596).

88. Riley uses the passage as an epigraph in *The Reader*.

89. Prynne, "Poetic Thought," 598.

90. See Althusser, "Ideology and Ideological State Apparatuses."

91. Thoreau, *Walden*, 8.

92. For a discussion of Prynne's development over his career, and especially the transition from *The White Stones* (1969) to *Brass* (1971), see Sutherland, "XL Prynne."

93. Google poses two threats to Prynne's poetry. First, it reduces the work required to read his poems and thus neutralizes their efficacy. Second, it implicates the poems in the

culture they oppose. (Is there a better representative of global capitalism than Google?) The increasing difficulty of Prynne's poetry over the last fifteen years might be read as a response to these two threats. The volume *Streak~~~Willing~~~Entourage / "Artesian"* (2009), for example, seems designed to outstrip Google's search capabilities. For a brief discussion of Prynne and search engines, see Jarvis, "The Poetry of Keston Sutherland," 142. Prynne's work, Jarvis writes, is now "far too easy to make sense of, because relevant linked chunks of information can be called up with a few passes of the search engine."

94. Nagel, *Equality and Partiality*, 21.

95. One of the many relevant contexts for *Not-You* is the failure of Maoism and Deng Xiaoping's subsequent market reforms. In the late 1970s, Deng reintroduced monetary incentives to spur productivity. In the countryside, farms were decollectivized and families allowed to sell above-quota output at a profit. Production increased, and Deng's "socialist market economy" began to represent the inferiority of Mao's utopianism. But Deng's reforms also gave life to various strands of utopianism, which found an outlet at the Tiananmen Square protests in 1989.

96. In "XL Prynne" (2007), Keston Sutherland writes, "Prynne is the only poet in English whose language is permanently impacted not only by the truth of this intellectual disinheritance, but also by the *trauma* of its necessity" (123).

97. Amy Lowell, preface to *Fir-Flower Tablets*, v.

98. Adorno, *Essays on Music*, 133.

99. Sutherland, "J. H. Prynne and Philology," 212–46.

100. Dobran is the coeditor of *Glossator*, which is subtitled, *Practice and Theory of Commentary*. For a discussion of Prynne and the commentary as a genre, see Kotin, review of *Concepts and Conception in Poetry*.

101. "The usual way of reading a traditional Chinese poem," Li explains, "is from right to left vertically downwards . . . However, Mr Prynne's poem refuses to be exhausted by a single reading: so that a second reading, following the English reading way, also the modern Chinese way, from left to right horizontally, may also be attempted." Li reads (and translates) the poem in two additional ways as well: "the traditional Chinese-right-to-left and English-horizontal way," and "the English-left-to-right and traditional Chinese-vertical way." See Li Zhimin, "Four Different Ways," 15.

102. Ibid.

103. Ibid., 17.

104. Robin Purves, in a response to an essay by John Wilkinson on *Not-You* (entitled "Counterfactual Prynne") in *Parataxis*, recognizes a version of this contradiction. "[T]he 'trust' which sustains the reader-critic in his labour," Purves writes, "has been seen to precede any apprehension of that writing's 'meaning.' The 'trust' may have its roots in perceived qualities of the poet himself (many writers on Prynne's poetry are his loyal ex-students) or qualities perceived to belong to previous works by Prynne which are then projected forward so that whatever he *might* do is already considered . . . perfect *a priori*" ("Apprehension," 48–49).

105. Negative reviews of Prynne's work invariably include a charge of exclusivity. An extreme example—a review of *Poems* (1999) from the *Daily Telegraph*: "Reading Prynne," the anonymous reviewer writes, "can feel like being seated at High Table next to a thundering bore determined to hold forth on all academic subjects. . . . If Prynne is its true representative, then Cambridge poetry is now happening in its own private universe, having lost all interest in talking to the wider world." See "Now Available outside Cambridge."

106. Lerner, *The Hatred of Poetry*, 53. Robert von Hallberg makes a similar point: "Poets look for trouble, taking only the long shots," he writes, "[a]nd they plan to lose" (*Lyric Powers*, 14).

Conclusion: Utopias of Two

1. Dickinson, *The Poems of Emily Dickinson: Reading Edition*, 261.

2. For an account of these changes, see Dickinson, *The Poems of Emily Dickinson: Variorum Edition*, 2:578–79.

3. Hirsch, *How to Read a Poem*, 254–55.

4. Ibid., 256.

5. Ibid.

6. Ibid.

7. Ibid., 255.

8. Ibid., 256.

9. Arendt, "What Is Freedom?," 145.

10. Arendt criticizes Epictetus's valorization of "freedom within confinement." "'[I]nner freedom,'" she writes, is "the inward space into which men may escape from external coercion and *feel* free. This inner feeling remains without outer manifestations and hence is by definition politically irrelevant" (ibid.).

11. Cameron, *Choosing Not Choosing*, 3. Cameron continues: "The phrase ['revoked . . . referentiality'] is from Geoffrey Hartman's *Criticism in the Wilderness*, but one thinks also of Jay Leyda's description of Dickinson as writing 'riddle[s],' poems of the 'omitted center . . .'; of Robert Weisbuch's characterization of this poetry as 'sceneless,' producing 'analogical language which exists in parallel to a world of experience, as its definition'; of David Porter's assessment that 'here is the verbal equivalent of *sfumato*, the technique in expressionistic painting whereby information . . . on a canvas is given only piecemeal and thereby necessarily stimulates the imaginative projection of the viewer, who, out of his own experience, supplies the missing . . . context'; of an earlier claim of my own that the poems 'excavate the territory that lies past the range of all phenomenal sense'" (ibid.).

12. Hirsch, *How to Read a Poem*, 256.

13. Cathy Slovensky, the copy editor of this book, perceptively notes that Dickinson may be "ruminating upon the civil war within, which every human being experiences, and possibly intimating that we have to be a utopia of one before we can be a utopia communally" (e-mail message to author, December 5, 2016).

14. Hirsch, *How to Read a Poem*, 254. "One could make a wonderful little anthology of Dickinson's images of the soul," Hirsch writes. "Some of these images bear traces of Jonathan Edwards's sermons, or Emerson's essays, or the Protestant hymns of her childhood. Others are all her own. She writes of the soul as a lost boat, an internal lamp, a storm within, an emperor; she characterizes her soul numb and her soul ripening, her soul entombed and her soul released, her soul as an adventure unto itself. She writes of 'The Cellars of the Soul' and the 'electric gale' of that same soul, and thus the soul becomes the image for her plunges into the psychological depths as well as a sign of her flight to the celestial heights. She asks, 'Dare you see a Soul *at the White Heat*?' She speaks of the soul admitted to itself as a site of 'polar privacy' and 'Finite infinity.' She directs her soul to 'Take thy risk'" (ibid.).

15. Ibid.

16. Dickinson, *The Poems of Emily Dickinson: Reading Edition*, 256.

17. Mallarmé, "The White Waterlily," 35.

18. Bushnell, *Sermons*, 61. This is the specific edition Dickinson's family owned.

19. Emerson, *Essays*, 224. Dickinson's family owned this particular edition, published just one year (more or less) before Dickinson wrote "The Soul unto Itself."

20. Toward the end of "The Over-Soul," Emerson writes, "The simplest person, who in his integrity worships God, becomes God; yet forever and ever the influx of this better

and universal self is new and unsearchable. Ever it inspires awe and astonishment." See Emerson, *Essays*, 241.

21. Dickinson, *The Letters of Emily Dickinson*, 2:423.

22. Ibid., 2:424.

23. Ibid.

24. Higginson, "Emily Dickinson's Letters," 449.

25. Higginson, "The Procession of the Flowers," 656. In 1865, Harriet Prescott married Richard S. Spofford and became Harriet Prescott Spofford.

26. The manuscript version of "The Robin is the One" that Dickinson sent to Higginson is no longer extant. Dickinson also sent a version to Susan Dickinson in 1863. That manuscript is lost as well. In 1865, Dickinson made a third copy. See Dickinson, *The Poems of Emily Dickinson: Variorum Edition*, 1:511–12.

27. The poem, despite its off-rhyme of "since" and "peace," is not included in William H. Schurr's *New Poems of Emily Dickinson* (1993).

28. For an account of Dickinson's relationship with Susan, see Smith, "Susan and Emily Dickinson." Other contexts are also relevant, of course. See, for example, David S. Reynolds's arguments about Dickinson's connection to contemporary women's writing in *Beneath the American Renaissance*, 387–437.

29. Jackson, *Dickinson's Misery*, 38.

30. In "On the Teaching of Modern Literature" (1961), Lionel Trilling describes the importance of attending to what a poet "wants to happen outside the poem as a result of the poem": "A couple of decades ago, the discovery was made that a literary work is a structure of words: this doesn't seem a surprising thing to have learned except for its polemical tendency, which is to urge us to minimize the amount of attention we give to the poet's social and personal will, to what he wants to happen outside the poem as a result of the poem. For me this polemical tendency has been of the greatest usefulness, for it has corrected my inclination to pay attention chiefly to what the poet *wants*. For two or three years I directed my efforts toward dealing with [poems] chiefly as structures of words . . . But it went against the grain. It went against my personal grain. It went against the grain of the classroom situation . . . And it went against the grain of the authors themselves—structures of words they may indeed have created, but these structures were not pyramids or triumphal arches, they were manifestly contrived to be not static and commemorative but mobile and aggressive, and one does not describe a quinquereme or a howitzer or a tank without estimating how much *damage* it can do" (388).

31. Higginson, preface to *Poems*, v.

32. Blackmur, "Emily Dickinson's Notation," 227.

33. Susan Howe, "These Flames and Generosities of the Heart," 136.

34. Ibid., 140.

35. Ibid., 141.

36. Ben Lerner writes, "it's worth noting that the unusual nature of her manuscript pages makes the status of a Dickinson composition difficult to determine: Is it a poem or some other kind of object? A work of visual art? What about, for instance, her 'envelope writings'—gently pried apart envelopes whose physical shapes, some have argued, interact purposefully with Dickinson's language? Are her letters poems? What about her notes on advertising flyers?" (*The Hatred of Poetry*, 33–34).

37. Cameron, *Choosing Not Choosing*, 20, 19.

38. Ibid., 18.

39. Ibid., 41.

40. Ibid., 40.

41. Rancière, *Politics of Aesthetics*, 40.

42. Unlike the aims of the other writers I discuss in this book, Dickinson's aims might simply be epistemological. Perhaps she is exploring different accounts of "inner spiritual division" in the poem, rather than attempting to achieve her own "inner spiritual division." Some of the best recent Dickinson criticism details the epistemological value of her poems. See, for example, Clune, "How Poems Know What It's Like to Die."

43. Susan Howe, "These Flames and Generosities of the Heart," 137.

44. Discussing Dickinson's variants, Cameron writes, "What is more radically revealed is a question about what constitutes the identity of the poem. . . . The question raised is: If this word—or this second poem—conventionally understood to be *outside* the poem is rather *integral* to the poem, how is the poem delimited? What *is* the poem?" (*Choosing Not Choosing*, 4, 5).

45. An example: in 2013–14, I participated in a reading group at Princeton University that read Prynne's *Wound Response* over a year, one poem every two weeks. The group came close to realizing the demands of Prynne's poetry, and, in the process, began to illuminate the promise of collective life at a local (and radically privileged) level.

BIBLIOGRAPHY

Adorno, Theodor W. *Aesthetic Theory*. Edited by Gretel Adorno and Rolf Tiedemann. Translated by Robert Hullot-Kentor. Minneapolis: University of Minnesota Press, 1997.

———. *Essays on Music*. Edited by Richard Leppert. Translated by Susan H. Gillespie. Berkeley: University of California Press, 2002.

Akhmatova, Anna. *Sobranie sochinenii*. 8 vols. Moscow: Ellis Lak, 1998–2005.

———. *Stikhotvoreniia*. Moscow: Gosudarstvennoe Izdatel'stvo Khudozhestvennoi Literatury, 1958.

———. *The Word that Causes Death's Defeat: Poems of Memory*. Translated, with an introductory biography, critical essays, and commentary, by Nancy K. Anderson. New Haven, CT: Yale University Press, 2004.

Alter, Robert. "Osip Mandelstam: The Poet as Witness." In *Defenses of the Imagination: Jewish Writers and Modern Historical Crisis*, 25–46. Philadelphia: Jewish Publication Society of America, 1977.

Althusser, Louis. "Ideology and Ideological State Apparatuses (Notes towards an Investigation)." In *Lenin and Philosophy and Other Essays*, translated by Ben Brewster, 121–73. London: NLB, 1971.

Altieri, Charles. *Wallace Stevens and the Demands of Modernity: Toward a Phenomenology of Value*. Ithaca, NY: Cornell University Press, 2013.

Alvarez, A. Review of *Section: Rock-Drill de los Cantares*, by Ezra Pound. In *Ezra Pound: The Critical Heritage*, ed. Eric Homberger, 441–43. London: Routledge & Kegan Paul, 1972.

———. *Stewards of Excellence: Studies in Modern English and American Poets*. New York: Scribner, 1958.

Amert, Susan. *The Later Poetry of Anna Akhmatova*. Stanford, CA: Stanford University Press, 1992.

Anderson, Nancy K., trans. Introduction to *The Word that Causes Death's Defeat: Poems of Memory*. Introductory biography, critical essays, and commentary by Nancy K. Anderson. New Haven, CT: Yale University Press, 2004.

Andrews, William L. "Checklist of Du Bois's Autobiographical Writings." In *Critical Essays on W.E.B. Du Bois*, edited by William L. Andrews, 226–29. Boston: G. K. Hall, 1985.

Aptheker, Herbert. *Annotated Bibliography of the Published Writings of W.E.B. Du Bois*. Millwood: Kraus-Thomson Organization, 1973.

———. *History and Reality*. New York: Cameron Associates, 1955.

———. "The Souls of Black Folk: A Comparison of the 1903 and 1952 Editions." *Negro History Bulletin* 34.1 (January 1971): 15–17.

Arendt, Hannah. "What Is Freedom?" In *Between Past and Future: Eight Exercises in Political Thought*, 142–69. London: Penguin, 2006.

Arsić, Branka. *Bird Relics: Grief and Vitalism in Thoreau*. Cambridge, MA: Harvard University Press, 2016.

Auden, W. H. "In Memory of W. B. Yeats." In *The English Auden: Poems, Essays, and Dramatic Works, 1927–1939*, edited by Edward Mendelson, 241–42. New York: Random House, 1977.

Baines, Jennifer. *Mandelstam: The Later Poetry*. Cambridge: Cambridge University Press, 1977.

Bakhtin, Mikhail. *The Dialogic Imagination: Four Essays*. Translated by Caryl Emerson and Michael Holquist. Austin: University of Texas Press, 1992.

Baldwin, Kate A. *Beyond the Color Line and the Iron Curtain: Reading Encounters between Black and Red, 1922–1963*. Durham, NC: Duke University Press, 2002.

Balfour, Lawrie. *Democracy's Reconstruction: Thinking Politically with W.E.B. Du Bois*. New York: Oxford University Press, 2011.

Balibar, Étienne. "Subjection and Subjectivation." In *Supposing the Subject*, edited by Joan Copjec, 1–15. London: Verso, 1994.

Barnhisel, Greg. *Cold War Modernists: Art, Literature, and American Cultural Diplomacy*. New York: Columbia University Press, 2015.

Baron, Nick. "Conflict and Complicity: The Expansion of the Karelian Gulag, 1923–1933." *Cahiers du Monde russe* 42.2–4 (April–December 2001): 615–48.

Barringer, Felicity. "Anti-Stalin Poem of the 30's Appears." *New York Times*, March 25, 1987.

Barthes, Roland. *The Neutral*. Translated by Rosalind E. Krauss and Denis Hollier. New York: Columbia University Press, 2005.

———. *The Rustle of Language*. Translated by Richard Howard. Berkeley: University of California Press, 1989.

Baudrillard, Jean. "Utopia deferred . . ." In *Utopia Deferred: Writings for Utopie (1967–1978)*, translated by Stuart Kendall, 61–63. New York: Semiotext(e), 2006.

Bennett, Jane. *Thoreau's Nature: Ethics, Politics, and the World*. 2nd ed. Lanham: Rowman & Littlefield, 2002.

Berger, Charles. *Forms of Farewell: The Late Poetry of Wallace Stevens*. Madison: University of Wisconsin Press, 1985.

Berlant, Lauren. "Cruel Optimism." *Differences: A Journal of Feminist Cultural Studies* 17.3 (2006): 20–36.

———. "Remembering Love, Forgetting Everything Else: *Now, Voyager*." In *The Female Complaint: The Unfinished Business of Sentimentality in American Culture*, 169–205. Durham, NC: Duke University Press, 2008.

———. "Trauma and Ineloquence." *Cultural Values* 5.1 (January 2001): 41–58.

Berlin, Isaiah. "Conversations with Akhmatova and Pasternak." *New York Review of Books* (November 20, 1980). http://www.nybooks.com/articles/1980/11/20/conversations-with-akhmatova-and-pasternak/.

———. "A Great Russian Writer." *New York Review of Books* (December 23, 1965). http://www.nybooks.com/articles/1965/12/23/a-great-russian-writer/.

———. Two Concepts of Liberty." In *Four Essays on Liberty*, 118–72. London: Oxford University Press, 1969.

Bersani, Leo. *The Culture of Redemption*. Cambridge, MA: Harvard University Press, 1990.

Bird, Robert. "Voices of Silence: Antigone and Niobe in Akhmatova's *Requiem*." In *Poetics. Place. Self: Essays in Honor of Anna Lisa Crone*, edited by Catherine O'Neil, Nicole Boudreau, and Sarah Krive, 331–49. Bloomington, IN: Slavica, 2007.

Birrell, Anne, ed. *New Songs from a Jade Terrace: An Anthology of Early Chinese Love Poetry*. Harmondsworth, UK: Penguin, 1986.

Blackmur, R. P. "Emily Dickinson's Notation." *Kenyon Review* 18.2 (1956): 224–37.

Bloch, Ernst, and Theodor W. Adorno. "Something's Missing: A Discussion between Ernst Bloch and Theodor W. Adorno on the Contradictions of Utopian Longing." In *The Utopian Function of Art and Literature: Selected Essays*, by Ernst Bloch, translated by Jack Zipes and Frank Mecklenburg, 1–17. Cambridge, MA: MIT Press, 1987.

Bloom, Harold. *Wallace Stevens: The Poems of Our Climate*. Ithaca, NY: Cornell University Press, 1977.

Boone, Joseph Allen. "Delving and Diving for Truth: Breaking through to Bottom in Thoreau's *Walden*." *ESQ: A Journal of the American Renaissance* 27 (1981): 135–46.

Booth, Stephen, ed. *Shakespeare's Sonnets*. New Haven, CT: Yale, 1977.

Bornstein, George. "W.E.B. Du Bois and the Jews: Ethics, Editing, and *The Souls of Black Folk*." *Textual Cultures* 1.1 (Spring 2006): 64–74.

Boym, Svetlana. *Another Freedom: The Alternative History of an Idea*. Chicago: University of Chicago Press, 2012.

———. *Death in Quotation Marks: Cultural Myths of the Modern Poet*. Cambridge, MA: Harvard University Press, 1991.

Brodsky, Joseph. "Beyond Consolation." Translated by Barry Rubin. *New York Review of Books* (February 7, 1974). http://www.nybooks.com/articles/1974/02/07/beyond-consolation/.

———. *Less than One: Selected Essays*. New York: Farrar, Straus and Giroux, 1986.

Brown, Clarence. "Mandelshtam's Acmeist Manifesto," *Russian Review* 24.1 (January 1965): 46–51.

———. "Memories of Nadezhda." *Russian Review* 61.4 (October 2002): 485–88.

Buck-Morss, Susan. *Dreamworld and Catastrophe: The Passing of Mass Utopia in East and West*. Cambridge, MA: MIT Press, 2000.

Budé, Guillaume. Guillaume Budé to Thomas Lupset, July 31, 1517. In *Utopia*, by Thomas More, edited by George M. Logan and Robert M. Adams, translated by Robert M. Adams, 115–21. Cambridge: Cambridge University Press, 1996.

Buell, Lawrence. *The Environmental Imagination: Thoreau, Nature Writing, and the Formation of American Culture*. Cambridge, MA: Harvard University Press, 1995.

Bukharin, Nikolai. *Poetry, Poetics and the Problems of Poetry in the U.S.S.R.* In *Problems of Soviet Literature: Reports and Speeches at the First Soviet Writers' Congress*, edited by H. G. Scott, 183–258. Westport, CT: Hyperion Press, 1981.

Bushnell, Horace. *Sermons for the New Life*. 6th ed. New York: Scribner, 1860.

Butler, Judith. *Undoing Gender*. New York: Routledge, 2004.

Byerman, Keith E. "The Children Ceased to Hear My Name: Recovering the Self in *The Autobiography of W.E.B. Du Bois*." In *Multicultural Autobiography: American Lives*, edited by James Robert Payne, 64–93. Knoxville: University of Tennessee Press, 1992.

Cafaro, Philip. *Thoreau's Living Ethics: Walden and the Pursuit of Virtue*. Athens: University of Georgia Press, 2004.

Cameron, Sharon. *Choosing Not Choosing: Dickinson's Fascicles*. Chicago: University of Chicago Press, 1992.

———. "The Way of Life by Abandonment: Emerson's Impersonal." In *The Other Emerson*, edited by Branka Arsić and Cary Wolfe, 3–40. Minneapolis: University of Minnesota Press, 2010.

Carne-Ross, D. S. "The Music of Lost Dynasty: Pound in the Classroom." In *Ezra Pound's Cantos: A Casebook*, edited by Peter Makin, 181–203. Oxford: Oxford University Press, 2006.

Cavanagh, Clare. *Lyric Poetry and Modern Politics: Russia, Poland, and the West*. New Haven, CT: Yale University Press, 2009.

Cavell, Stanley. *The Claim of Reason: Wittgenstein, Skepticism, Morality, and Tragedy*. New York: Oxford University Press, 1999.

———. *Contesting Tears: The Hollywood Melodrama of the Unknown Woman*. Chicago: Chicago University Press, 1996.

———. *Senses of Walden*. Chicago: University of Chicago Press, 1992.

Chandler, Nahum Dimitri. *X: The Problem of the Negro as a Problem for Thought*. New York: Fordham University Press, 2013.

Chatwin, Bruce. Introduction to *Journey to Armenia*, by Osip Mandelstam, 8–11. London: Next Editions, 1980.

Cheetham, Mark A. *The Rhetoric of Purity: Essentialist Theory and the Advent of Abstract Painting*. Cambridge: Cambridge University Press, 1994.

Chou King: Les annales de la Chine. Translated by Séraphin Couvreur. Paris: Cathasia, 1950.

Chukovskaia, Lidiia. [Lydia Chukovskaya]. *The Akhmatova Journals*. Translated by Milena Michalski and Sylva Rubashova. London: Harvill, 1994.

———. *Zapiski ob Anne Akhmatovoi*. 3 vols. Moscow: Vremia, 2007.

Chukovskii, Kornei. [Korney Chukovsky]. "Akhmatova and Mayakovsky." Translated by John Pearson. In *Major Soviet Writers: Essays in Criticism*, edited by Edward J. Brown, 33–53. London: Oxford University Press, 1973.

Clapper, Ronald Earl. "The Development of *Walden*: A Genetic Text." PhD diss., University of California, Los Angeles, 1967.

Clark, Katerina. "'The History of the Factories' as a Factory of History: A Case Study on the Role of Soviet Literature in Subject Formation." In *Autobiographical Practices in Russia—Autobiographische Praktiken in Russland*, edited by Jochen Hellbeck and Klaus Heller, 251–77. Gottingen: V&R Unipress, 2004.

———. *The Soviet Novel: History as Ritual*. 3rd ed. Bloomington: Indiana University Press, 2000.

———. "Utopian Anthropology as a Context for Stalinist Literature." In *Stalinism: Essays in Historical Interpretation*, edited by Robert Tucker, 180–98. New York: Norton, 1977.

Clark, Katerina, and Evgeny Dobrenko, eds. *Soviet Culture and Power: A History in Documents, 1917–1953*. New Haven, CT: Yale University Press, 2007.

Clover, Joshua, and Keston Sutherland. "Always Totalize: Poetry and Revolution." *Claudius App* 5 (2013). http://theclaudiusapp.com/5-clover-sutherland.html.

Clune, Michael. "Bernhard's Way." Nonsite.org 9 (2013). http://nonsite.org/feature/bernhards-way.

———. "How Poems Know What It's Like to Die." *ELH* 83 (2016): 633–54.

[Clutton-Brock, Arthur]. "The Poems of Mr. Ezra Pound." *Times Literary Supplement* (November 16, 1916): 545.

Coetzee, J. M. "Osip Mandelstam and the Stalin Ode." *Representations* 35 (Summer 1991): 72–83.

Cook, Eleanor. *A Reader's Guide to Wallace Stevens*. Princeton, NJ: Princeton University Press, 2007.

———. "Wallace Stevens and the King James Bible." *Essays in Criticism: A Quarterly Journal of Literary Criticism* 41.3 (1991): 240–52.

Costello, Bonnie. *Shifting Ground: Reinventing Landscape in Modern American Poetry*. Cambridge, MA: Harvard University Press, 2003.

Cramer, Jeffrey S., ed. *Walden: A Fully Annotated Edition*, by Henry David Thoreau. New Haven, CT: Yale University Press, 2004.

Critchley, Simon. *Things Merely Are: Philosophy in the Poetry of Wallace Stevens*. Abingdon, UK: Routledge, 2005.

Crone, Anna L. "Antimetabole in *Rekviem*: The Structural Disposition of Themes and Motifs." In *The Speech of Unknown Eyes: Akhmatova's Readers on Her Poetry*, edited by Wendy Rosslyn, 1:27–41. Nottingham, UK: Astra Press, 1990.

Culler, Jonathan. *Theory of the Lyric*. Cambridge, MA: Harvard University Press, 2015.

Cunningham, J. V. "The Styles and Procedures of Wallace Stevens." In *The Collected Essays of J. V. Cunningham*, 379–98. Chicago: Swallow, 1976.

Dalos, György. *The Guest from the Future: Anna Akhmatova and Isaiah Berlin*. Translated by Antony Wood. New York: Farrar, Straus and Giroux, 1999.

Davenport, Guy. "The Man without Contemporaries." *Hudson Review* 27.4 (Summer 1974): 296–302.

Davie, Donald. "Bed-Rock." Review of *Section: Rock-Drill, 85–95, de Los Cantares*, by Ezra Pound. *New Statesman and Nation* 53 (March 9, 1957): 316–17.

——. *Ezra Pound.* New York: Viking, 1975.

——. *Ezra Pound: Poet as Sculptor.* Oxford: Oxford University Press, 1964.

Dean, Bradley P., and Ronald Wesley Hoag. "Thoreau's Lectures before *Walden*: An Annotated Calendar." *Studies in the American Renaissance* (1995): 127–228.

Delano, Sterling F. *Brook Farm: The Dark Side of Utopia.* Cambridge, MA: Belknap Press of Harvard University Press, 2004.

Deleuze, Gilles, and Félix Guattari. "Percept, Affect, and Concept." In *What Is Philosophy?*, translated by Hugh Tomlinson and Graham Burchell, 163–99. New York: Columbia University Press, 1996.

Dickinson, Emily. *The Letters of Emily Dickinson.* 3 vols. Edited by Thomas H. Johnson. Cambridge: Belknap Press of Harvard University Press, 1955.

——. *The Poems of Emily Dickinson: Reading Edition.* Edited by R. W. Franklin. Cambridge, MA: Belknap Press of Harvard University Press, 2005.

——. *The Poems of Emily Dickinson: Variorum Edition.* 3 vols. Edited by R. W. Franklin. Cambridge, MA: Belknap Press of Harvard University Press, 1998.

Dimock, Wai Chee. "Literature for the Planet." *PMLA* 116.1 (January 2001): 173–88.

Dobrenko, Evgeny. *The Making of the State Writer: Social and Aesthetic Origins of Soviet Literary Culture.* Translated by Jesse M. Savage. Stanford, CA: Stanford University Press, 2001.

Doggett, Frank, and Dorothy Emerson. "A Primer of Possibility for 'The Auroras of Autumn.'" *Wallace Stevens Journal* 13.1 (1989): 53–66.

Doherty, Justin. *The Acmeist Movement in Russian Poetry: Culture and the Word.* Oxford: Oxford University Press, 1995.

Duberman, Martin. "Du Bois as Prophet." *New Republic* (March 23, 1968): 36–39.

Du Bois, W.E.B. [W. E. Burghardt DuBois]. "The Atlanta Conferences." *Voice of the Negro* 1.3 (March 1904): 85–90.

——. *The Autobiography of W.E.B. Du Bois: A Soliloquy on Viewing My Life from the Last Decade of Its First Century.* New York: Oxford University Press, 2007.

——. *The Correspondence of W.E.B. Du Bois.* Vol. 3, *Selections, 1944–1963.* Edited by Herbert Aptheker. Amherst: University of Massachusetts Press, 1978.

——. *Darkwater: Voices from Within the Veil.* New York: Oxford University Press, 2007.

——. *Dusk of Dawn: An Essay toward an Autobiography of a Race Concept.* New York: Oxford University Press, 2007.

——. *In Battle for Peace: The Story of My 83rd Birthday.* New York: Oxford University Press, 2007.

——. "I Won't Vote." *Nation* 183.16 (October 20, 1956). https://www.thenation.com/article/i-wont-vote/.

——. [W.E. Burghardt Du Bois] "My Evolving Program for Negro Freedom." *Clinical Sociology Review* 8.1 (1990): 27–57.

——. "A Negro Student at Harvard at the End of the 19th Century." *Massachusetts Review* 1.3 (Spring 1960): 439–58.

——. "On Stalin." *National Guardian* (March 16, 1953). https://www.marxists.org/reference/archive/stalin/biographies/1953/03/16.htm.

——. Papers (MS 312). Special Collections and University Archives, University of Massachusetts Amherst Libraries.

——. "The Shadow of Years." *Crisis* 15.4 (February 1918): 167–71.

——. *The Souls of Black Folk.* Oxford: Oxford University Press, 2007.

——. [W. E. Burghardt Du Bois]. *The Souls of Black Folk: Essays and Sketches.* New York: Blue Heron Press, 1953.

——. [U.E.B. Diubua]. *Vospominania.* Moscow: Izdatel'stvo Inostrannoi Literatury, 1962.

———. *W.E.B. DuBois: A Recorded Autobiography; Interview with Moses Asch*. New York: Folkways Records, 1961.

Edwards, Jonathan. "A Faithful Narrative of the Surprising Work of God." In *A Jonathan Edwards Reader*, edited by John E. Smith, Harry S. Stout, and Kenneth P. Minkema, 57–87. New Haven, CT: Yale University Press, 2003.

Eeckhout, Bart. "Stevens and Philosophy." In *The Cambridge Companion to Wallace Stevens*, edited by John N. Serio, 103–17. Cambridge: Cambridge University Press, 2007.

Eitzen, Dirk. "When Is a Documentary? Documentaries as a Mode of Reception." *Cinema Journal* 35.1 (Autumn 1995): 81–102.

Eliot, T. S. Introduction to *Selected Poems*, by Ezra Pound, vii–xxv. London: Faber and Faber, 1934.

———. "Poetry and Propaganda." *The Bookman: A Review of Books and Life* 70.6 (February 1930): 595–602.

———. "Tradition and the Individual Talent." In *Selected Essays*, 3–11. New York: Harcourt, Brace and World, 1964.

Emerson, Ralph Waldo. *Essays*. Boston: James Munroe and Company, 1861.

———. *Essays and Lectures*. Edited by Joel Porte. New York: Library of America, 1983.

Empson, William. *Some Versions of Pastoral*. London: Hogarth, 1986.

Engels, Frederick. *Engels*. In *Collected Works*, by Karl Marx and Frederick Engels, vol. 25. New York: International Publishers, 1987.

———. *Engels: 1892–1895*. In *Collected Works*, by Karl Marx and Frederick Engels, vol. 50. New York: International Publishers, 2004.

Erenburg, Il'ia. *Portrety sovremennykh poetov*. St. Petersburg: Nauka, 2002.

Euchner, Charles. *Nobody Turn Me Around: A People's History of the 1963 March on Washington*. Boston: Beacon Press, 2010.

Evtushenko, Evgenii. "Reigan i Akhmatova." *Itogi* 5 (January 26, 2009). http://dlib.eastview.com/browse/doc/19510272.

Feddersen, Timothy J. "Rational Choice Theory and the Paradox of Not Voting." *Journal of Economic Perspectives* 18.1 (Winter 2004): 99–112.

Fenollosa, Ernest, and Ezra Pound. *The Chinese Written Character as a Medium for Poetry: A Critical Edition*. Edited by Haun Saussy, Jonathan Stalling, and Lucas Klein. New York: Fordham University Press, 2008.

Fernandez, Ramon. "Lettre ouverte à André Gide." *La Nouvelle Revue Française* 247 (April 1934): 703–8.

Fitzpatrick, Sheila. *Stalin's Peasants: Resistance and Survival in the Russian Village after Collectivization*. New York: Oxford University Press, 1996.

Flory, Wendy Stallard. *Ezra Pound and "The Cantos": A Record of Struggle*. New Haven, CT: Yale University Press, 1980.

Forrest-Thomson, Veronica. *Poetic Artifice: A Theory of Twentieth-Century Poetry*. New York: St. Martin's, 1978.

Francis, Richard. *Transcendental Utopias: Individual and Community at Brook Farm, Fruitlands, and Walden*. Ithaca, NY: Cornell University Press, 1997.

Freidin, Gregory. *A Coat of Many Colors: Osip Mandelstam and His Mythologies of Self-Presentation*. Berkeley: University of California Press, 1987.

Freire, Paulo. *Pedagogy of the Oppressed*. Translated by Myra Bergman Ramos. New York: Continuum, 1993.

Frost, Robert. *The Letters of Robert Frost*. Vol. 1, *1886–1920*. Edited by Donald Sheehy, Mark Richardson, and Robert Faggen. Cambridge, MA: Belknap Press of Harvard University Press, 2014.

Gaddis, John Lewis. *George F. Kennan: An American Life*. New York: Penguin, 2011.

Galenson, David W. “Literary Life Cycles: Measuring the Careers of Modern American Poets.” In *Artistic Capital*, 145–70. New York: Routledge, 2006.

Gardner, Sebastian. “Wallace Stevens and Metaphysics: The Plain Sense of Things.” *European Journal of Philosophy* 2.3 (1994): 322–44.

Garrison, William Lloyd. Preface to *Narrative of the Life of Frederick Douglass: An American Slave*, by Frederick Douglass, edited by Deborah E. McDowell, 3–11. New York: Oxford University Press, 1999.

Gasparov, M. L. *O. Mandel'shtam: Grazhdanskaia lirika 1937 goda*. Moscow: Rossiiskii Gosudarstvennyi Gumanitarnyi Universitet, 1996.

Gates, Henry Louis, Jr. “Bad Influence.” *New Yorker* (March 7, 1994): 94–99.

———. “The Black Letters on the Sign: W.E.B. Du Bois and the Canon.” In *The Souls of Black Folk*, by W.E.B. Du Bois. New York: Oxford University Press, 2007.

Gerould, Gordon Hall. “The Ballad of *The Bitter Withy*.” *PMLA* 23.1 (1908): 141–67.

Gershtein, Emma. *Memuary*. Moscow: Zakharov, 2002.

———. [Emma Gerstein]. *Moscow Memoirs*. Translated by John Crowfoot. London: Harvill Press, 2004.

Giles, Herbert A. *A History of Chinese Literature*. New York: Appleton, 1901.

Gilroy, Paul. *The Black Atlantic: Modernity and Double Consciousness*. Cambridge, MA: Harvard University Press, 1993.

Golovnikova, O. V., and N. S. Tarkhova. “‘Iosif Vissarionovich! Spasite sovetskogo istorika . . .’ (O neizvestnom pis'me Anny Akhmatovoi Stalinu).” *Otechestvennaia Istoria* 3 (2001): 149–57.

Gooding-Williams, Robert. “Evading Narrative Myth, Evading Prophetic Pragmatism: Cornel West's *The Evasion of American Philosophy*.” *Massachusetts Review* 32.4 (Winter 1991): 517–42.

———. Review of *Dark Voices*, by Shamoon Zamir. *American Literature* 69.4 (1997): 855–56.

Goodman, Nelson. *Ways of Worldmaking*. Cambridge, MA: Hackett, 1978.

Gor'kii, M., L. L. Averbakh, and S. G. Firin, eds. [Maxim Gorky, L. Auerbach, and S. G. Firin, eds.] *Belomor: An Account of the Construction of the New Canal between the White Sea and the Baltic Sea*. New York: Harrison Smith and Robert Haas, 1935.

———. *Belomorsko-Baltiiskii Kanal imeni Stalina: Istoriia stroitel'stva*. [Moscow]: Gosudarstvennoe izdatel'stvo “Istoriia fabrik i zavodov,” 1934.

Greeley, Horace. Editorial comments. *New-York Daily Tribune*, April 7, 1849.

Groys, Boris. *The Total Art of Stalinism: Avant-Garde, Dictatorship, and Beyond*. Translated by Charles Rougle. Princeton, NJ: Princeton University Press, 1992.

Gusdorf, Georges. “Conditions and Limits of Autobiography.” Translated by James Olney. In *Autobiography: Essays Theoretical and Critical*, edited by James Olney, 28–48. Princeton, NJ: Princeton University Press, 1980.

Haight, Amanda. *Akhmatova: A Poetic Pilgrimage*. Oxford: Oxford University Press, 1990.

Halfin, Igal. *Terror in My Soul: Communist Autobiographies on Trial*. Cambridge, MA: Harvard University Press, 2003.

Hall, James C. *Mercy, Mercy Me: African-American Culture and the American Sixties*. New York: Oxford University Press, 2001.

Harding, Walter, and Michael Meyer. “Thoreau's Reputation.” In *The New Thoreau Handbook*, edited by William Harding and Michael Meyer, 202–24. New York: New York University Press, 1980.

Hartman, Saidiya V. *Scenes of Subjection: Terror, Slavery, and Self-Making in Nineteenth-Century America*. New York: Oxford University Press, 1997.

Harvey, David. *Spaces of Hope*. Berkeley: University of California Press, 2000.

Havelock, Eric. *Preface to Plato*. Oxford: Oxford University Press, 1963.

Hayot, Eric. *Chinese Dreams: Pound, Brecht, Tel Quel*. Ann Arbor: University of Michigan Press, 2004.

Heaney, Seamus. "Osip and Nadezhda Mandelstam." In *Government of the Tongue: Selected Prose, 1978–1987*, 71–88. New York: Farrar, Straus and Giroux, 1989.

Hejinian, Lyn. "The Rejection of Closure." In *The Language of Inquiry*, 40–58. Berkeley: University of California Press, 2000.

Hellbeck, Jochen. "Working, Struggling, Becoming: Stalin-Era Autobiographical Texts." *Russian Review* 60.3 (2001): 340–59.

Hermans, Theo. *The Structure of Modernist Poetry*. London: Croom Helm, 1982.

Higginson, Thomas Wentworth. "Emily Dickinson's Letters." *Atlantic Monthly* (December 1862): 444–56.

——. Preface to *Poems*, by Emily Dickinson, edited by Mabel Loomis Todd and T. W. Higginson. Boston: Roberts Brothers, 1890.

——. "The Procession of the Flowers." *Atlantic Monthly* (October 1891): 649–57.

Hirsch, Edward. *How to Read a Poem and Fall in Love with Poetry*. New York: Harcourt, Brace, 1999.

Hohn, Donovan. "Everybody Hates Henry: Literary Saint or Arrogant Fraud—Why Do We Need Thoreau to Be One or the Other?" *New Republic* (October 21, 2015). https://newrepublic.com/article/123162/everybody-hates-henry-david-thoreau.

Holmgren, Beth. *Women's Works in Stalin's Time: On Lidiia Chukovskaia and Nadezhda Mandelstam*. Bloomington: Indiana University Press, 1993.

Horne, Gerald. *Race Woman: The Lives of Shirley Graham Du Bois*. New York: New York University Press, 2000.

Horst, R. Kenneth. *Westcott's Plant Disease Handbook*. 7th ed. Berlin: Springer-Verlag, 2008.

Howe, Irving. "Remarkable Man, Ambiguous Legacy." *Harper's Magazine* (March 1968): 143–49.

Howe, Susan. "These Flames and Generosities of the Heart: Emily Dickinson and the Illogic of Sumptuary Values." In *The Birth-Mark: Unsettling the Wilderness in American Literary History*, 131–53. Middleton, CT: Wesleyan University Press, 1993.

Huggins, Nathan, ed. *Writings*, by W.E.B. Du Bois. New York: Library of America, 1986.

Hume, David. *An Enquiry concerning the Principles of Morals*. Edited by Tom L. Beauchamp. Oxford: Oxford University Press, 1998.

Ilgunas, Ken. "Thoreau's Disciple." *Spartan Student* (blog), January 14, 2009. http://www.kenilgunas.com/2009/01/thoreaus-disciple.html.

Isenberg, Arnold. "Deontology and the Ethics of Lying." *Philosophy and Phenomenological Research* 24.4 (June 1964): 463–80.

Ivinskaia, Ol'ga. [Olga Ivinskaya]. *A Captive of Time*. Translated by Max Hayward. Garden City: Doubleday, 1978.

Izenberg, Oren. *Being Numerous: Poetry and the Ground of Social Life*. Princeton, NJ: Princeton University Press, 2011.

Jackson, Virginia. *Dickinson's Misery: A Theory of Lyric Reading*. Princeton, NJ: Princeton University Press, 2005.

Jackson, Virginia, and Yopie Prins, eds. General introduction to *The Lyric Theory Reader: A Critical Anthology*, edited by Virginia Jackson and Yopie Prins, 1–8. Baltimore: Johns Hopkins University Press, 2013.

Jakobson, Roman. "Two Aspects of Language and Two Types of Aphasic Disturbances." In *Language in Literature*, 95–114. Cambridge, MA: Belknap Press of Harvard University Press, 1987.

James, William. "The Dilemma of Determinism." In *The Will to Believe and Other Essays in Popular Philosophy*, edited by Frederick H. Burkhardt, Fredson Bowers, and Ignas K. Skrupskelis, 114–40. Cambridge, MA: Harvard University Press, 1979.

——. *Pragmatism*. In *Writings, 1902–1910*, edited by Bruce Kuklick, 479–624. New York: Library of America, 1987.

Jameson, Fredric. *Archaeologies of the Future: The Desire Called Utopia and Other Science Fictions*. London: Verso, 2005.

——. "Exoticism and Structuralism in Wallace Stevens." In *The Modernist Papers*, 207–22. New York: Verso, 2007.

Jangfeldt, Bengt. "Osip Mandel'štam's Ode to Stalin." *Scando-Slavica* 22.1 (1976): 35–41.

Jarrell, Randall. "Reflections of Wallace Stevens." In *Poetry and the Age*, 116–29. London: Faber, 1993.

Jarvis, Simon. "The Poetry of Keston Sutherland." *Chicago Review* 53.1 (Spring 2007): 139–45.

——. "Soteriology and Reciprocity." *Parataxis* 5 (Winter 1993–94): 30–39.

Johnson, Barbara. "A Hound, a Bay Horse, and a Turtle Dove: Obscurity in *Walden*." In *The Barbara Johnson Reader: The Surprise of Otherness*, edited by Melissa Feurstein, Bill Johnson Gonzalez, Lili Porten, and Keja Valens, 36–43. Durham, NC: Duke University Press, 2014.

Kant, Immanuel. *Critique of Pure Reason*. Edited and translated by Paul Guyer and Allen W. Wood. Cambridge: Cambridge University Press, 1998.

——. *Critique of the Power of Judgment*. Edited by Paul Guyer. Translated by Paul Guyer and Eric Matthews. Cambridge: Cambridge University Press, 2000.

Katko, Justin. "Relativistic Phytosophy: Towards a Commentary on 'The *Plant Time Manifold* Transcripts.'" *Glossator* 2 (2010): 245–94.

Kenner, Hugh. *A Homemade World: The American Modernist Writers*. Baltimore: Johns Hopkins University Press, 1989.

——. *The Poetry of Ezra Pound*. Norfolk, CT: New Directions, [1951].

——. *The Pound Era*. Berkeley: University of California Press, 1971.

——. "Under the Larches of Paradise." In *Gnomon*, 280–96. New York: McDowell, Obolensky, 1958.

Kern, Robert. *Orientalism, Modernism, and the American Poem*. Cambridge: Cambridge University Press, 1996.

Kindellan, Michael, and Joshua Kotin. "*The Cantos* and Pedagogy." *Modernist Cultures*, forthcoming.

King, Martin Luther, Jr. "Honoring Dr. Du Bois." In *Freedomways Reader: Prophets in Their Own Country*, edited by Esther Cooper Jackson with Constance Pohl, 31–39. Boulder, CO: Westview, 2000.

——. "I Have a Dream." In *I Have a Dream: Writing and Speeches that Changed the World*, edited by James Melvin Washington, 101–6. New York: HarperCollins, 1992.

Klagge, James C., and Alfred Nordmann, eds. *Ludwig Wittgenstein: Public and Private Occasions*. Lanham, MD: Rowman & Littlefield, 2003.

Klein, Robert. *Form and Meaning: Writings on Renaissance and Modern Art*. New York: Viking, 1979.

Kotin, Joshua. Review of *Concepts and Conception in Poetry*, by J. H. Prynne. *Wallace Stevens Journal* 39.1 (Spring 2015): 128–30.

Kumar, Krishan. *Utopia and Anti-Utopia in Modern Times*. London: Blackwell, 1987.

Kuzmin, Mikhail. *Selected Writings*. Translated by Michael A. Green and Stanislav A. Shvabrin. Lewisburg, PA: Bucknell University Press, 2005.

Lekmanov, Oleg. *Mandelstam*. Translated by Tatiana Retivov. Boston: Academic Studies Press, 2010.

Lerner, Ben. *The Hatred of Poetry*. New York: Farrar, Straus and Giroux, 2016.

Lewis, David. "Languages and Language." In *Philosophical Papers*. Vol. 1, 163–88. New York: Oxford University Press, 1983.

Lewis, David Levering. *W.E.B. Du Bois: Biography of a Race, 1868–1919*. New York: Henry Holt, 1993.

——. *W.E.B. Du Bois: The Fight for Equality and the American Century, 1919–1963*. New York: Henry Holt, 2000.

Littell, Robert. *The Stalin Epigram*. New York: Simon and Schuster, 2009.

Li Zhimin. "Four Different Ways of Looking at J. H. Prynne's Chinese Poem—A Harmony of English and Chinese Cultures." *Quid* 7a ([2001]): 14–18.

Lockwood, Charles. *Manhattan Moves Uptown: An Illustrated History*. Boston: Houghton Mifflin, 1976.

Lodge, David. *Modes of Modern Writing: Metaphor, Metonymy, and the Typology of Modern Literature*. Chicago: University of Chicago Press, 1977.

Longenbach, James. *Wallace Stevens: The Plain Sense of Things*. New York: Oxford University Press, 1991.

Loseff, Lev. "Who Is the Hero of the Poem without One?" *Essays in Poetics* 11–12 (1986): 91–104.

Lowance, Mason. General introduction to *Against Slavery: An Abolitionist Reader*, edited by Mason Lowance, xiii–xxxvi. New York: Penguin, 2000.

Lowell, Amy. Preface to *Fir-Flower Tablets, Poems from the Chinese*, by Florence Ayscough and Amy Lowell, v–x. Boston: Houghton Mifflin, 1921.

Lowell, Robert. *Collected Poems*. Edited by Frank Bidart and David Gewanter. New York: Farrar, Straus and Giroux, 2003.

Macpherson, C. B. *The Political Theory of Possessive Individualism: Hobbes to Locke*. Don Mills, ON: Oxford University Press, 2011.

Mallarmé, Stéphane. "The White Waterlily." In *Divagations*, translated by Barbara Johnson, 33–36. Cambridge, MA: Harvard University Press, 2007.

Mandel'shtam, Nadezhda. [Nadezhda Mandelstam]. *Hope Abandoned*. Translated by Max Hayward. New York: Atheneum, 1974.

——. [Nadezhda Mandelstam]. *Hope against Hope*. Translated by Max Hayward. New York: Modern Library, 1999.

——. *Kniga Tret'ia*. Paris: YMCA-Press, 1987.

——. [N. Ya. Mandel'shtam] *Vospominaniia*. Moscow: Kniga, 1989.

Mandel'shtam, Osip. [Osip Mandelstam]. *Critical Prose and Letters*. Edited by Jane Gary Harris. Translated by Jane Gary Harris and Constance Link. Woodstock: Ardis, 2003.

——. *Polnoe sobranie sochinenii i pisem v trekh tomakh*. 3 vols. Moscow: Progress-Pleiada, 2009–11.

——. *Sobranie sochinenii*. Vol. 1. Edited by G. P. Struve and B. A. Filippova. [Washington, DC]: Mezhdunarodnoe Literaturnoe Sodruzhestvo, 1967.

Manuel, Frank E., and Fritzie P. Manuel. *Utopian Thought in the Western World*. Cambridge, MA: Belknap Press of Harvard University Press, 1979.

Mao, Douglas. *Solid Objects: Modernism and the Test of Production*. Princeton, NJ: Princeton University Press, 1998.

Mao Tse-Tung. *Four Philosophical Essays*. Peking: Foreign Language Press, 1968.

Marshall, Mason. "Freedom through Critique: Thoreau's Service to Others." *Transactions of the Charles S. Peirce Society* 41.2 (Spring 2005): 395–427.

Marx, Karl. *Capital*. Vol. 1. Translated by Ben Fowkes. London: Penguin 1990.

Marx, Karl, and Frederick Engels. *The Communist Manifesto*. Boston: Bedford, 1999.

Marx, Leo. *The Machine in the Garden: Technology and the Pastoral Ideal in America*. New York: Oxford University Press, 2000.

McDowell, John. *Mind and World*. Cambridge, MA: Harvard University Press, 1996.

———. "Sellars and the Space of Reasons." Last modified September 14, 2009. Microsoft Word file. http://www.pitt.edu/~brandom/me-core/downloads/McD%20Cape%20Town%20talk--Sellars%20EPM.doc.

McFadden, Robert D. "Joseph Brodsky, Exiled Poet Who Won Nobel, Dies at 55." *New York Times*, January 29, 1996.

McGarry, Matthew. "'Ode to the Great Leader' or 'Ode to the Poet': Identifying the Hero in Osip Mandel'shtam's 'Poems about Stalin.'" *Studies in Slavic Cultures* 6 (May 2007): 67–81.

Melamed, Jodi. "W.E.B. Du Bois's UnAmerican End." *African American Review* 40.3 (2006): 67–81.

Michaels, Walter Benn. "Walden's False Bottoms." *Glyph* 1 (1977): 132–49.

Middleton, Peter. "Dirigibles." *Quid* 8ii ([2001]): 28–49.

Miller, J. Hillis. *Poets of Reality: Six Twentieth-Century Writers*. Cambridge, MA: Harvard University Press, 1965.

Miłosz, Czesław. *A Year of the Hunter*. Translated by Madeline G. Levine. New York: Farrar, Straus and Giroux, 1994.

Miner, Earl. *The Japanese Tradition in British and American Literature*. Princeton, NJ: Princeton University Press, 1966.

Moody, A. David. *Ezra Pound: Poet; A Portrait of the Man and His Work*. Vol. 1, *The Young Genius, 1885–1920*. Oxford: Oxford University Press, 2007.

———. [A. D. Moody]. "Pound's Allen Upward." *Paideuma* 4.1 (Spring 1975): 55–70.

Morris, Alden. *The Scholar Denied: W.E.B. Du Bois and the Birth of Modern Sociology*. Berkeley: University of California Press, 2015.

Morukov, Mikhail. "The White Sea–Baltic Canal." In *The Economics of Forced Labor: The Soviet Gulag*, edited by Paul R. Gregory and Valery V. Lazarev, 151–62. Stanford, CA: Hoover Institute, 2003.

Mostern, Kenneth. *Autobiography and Black Identity Politics: Racialization in Twentieth-Century America*. Cambridge: Cambridge University Press, 1999.

Mullan, John. "Prynne's Progress." *Guardian*, February 24, 2004.

Mullen, Bill V. *Un-American: W.E.B. Du Bois and the Century of World Revolution*. Philadelphia: Temple University Press, 2015.

Nagel, Thomas. *Equality and Partiality*. New York: Oxford University Press, 1991.

Naiman, Anatolii. [Anatoly Nayman]. *Remembering Anna Akhmatova*. Translated by Wendy Rosslyn. New York: John Macrae-Henry Holt, 1991.

Nealon, Christopher. "The Poetic Case." *Critical Inquiry* 33 (Summer 2007): 865–86.

Nelson, Truman. "W.E.B. DuBois: Prophet in Limbo." *Nation* 186.4 (January 25, 1958): 76–79.

Nersessian, Anahid. *Utopia, Limited: Romanticism and Adjustment*. Cambridge, MA: Harvard University Press, 2015.

Nicholls, Peter. *Ezra Pound: Politics, Economics and Writing*. Atlantic Highlands, NJ: Humanities Press, 1984.

Nietzsche, Friedrich. *The Gay Science*. Edited by Bernard Williams. Translated by Josefine Nauckhoff. Cambridge: Cambridge University Press, 2001.

"Now Available outside Cambridge." *Daily Telegraph*, October 2, 1999.

Orwell, George. *The Collected Essays, Journalism, and Letters*. Vol. 3, *As I Please: 1943–1946*, edited by Sonia Orwell and Ian Angus. Boston: Nonpareil Books, 2000.

Osofsky, Gilbert. "The Master of the Grand Vision." *Saturday Review* (February 24, 1968): 42.

Oushakine, Serguei Alex. "The Terrifying Mimicry of Samizdat." *Public Culture* 13.2 (Spring 2001): 191–214.

Owen, Stephen. *Traditional Chinese Poetry and Poetics: Omen of the World*. Madison: University of Wisconsin Press, 1985.

Paglia, Camille. "Final Cut: The Selection Process for Break, Blow, Burn." *Arion* 16.2 (2008): 1–23.

Paperno, Irina. "Personal Accounts of the Soviet Experience." *Kritika* 3.4 (Fall 2002): 577– 610.

——. *Stories of the Soviet Experience: Memoirs, Diaries, Dreams*. Ithaca, NY: Cornell University Press, 2009.

Partington, Paul G. *W.E.B. Du Bois: A Bibliography of His Published Writings*. Revised ed. Whittier, CA: Paul G. Partington, 1979.

Peirce, C. S. "Some Consequences of Four Incapacities." *Journal of Speculative Philosophy* 2.3 (1868): 140–57.

Pelletreau, William Smith. *Early New York Houses*. New York: Francis P. Harper, 1900.

Perloff, Marjorie. *The Poetics of Indeterminacy: Rimbaud to Cage*. Evanston, IL: Northwestern University Press, 1981.

Platt, John. "Social Traps." *American Psychologist* 28.8 (August 1973): 641–51.

Posnock, Ross. "Going Astray, Going Forward: Du Boisian Pragmatism and Its Lineage." In *The Revival of Pragmatism: New Essays on Social Thought, Law, and Culture*, edited by Morris Dickstein, 176–89. Durham, NC: Duke University Press, 1998.

Pound, Ezra. *ABC of Reading*. New York: New Directions, 1960.

——. "The Art of Poetry." An interview with Ezra Pound, by Donald Hall. In *The Paris Review Interviews*. Vol. 4, 49–78. New York: Picador, 2009.

——. *The Cantos*. New York: New Directions, 1970.

——. *Cathay*. London: Elkin Mathews, 1915.

——. *Early Writings: Poetry and Prose*. Edited by Ira B. Nadel. New York: Penguin, 2005.

——. *Ezra Pound and Japan: Letters and Essays*. Edited by Sanehide Kodama. Redding Ridge: Black Swan Books, 1987.

——. "A Few Don'ts by an Imagiste." *Poetry* 1.6 (March 1913): 200–206.

——. *Guide to Kulchur*. New York: New Directions, 1968.

——. "Imagisme and England: A Vindication and an Anthology." *T. P's Weekly* 25 (February 20, 1915): 185.

——. *Lustra*. New York: [Privately printed], 1916.

——. "Praefatio." In *Active Anthology*, edited by Ezra Pound. London: Faber and Faber, 1933.

——. Review of *A Boy's Will*, by Robert Frost. *Poetry* 2.2 (May 1913): 72–74.

——. Review of *Helen Redeemed and Other Poems*, by Maurice Hewlett. *Poetry* 2.2 (May 1913): 74–76.

Pound, Ezra, and E. E. Cummings. *Pound/Cummings: The Correspondence of Ezra Pound and E. E. Cummings*. Edited by Barry Ahearn. Ann Arbor: University of Michigan Press, 1996.

Prieto, José Manuel. "Reading Mandelstam on Stalin." Translated by Esther Allen. *New York Review of Books* (June 10, 2010). http://www.nybooks.com/articles/2010/06/10/reading-mandelstam-stalin/.

Proffer, Carl R. "The Attack on Mme. Mandelstam." *New York Review of Books* (February 21, 1974). http://www.nybooks.com/articles/1974/02/21/the-attack-on-mme-mandelstam/.

Prynne, J. H. Afterword to "Original: Chinese Language-Poetry Group." Special issue, *Parataxis: Modernism and Modern Writing* 7 (1995): 121–24.

——. "China Figures." In *New Songs from a Jade Terrace: An Anthology of Early Chinese Love Poetry*, edited by Anne Birrell, 363–92. Harmondsworth, UK: Penguin, 1986.

——. [*Jie ban mi Shi Hu*]. Cambridge: Poetical Histories, 1992.

——. *Not-You*. Cambridge: Equipage, 1993.

——. *Poems*. Northumberland: Bloodaxe, 2015.

——. "Poetic Thought." *Textual Practice* 24.4 (2010): 595–606.

——. *They That Haue Powre to Hurt: A Specimen of a Commentary on Shake-speares Sonnets, 94*. Cambridge: Privately published, 2001.

Purves, Robin. "Apprehension; or, J. H. Prynne, His Critics, and the Rhetoric of Art." *Gig* 2 (March 1999): 45–60.

Putnam, Hilary. *"The Collapse of the Fact/Value Dichotomy" and Others Essays*. Cambridge, MA: Harvard University Press, 2004.

Qian, Zhaoming. *Orientalism and Modernism: The Legacy of China in Pound and Williams*. Durham, NC: Duke University Press, 1995.

Qian Zhongshu. "The Corruption of Consciousness." In *Limited Views*, translated by Ronald Egan, 56–60. Cambridge, MA: Harvard University Asia Center, 1998.

Rampersad, Arnold. *The Art and Imagination of W.E.B. Du Bois*. New York: Schocken Books, 1990.

Rancière, Jacques. *The Politics of Aesthetics: The Distribution of the Sensible*. Translated by Gabriel Rockhill. London: Continuum, 2004.

Rasberry, Vaughn. *Race and the Totalitarian Century: Geopolitics in the Black Literary Imagination*. Cambridge, MA: Harvard University Press, 2016.

Reagan, Ronald. "Remarks at a Luncheon Hosted by Artists and Cultural Leaders in Moscow." Speech, Moscow, May 31, 1988. http://www.reagan.utexas.edu/archives/speeches/1988/053188a.htm.

Redding, J. Saunders. "Portrait: W. E. Burghardt Du Bois." *American Scholar* 18.1 (Winter 1948–49): 93–96.

Redman, Tim. *Ezra Pound and Italian Fascism*. Cambridge: Cambridge University Press, 1991.

Reed, Adolph L., Jr. *W.E.B. Du Bois and American Political Thought: Fabianism and the Color Line*. New York: Oxford University Press, 1997.

Reed, Brian M. "Ezra Pound's Utopia of the Eye." In *Phenomenal Reading: Essays on Modern and Contemporary Poetics*, 61–68. Tuscaloosa: University of Alabama Press, 2012.

Reeder, Roberta. *Anna Akhmatova: Poet and Prophet*. New York: Picador, 1994.

Review of Thoreau lecture "Economy." *New-York Daily Tribune*, April 2, 1849.

Reynolds, David S. *Beneath the American Renaissance: The Subversive Imagination in the Age of Emerson and Melville*. Oxford: Oxford University Press, 2011.

Rich, Adrienne. "What Would We Create?" In *What Is Found There: Notebooks on Poetry and Politics*, 14–21. New York: Norton, 1993.

Richardson, Robert D., Jr. "The Social Ethics of *Walden*." In *Critical Essays on Henry David Thoreau's "Walden,"* edited by Joel Myerson. Boston: G. K. Hall, 1988.

Riddel, Joseph. *The Clairvoyant Eye: The Poetry and Poetics of Wallace Stevens*. Baton Rouge: Louisiana State University Press, 1965.

Riley, Peter. "Bibliography (b): Poetical Histories; The Whole Story." April Eye. Last modified May 18, 2016. http://www.aprileye.co.uk/histories.html.

——. *The Reader*. London: Shacklewell Lane, 1992.

Robbins, Michael. *Equipment for Living: Poetry and Popular Music*. New York: Simon and Schuster, forthcoming.

Rorty, Richard. Introduction to *Empiricism and the Philosophy of Mind*, by Wilfrid Sellars, 1–12. Cambridge, MA: Harvard University Press, 1997.

Rosenwald, Lawrence. "The Theory, Practice, and Influence of Thoreau's Civil Disobedience." In *The Oxford Historical Companion to Henry David Thoreau*, edited by William E. Cain, 153–79. Oxford: Oxford University Press, 2000.

Rosslyn, Wendy. "*Requiem*." In *Encyclopedia of Literary Translation into English*, vol. 1, edited by Olive Classe, 24–28. Chicago: Fitzroy Dearborn, 2000.

Ruder, Cynthia. *Making History for Stalin: The Story of the Belomor Canal*. Gainesville: University of Florida Press, 1998.

Rushdie, Salman. "Whither Moral Courage?" *New York Times*, April 28, 2013.

Rylkova, Galina S. *The Archaeology of Anxiety: The Russian Silver Age and Its Legacy*. Pittsburgh: University of Pittsburgh Press, 2007.

———. Review of *Memuary*, by Emma Gershtein, and *Vospominaniia*, by Nadezhda Mandel'shtam. *Kritika: Explorations in Russian and Eurasian History* 1.1 (Winter 2000): 224–30.

The Sacred Books of China: The Texts of Confucianism. Part 1, *The Shû King, The Religious Portions of the Shih King, The Hsiâo King*. Translated by James Legge. Oxford: Clarendon Press, 1879.

Said, Edward. *On Late Style: Music and Literature against the Grain*. New York: Vintage Books, 2007.

Sarnov, Benedikt. *Stalin i pisateli*. Vol. 1. Moscow: Eksmo, 2008.

———. *Stalin i pisateli*. Vol. 2. Moscow: Eksmo, 2008.

Sartre, Jean-Paul. *Existentialism Is a Humanism*. Translated by Carol Macomber. New Haven, CT: Yale University Press, 2007.

Sattelmeyer, Robert. "The Remaking of Walden." In *Walden, Civil Disobedience, and Other Writings*, by Henry David Thoreau, 3rd ed., edited by William Rossi, 489–507. New York: Norton, 2008.

Saunders, Frances Stonor. *The Cultural Cold War: The CIA and the World of Arts and Letters*. New York: New Press, 1999.

Saussy, Haun. "Fenollosa Compounded: A Discrimination." In *The Chinese Written Character as a Medium for Poetry: A Critical Edition*, edited by Haun Saussy, Jonathan Stalling, and Lucas Klein, 1–40. New York: Fordham University Press, 2008.

Schopenhauer, Arthur. *The World as Will and Presentation*. Vol. 2. Translated by David Carus and Richard E. Aquila. Boston: Prentice, 2011.

Schulz, Kathryn. "Pond Scum: Henry David Thoreau's Moral Myopia." *New Yorker* (October 19, 2015). http://www.newyorker.com/magazine/2015/10/19/pond-scum.

Searle, John. "The Logical Status of Fictional Discourse." In *Expression and Meaning: Studies in the Theory of Speech Acts*, 58–75. Cambridge: Cambridge University Press, 1979.

Sellars, Wilfrid. *Empiricism and the Philosophy of Mind*. Cambridge, MA: Harvard University Press, 1997.

Seneca. *Letters from a Stoic*. Translated by Robin Campbell. London: Penguin, 2004.

Shamir, Milette. *Inexpressible Privacy: The Interior Life of Antebellum American Literature*. Philadelphia: University of Pennsylvania Press, 2006.

Shanley, J. Lyndon. *The Making of "Walden."* Chicago: University of Chicago Press, 1957.

Shaw, Peter. "The Uses of Autobiography." *American Scholar* 38 (Winter 1968–69): 136, 138, 140, 142, 144, 146.

Shelley, Percy Bysshe. *Shelley's Poetry and Prose*. Edited by Donald H. Reiman and Neil Fraistat. New York: Norton, 2002.

Shentalinskii, Vitalii. [Vitaly Shentalinsky]. *The KGB's Literary Archive*. Translated by John Crowfoot. London: Harvill Press, 1995.

Siraganian, Lisa. *Modernism's Other Work: The Art Object's Political Life*. New York: Oxford University Press, 2012.

Smith, Martha Nell. "Susan and Emily Dickinson: Their Lives, in Letters." In *The Cambridge Companion to Emily Dickinson*, edited by Wendy Martin, 51–73. Cambridge: Cambridge University Press, 2002.

Sollors, Werner. Introduction to *The Autobiography of W.E.B. Du Bois: A Soliloquy on Viewing My Life from the Last Decade of Its First Century*, by W.E.B. Du Bois. New York: Oxford University Press, 2007.

Solzhenitsyn, Aleksandr I. *The Gulag Archipelago: 1918–1956; An Experiment in Literary Investigation*. Vol. 1: Parts 1–2. Translated by Thomas P. Whitney. New York: Harper & Row, 1974.

——. *The Gulag Archipelago: 1918–1956; An Experiment in Literary Investigation*. Vol. 2: Parts 3–4. Translated by Thomas P. Whitney. New York: Harper & Row, 1975.

Sontag, Susan. *Conversations with Susan Sontag*. Edited by Leland Poague. Oxford: University Press of Mississippi, 1995.

Stalin, J[osef]. *Dialectical and Historical Materialism*. Moscow: Foreign Languages Publishing House, 1949.

Steiner, George. *After Babel: Aspects of Language and Translation*. London: Oxford University Press, 1975.

——. "Death of a Poet." *New Yorker* (December 26, 1970): 59–63.

Stetskii, A. I. [A. I. Stetsky]. "Under the Flag of the Soviets, Under the Flag of Socialism." In *Problems of Soviet Literature: Reports and Speeches at the First Soviet Writers' Congress*, edited by H. G. Scott, 183–258. Westport, CT: Hyperion Press, 1981.

Stevens, Wallace. *Collected Poetry and Prose*. Edited by Frank Kermode and Joan Richardson. New York: Library of America, 1997.

——. *Letters of Wallace Stevens*. Edited by Holly Stevens, 823. Berkeley: University of California Press, 1966.

——. *Voice of the Poet*. Read by the author. New York: Random House Audio, 2002.

Stewart, Susan. *The Poet's Freedom: A Notebook on Making*. Chicago: University of Chicago Press, 2011.

Struve, Nikita. *Osip Mandel'shtam*. Moscow: Russkii put', 2011.

Surette, Leon. *The Modern Dilemma: Wallace Stevens, T. S. Eliot, and Humanism*. Montreal: McGill-Queen's University Press, 2008.

Sutherland, Keston. "J. H. Prynne and Philology." PhD diss., Cambridge University, 2004.

——. "XL Prynne." In *A Matter of Utterance: The Poetry of J. H. Prynne*, edited by Ian Brinton, 104–32. Exeter, UK: Shearsman Books, 2009.

Szalay, Michael. *New Deal Modernism*. Durham, NC: Duke University Press, 2000.

[Thompson, Dunstan]. "The Poetry of Wallace Stevens." *Times Literary Supplement* (June 19, 1953): 396.

Thoreau, Henry David. "Resistance to Civil Government." In *The American Transcendentalists: Essential Writings*, edited by Lawrence Buell, 257–77. New York: Modern Library, 2006.

——. *Walden*. Princeton, NJ: Princeton University Press, 2004.

Thorough, Timothy. Letter to the editor. *New-York Daily Tribune*, April 7, 1849.

Tiffany, Daniel. *Infidel Poetics: Riddles, Nightlife, Substance*. Chicago: University of Chicago Press, 2009.

Trilling, Lionel. "On the Teaching of Modern Literature." In *The Moral Obligation to Be Intelligent: Selected Essays*, edited by Leon Wieseltier, 381–401. Evanston, IL: Northwestern University Press, 2008.

Twitchell, Jeffrey, and Huang Fan. "Avant-Garde Poetry in China: The Nanjing Scene, 1981–1992." *World Literature Today* 71.1 (Winter 1997): 29–35.

Vaingurt, Julia. "Introduction: Mastery and Method in Poetry; Osip Mandel'shtam's 'Conversation about Dante.'" *Slavic Review* 73.3 (Fall 2014): 457–70.

Vendler, Helen. *On Extended Wings: Wallace Stevens' Longer Poems*. Cambridge, MA: Harvard University Press, 1969.

———. *Wallace Stevens: Words Chosen Out of Desire*. Knoxville: University of Tennessee Press, 1984.

Vogler, Candace. "The Moral of the Story." *Critical Inquiry* 34 (Autumn 2007): 5–35.

von Hallberg, Robert. *Lyric Powers*. Chicago: Chicago University Press, 2008.

———. *Charles Olson: A Scholar's Art*. Cambridge, MA: Harvard University Press, 1978.

Wain, John. "The Shadow of an Epic." In *Ezra Pound: The Critical Heritage*, edited by Michael Homberger, 453–56. London: Routledge and Kegan Paul, 1972.

Walls, Laura Dassow. "*Walden* as Feminist Manifesto." *ISLE: Interdisciplinary Studies in Literature and Environment* 1.1 (Spring 1993): 137–44.

Warner, Michael. "Thoreau's Bottom." *Raritan* 11.3 (Winter 1992): 53–79.

Warren, Kenneth W. *What Was African American Literature?* Cambridge, MA: Harvard University Press, 2011.

Wells, David N. *Anna Akhmatova: Her Poetry*. Oxford: Berg, 1996.

West, Cornel. *The American Evasion of Philosophy: A Genealogy of Pragmatism*. Madison: University of Wisconsin Press, 1989.

White, E. B. "A Slight Sound at Evening." In *The Essays of E. B. White*, 292–302. New York: HarperCollins, 1977.

Whitman, Walt. *Complete Poetry and Collected Prose*. Edited by Justin Kaplan. New York: Library of America, 1982.

Wiggins, David. "Truth, Invention, and the Meaning of Life." In *Needs, Values, Truth: Essays in the Philosophy of Value*, 3rd ed., 87–137. Oxford: Oxford University Press, 1998.

Wilkinson, John. "Counterfactual Prynne: An Approach to *Not-You*." *Parataxis* 8/9 (1996): 190–202.

Williams, Bernard. "The Makropulos Case: Reflections on the Tedium of Immortality." In *Problems of the Self: Philosophical Papers, 1956–1972*, 82–100. Cambridge: Cambridge University Press, 1973.

Wimsatt, W. K., Jr., and Monroe C. Beardsley. "The Intentional Fallacy." In *The Verbal Icon: Studies in the Meaning of Poetry*, by W. K. Wimsatt Jr., 3–18. Lexington: University of Kentucky Press, 1967.

Winter, Jay. "Minor Utopias and the British Literary Temperament, 1880–1945." In *Utopian Spaces of Modernism: British Literature and Culture, 1885–1945*, edited by Rosalyn Gregory and Benjamin Kohlmann, 71–84. Houndmills, UK: Palgrave, 2012.

Winters, Yvor. *In Defense of Reason*. Athens: Swallow Press, 1987.

Wittgenstein, Ludwig. "A Lecture on Ethics." *Philosophical Review* 74.1 (1965): 3–12.

———. *Philosophical Investigations*. 4th ed. Translated by G.E.M. Anscombe, P.M.S. Hacker, and Joachim Schulte. Chichester, UK: John Wiley, 1958.

Woolf, Virginia. "Thoreau." In *The Essays of Virginia Woolf*, vol. 2, *1912–1918*, edited by Andrew McNeillie, 132–40. San Diego: Harcourt Brace Jovanovich, 1987.

Yousef, Nancy. *Isolated Cases: The Anxieties of Autonomy in Enlightenment Philosophy and Romantic Literature*, 12. Ithaca, NY: Cornell University Press, 2004.

Yurchak, Alexei. *Everything Was Forever, Until It Was No More*. Princeton, NJ: Princeton University Press, 2006.

"Zametki o peresechenii biografii Osipa Mandel'shtama i Borisa Pasternaka." *Pamiat'* 4 (1979/1981): 283–337.

Zamir, Shamoon. *Dark Voices: W.E.B. Du Bois and American Thought, 1888–1903*. Chicago: University of Chicago Press, 1995.

Zhdanov, Andrei. *The Central Committee Resolution and Zhdanov's Speech on the Journals "Zvezda" and "Leningrad": Bilingual Edition*. Translated by Felicity Ashbee and Irina Tidmarsh. Royal Oak: Strathcona, 1978.

Zholkovsky, Alexander. "The Obverse of Stalinism: Akhmatova's Self-Serving Charisma of Selflessness." In *Self and Story in Russian History*, edited by Lara Engelstein and Stephanie Sandler, 46–68. Ithaca, NY: Cornell University Press, 2000.

Žižek, Slavoj. "A Prophetic Vision of Haiti's Past." *Los Angeles Review of Books* (April 17, 2016). https://lareviewofbooks.org/article/prophetic-vision-haitis-past/.

INDEX

A NOTE ON THE TYPE

THIS BOOK has been composed in Miller, a Scotch Roman typeface designed by Matthew Carter and first released by Font Bureau in 1997. It resembles Monticello, the typeface developed for The Papers of Thomas Jefferson in the 1940s by C. H. Griffith and P. J. Conkwright and reinterpreted in digital form by Carter in 2003.

Pleasant Jefferson ("P. J.") Conkwright (1905–1986) was Typographer at Princeton University Press from 1939 to 1970. He was an acclaimed book designer and AIGA Medalist.

The ornament used throughout this book was designed by Pierre Simon Fournier (1712–1768) and was a favorite of Conkwright's, used in his design of the *Princeton University Library Chronicle*.